CASE
MANAGEMENT
BY DESIGN

CASE MANAGEMENT BY DESIGN

Reflections on Principles and Practices

David P. Moxley

School of Social Work
Wayne State University

Nelson-Hall Publishers
Chicago

Senior Editor: Libby Rubenstein
Printer: Capital City Press
Cover Painting: Kathryn Pecard, *In A World So Uncertain*

Chapter 4, "A Framework for the Development of Case Management Programs," originally appeared as "Outpatient program development" and is reproduced with permission from *Outpatient Case Management: Strategies for a New Reality*, published by American Hospital Publishing, Inc., Copyright © 1994. All rights reserved.

Chapter 9, "A Model of Consumer-Driven Case Management in Psychiatric Rehabilitation," originally appeared as "A model of advocacy for promoting client self-determination in psychosocial rehabilitation" in the *Psychosocial Rehabilitation Journal*, Volume 14, Number 2, pages 69–82. It is reproduced with permission by the Boston University Center for Psychiatric Rehabilitation.

A version of Chapter 12, "Serious Mental Illness and the Concept of Recovery: Implications for Case Management in Social Work Practice," was originally published as a monograph by the Boston University Center for Psychiatric Rehabilitation. It is reproduced with permission by the Center.

Library of Congress Cataloging-in-Publication Data

Moxley, David
   Case management by design : reflections on principles and
     practices / David P. Moxley.
      p. cm.
   Includes bibliographical references and index.
   ISBN 0–8304–1353–7
   1. Social case work   Management.   I. Title.
HV43.M63   1997
361.3'2--DC20   96-35411
                                CIP

Manufactured in the United States of America

10 9 8 7 6 5 4 3 2 1

DEDICATION

I dedicate this volume to my dear friend, Shirley P. Thrasher, D.S.W., Assistant Professor of Social Work, at the Wayne State University School of Social Work. Dr. Thrasher was my valued colleague whose contributions to the chapters in this volume on homeless families and on advocacy reflect her great commitment to combating the many social ills and injustices facing poor people, children, and members of minority groups. Her untimely death took her from us before her many professional contributions and aspirations could be realized.

Shirley, you taught me much about the meaning of social work, and you helped me to expand my vistas and my understanding of the profession in ways I could have only dreamed of if you had not come into my life. Thank you, Dr. Thrasher, teacher, researcher, and advocate. Thank you, Shirley, dear friend, esteemed colleague. The diversity of people you brought together, through your affirmation of the human spirit, is a testimony to your own boundless spirit and to the very humanism animating your professional and personal work.

To the children who must go on without her, David and Leslie: Understand the great legacy both of you embody. Shirley once told me that parents can do only two things: Bring us into the world, and prepare us to carry on with the work of the world when they are no longer with us. She frequently told me about how unique and vital you are, and she recognized the two of you as the real product of her devotion, for being a loving parent had no rival in her life.

To the many friends and colleagues who must go on without her, let us emulate her commitment, and let us devote ourselves to the humanism she stood for. Her life is a testimony to the ideal that people of different races, ages, and backgrounds can come together and live in peace.

As Van Morrison sings: "Let grief be a falling leaf at the dawning of the day." I will miss you, dear friend. And so will many others. And yet, despite our grief, you taught us the importance of carrying on.

CONTENTS

PART I

THE ROLE OF CASE MANAGEMENT IN HUMAN SERVICES

PART II

DEVELOPING CASE MANAGEMENT PROGRAMS AND IMPROVING THEIR IMPLEMENTATION

Introduction to Part II 39

Contents

PART III

CONSUMERISM AND CASE MANAGEMENT

Chapter 8: Properties of Consumer-Driven Forms of Case Management

111

David P. Moxley and Michael Daeschlein

Contents

Contents

PART IV

EDUCATING CASE MANAGEMENT PERSONNEL

Chapter 14: Implications of Research on Homelessness and Serious Mental Illness for the Core Practice Competencies of Case Management Personnel

PART V

CONCLUSION

Chapter 15: The Organization of Human Services and the Future of Case Management

Contents

ACKNOWLEDGMENTS

The creation of effective case management programs is no easy task. Neither is the role of the case manager. Over the past five years, many case management programs, and their personnel, have offered me a plethora of opportunities to learn about case management directly. They have been warm and gracious hosts in welcoming me into their programs and into their professional lives. They have been astute observers of what is needed to offer good case management, and they have taught me well about those forces and factors they experience firsthand that can compromise the achievement of effective programs.

I want to acknowledge the gifts of knowledge and understanding these programs and their personnel have given me. To my colleagues in the Sioux City Region of the Iowa Department of Human Services: I have never met a group of more decent and committed human service professionals and public servants. Your efforts within child welfare to create an effective case management system based on principles of continuous improvement serve as a model of human service systems change for the nation. Your efforts also demonstrate what can be done when a group of committed professionals working within state government come together to create bottom-up change and to struggle with elevating the standards of service for children and families. I am so pleased that I have had the opportunity to work with all of you in crafting a case management model based on strengths, collaboration, and performance.

I also want to acknowledge those gifts given to me by the case management staff of Community Care Services, Taylor, Michigan. We have struggled with a number of the themes and issues discussed in this volume, and you have been pivotal in shaping my understanding of the challenges inherent in the achievement of good case management practice. I have been thrilled with our discussions and analyses as we moved from theory to practice, and from practice to theory.

Acknowledgments

A book like this cannot be written without considerable support from others. And so I want to thank both Drs. Leon Chestang and Phyllis Vroom, Dean and Associate Dean, respectively, of the Wayne State University School of Social Work, for their help in rearranging my teaching schedule during the Spring and Summer semesters of 1994. I can't adequately express my appreciation for this gift of time. It made this book possible. I also want to thank Dean Chestang for his continuing support.

Mr. Richard Meade of Nelson-Hall Publishers was instrumental in keeping this project alive. He was most gracious in giving me a generous extension on my initial deadline. I also want to thank Dr. Leonard Rosen, who taught me a great deal about how much I can learn from my direct experiences when I only take the time to listen carefully to what they have to offer me. I want to thank Dr. Wallace Gingerich of the Mandel School of Applied Social Sciences (MSASS) at Case Western Reserve University. His timely invitation several years ago to teach an intensive course on case management at MSASS served to maintain my focus on this area. The students who took my course at MSASS from 1992 to 1996 offered me considerable input on the themes and issues I identify and discuss in this volume. Thank you for your insight and for your critical observations about case management.

I thank all of you for your support. I readily take full responsibility for the quality of the chapters included in this volume. My only hope is that the content of these chapters reflects the quality of the support I have received from these many people during the course of this journey to discover more about case management: its design, organization, and practice.

ABOUT THE AUTHOR

David P. Moxley, Ph.D., is an associate professor in the School of Social Work at Wayne State University, Detroit, Michigan, where he also cochairs the graduate concentration on community practice. Dr. Moxley's consultation, technical assistance, and research work contribute to the content of this volume. His other substantive interests in social work and social welfare include the areas of psychiatric rehabilitation, developmental disabilities, and organizational analysis in human services.

ABOUT THE CONTRIBUTORS

Orman E. Hall, M.A., is executive director of the Fairfield County Alcohol Drug Addiction and Mental Health Services Board located in Lancaster, Ohio. His interests include mental health administration, program evaluation, and management information systems. He coauthored Chapter 5 in this volume.

D. Larry Branham is executive director of the Ohio Diversity Mental Health Resource Training Center of the Ohio Department of Mental Health. He has been involved in mental health systems change and in training and development of case management personnel. He coauthored Chapter 5 in this volume.

Sandra L. Taranto, M.S.N., is supervisor of extended services at Community Care Services, Taylor, Michigan. Her interests include the development of rehabilitation alternatives for people with serious mental illness. She coauthored Chapter 7 in this volume.

Michael Daeschlein, M.A., is affiliated with the Wayne State University Developmental Disabilities Institute, where he develops and implements demonstration research in supported employment and in supported community living. He is also a doctoral student in evaluation in the Wayne State University School of Education. He coauthored Chapter 8 in this volume.

Paul P. Freddolino, Ph.D., is professor in the School of Social Work at Michigan State University, East Lansing, Michigan. His interests include research in rights protection and advocacy, and in distance education. He coauthored Chapter 9 in this volume.

Shirley P. Thrasher, D.S.W., was assistant professor in the School of Social Work at Wayne State University, where she taught courses on family systems practice, family diversity, and interpersonal practice. At the time of her death, Dr. Thrasher was implementing research on homelessness among families. She coauthored Chapters 10 and 11 in this volume.

Carol T. Mowbray, Ph.D., is associate professor in the School of Social Work at the University of Michigan, Ann Arbor, Michigan. Dr. Mowbray has conducted extensive research in mental health systems, psychiatric rehabilitation, and the role of gender in mental health service delivery. She coauthored Chapter 14 in this volume.

CHAPTER 1

AN INTRODUCTION TO CASE MANAGEMENT BY DESIGN

It has been some time since the publication of my modest text on case manage-ment practice (Moxley, 1989). Since then several very good textbooks have been published, and these have elaborated case management as a distinctive field of human service practice (Rose, 1992; Vourlekis & Green, 1992; Raiff & Shore, 1993). In addition to the comprehensive and excellent text on case mangement published by Weil and Karls (1985), and the work on aging and case manage-ment by Steinberg and Carter (1983), over the past ten years these books, in con-junction with a growing body of journal articles, have dramatically expanded the knowledge base in this field, as well as the know-how concerning pitfalls in actu-al case management practice.

I never intended to prepare another book length treatment of case man-agement since I assumed that I had outlined most of what I had to say about its practice in the 1989 book. But both my research and consultation work in the case management field have continued throughout the early nineties. Many orga-nizations and human service systems have invited me to work with them in plan-ning, evaluating, and improving case management systems addressing a variety of social problems and recipient groups. I took advantage of these opportunities so I could advance my own learning about case management, about its imple-mentation in actual service settings, and about the organizational contexts of this human service technology. The chapters included in this book are an outcome of this work. They reflect what I have learned about case management from actual field work; that is, from the people who do case management, from the people who use case management, and from the organizations and systems that serve as the hosts of case management programs.

But I also became involved in these projects because they offered me a chance to see how human services were coping with the often conflicting demands created by a social welfare institution that increasingly seeks efficiency in the face of spiraling needs among many of our most disadvantaged or oppressed citizens—the people who are most often the principal recipients of case management services. The emergence of case management in the human services is indeed a limited reform. It reflects, however, a changing social welfare institution—one that is juggling diverse and often conflicting policy aims reflecting a plurality of stakeholders and their expectations (Gibelman & Demone, 1989). These aims include achievement of an efficient response to human needs in a society that is so very ambivalent about responding collectively to human problems, and achievement of an equitable response in which the delivery of services is seen as an important if not principal means of correcting many of the inequities created by the social structure. Case management embraces both of these aims and often struggles with trying to optimize both despite the seeming impossibility of this effort given the very real structural limitations of our social welfare institution. Thus, it is not surprising that the field and practice of case management are just as confusing as our entire system of social welfare.

LIMITATIONS OF MY EARLIER WORK

As I worked on these various projects I soon appreciated the limitations of the 1989 book. To be sure, it offered a narrow view of case management based on my own program development experience within a multiservice mental health agency. The conceptual model I presented in the 1989 book was legitimately criticized by a number of reviewers for failing to examine the variety of case management forms and applications as well as for failing to address many of the issues involved in case management implementation. My version of case management, according to several reviewers, was "stripped down" and "pulled out of context," or it failed to capture the richness of contemporary case management programs, their contradictions, and the proliferation of forms and practices that have been propagated under the rubric of case management. I certainly concur with these observations.

This book is composed of a variety of chapters that offer me considerable flexibility in capturing my experiences and work with case management programs. I use the chapters to organize and communicate what I have learned from my work as an educator, consultant, and researcher; to tease out and expand on the issues I have identified in field work, sometimes in collaboration with other colleagues. Hopefully I have captured some of the more important themes germane to contemporary case management and the contents of these chapters are meaningful and relevant to readers. As in my earlier work in case management, I still maintain my conceptual posture in this book, not only because this is indicative of my approach to scholarly work but because I have found that concepts and their organization into frameworks offer people from diverse audiences something they can perhaps contemplate and apply to their own situations.

CASE MANAGEMENT AS A LIMITED REFORM

Through these chapters I attempt to capture some of the richness of this field, which demands continued documentation and mapping, not merely because case management is an innovation, or a relatively novel program, but because case management as a programmatic form reflects some of the most important contemporary developments in the human services. The advent of managed care (Jacobs & Moxley, 1993; Anthony, 1993), local efforts to create collaborative support systems for the most vulnerable of our citizens (Anthony & Blanch, 1989; Berkowitz, Halfon, & Klee, 1992), continued efforts to integrate service delivery (Capitman, Haskins, & Berstein, 1986), and the emergence of so-called consumer-driven practice models (Moxley & Freddolino, 1990) are some of these developments, and they reflect the strong possibility that conflict and contradiction will characterize case management (Deitchman, 1980).

The multiple models of case management (Korr & Cloninger, 1991) and the multiple expectations linked to case management suggest that much has been projected onto this modest and limited reform. But its purpose within human service systems varies with the configuration of these systems and the adequacy of resources these systems possess to meet human needs (Moore, 1992). As I noted in previous work (Moxley, 1986), case management remains in "good currency": It has broad policy legitimacy (Ellison, Rogers, Sciarappa, Cohen, & Forbess, 1995), despite the absence of consistent research findings supporting its efficacy (Chamberlin & Rapp, 1991; Rubin, 1992); and it possesses some face validity, despite the existence of multiple and conflicting definitions of what case management is (Kirkhart & Ruffolo, 1993) and of its role in human services. Since it has emerged from many social forces within the greater society and within human services over the past thirty years, case management is a concrete representation of the considerable turbulence occurring in the field of social welfare over several decades.

But despite the emergence of a variety of case management alternatives within a number of different policy areas, and despite the recognition of case management as a legitimate means for achieving various prescriptive policy ends (such as the achievement of coordination, the achievement of access, or the attainment of efficiency) (Beatrice, 1981), case management systems have not proven to be a "panacea" for the resolution of some of our most enduring and vexing problems in responding to human needs—needs that are too often the outcome of the interplay among complex social problems (Austin, 1993; Netting, 1992). Case management reflects a contradiction in meeting human needs: We perhaps define who people are by what they lack (Ignatieff, 1984), not by what they want. The dichotomy created by differentiating need and want reflects the dramatic differences in how case management is formulated and how it is expressed in implementation (Kirkhart & Ruffolo, 1993).

In addition, as a modest reform, case management itself can create serious problems in the delivery of human services, as it amplifies what is most problematic about the provision of social, health, and human services (e.g., how to infuse prevention into the provision of services; how to prevent relatively autonomous agencies from working at cross purposes; how to allocate scarce resources among multiple groups with competing aims yet with perhaps similar needs). Case management systems can make salient many of the conflicts, strains, and difficulties operating in contemporary human services.

We should recognize and respect case management for what it is: a somewhat limited but nonetheless important way of trying to make human service delivery work better (Anthony, Cohen, Farkas, & Cohen, 1988)—hopefully for people who are the direct recipients of human services, those individuals who often bear the multiple effects of our most serious social problems. Unfortunately, defining what is meant by "better" service delivery is another vexing issue since there is so much controversy about what human services should achieve and the values that govern this achievement. Defining "better" must be provisional since the goal set of case management systems is so often complex and so often challenged by the threat of goal displacement. The chosen form of case management will be influenced by the value packages embraced by its creators and their version of what constitutes "better" service delivery (Meenaghan & Kilty, 1994).

Policy agents project so many expectations and aspirations onto case management that the people who do it can take on the character of Sisyphus, trying to push a boulder up a mountain only to have it roll back down the hill when he nears the summit. Case managers, like the legendary Sisyphus, may be crushed repeatedly by the huge rocks they are trying to push upward. However, unlike Sisyphus, who is condemned by the gods to engage in this activity for eternity, case managers can cope with the unclarity of their roles, the multiple expectations held by policy makers and overseers, and the multiple values undergirding these expectations and goals by merely leaving the field. They can either move on, move up, or move out. And many make this choice. This is a serious issue since many writers on case management have underscored the importance of forming and sustaining strong, enduring case management relationships with recipients.

TWO ARCHETYPES OF CASE MANAGEMENT

It is asserted in several of these chapters that these multiple expectations and their values cluster into two primary archetypes—both consistent with the history and evolution of social welfare and human services in the United States (Gibelman & Demone, 1989). One archetype is composed of a set of values consistent with a true "management" philosophy in which societal resources allocated for the purposes of health and human services must be rationed. Efficiency is the cardinal value to achieve here. People are seen as individual actors whose functioning will be sustained or improved through better designed and targeted services. Yet there is little appreciation for the systemic or structural causes of their problems. From my perspective, a case management system that embodies a response to these systemic or structural factors would indeed constitute a meaningful innovation.

In this archetype, the case manager mediates these social values and may serve as a technical agent for ostensibly achieving an efficient solution to the problems of people in need. I conceive of this form of case management as trusteeship. The principal aim of the trustee is to husband the resources of the greater society: to use these scarce resources to respond to those human needs that are defined as legitimate. In the language of street level bureaucracy (Lipsky, 1980), the case manager is the system's representative who mediates between the citizen and the greater society. The trustee assures that the person in need is worthy of societal beneficence, that the problem is technically and diagnostically defined, and that the solution appears (at least on face) to be an efficient one.

However, efficiency in the American welfare state has always been elusive. Case managers saddled by expectations to meet human needs while conserving resources often opt for the former and inadvertently escalate costs. In fact, some models of case management (e.g., brokering and linking approaches) require the case manager to be vigilant in identifying and meeting needs, so we should expect that the utilization of services, supports, and benefits will increase and so will costs.

Another archetype is composed of a set of values consistent with consumerism. Case management is in part a product of the broader consumer movement in social welfare and human services that emerged some twenty to twenty-five years ago. This movement defined social services as a right, and equity was seen as a cardinal value that should be achieved by human service systems. People damaged by systemic forces should be assisted to become "whole" through the provision of services, supports, and entitlements. Consumers and their advocates sought more responsive forms of service delivery and, in the fields of physical disabilities, developmental disabilities, and serious mental illness, case management emerged as one means of achieving responsiveness through the creation of services and supports, the achievement of access, and the formulation of "need" in a manner consistent with the qualities, preferences, and desires of consumers themselves. In this archtype the case manager becomes a steward of client needs. This archetype addresses the fulfillment of need in response to disenfranchisement (Doyal & Gough, 1991). Thus, in some service arenas, case management has been fused with advocacy, empowerment, and elaboration of entitlements and services (Anthony et al., 1988; Hodge & Draine, 1993; Raiff & Shore, 1993; Steinberg & Carter, 1983). It is a means of representing the perspectives of a consumer who is too often disempowered and overshadowed by seemingly monolithic bureaucracies.

THE MULTIPLE MEANINGS OF MANAGEMENT

"Management" remains a principal concept in the archetype of stewardship (Wolk, Sullivan, & Hartman, 1994), but it takes on a dramatically different meaning compared to its use within the context of what I call "systems-driven" case management. Management means that the case manager, in partnership with the consumer, or in following the lead of the consumer, attempts to manage a system of services on behalf of the recipient. Responsiveness as a cardinal value means that the system is responsive to consumers—their perspectives and issues. Rather than serving as a trustee of the system, the case manager is a steward of the perspectives and desires of consumers and may act independently of, or in conjunction with, the consumer to achieve consumer-defined ends.

I employ the term *case management* because this is the term used most widely in the literature as well as in program designations. Some people are offended by this term (Everett & Nelson, 1992), but I employ it as a way of remaining consistent with the corpus of literature that has developed around service coordination and integration and, more recently, within managed care. I extend my apologies to those who are offended by this term. The term itself raises the larger question of who or what is managed? From one perspective, it is a system wishing to manage a person and/or the behavior of a person. From another perspective, it is a person who is seeking to manage a system. Thus, we must keep at the forefront of our minds the observation that case management does not have a singular meaning or definition. As you, the reader, plunge into these chapters I hope that you will reflect on what we really mean by the construct of case management. More importantly, I hope you decide what case management means to you and to your practice.

THE INSTITUTIONAL MATRIX OF CASE MANAGEMENT

Much of the pain and frustration experienced by case managers, I have found, is linked to a duality of role created by the operation of essentially two conflicting archetypes found in trusteeship and stewardship. Each archetype is based on a different value set. These values can collide in action and can create considerable value conflict and role conflict for case managers as they try to sort our their purpose, mission, and principal goals (Dill, 1987). We find this conflict inherent in ambiguous policy messages given to case management systems and to their personnel: "reduce resource expenditures while you improve quality"; "treat the recipient as a customer but limit the range of services offered"; "work efficiently but respond in a sensitive manner to the recipient"; "meet needs comprehensively but control consumption." These messages create mischief. They can fill case management with considerable ambiguity despite arguments that cost efficiency and responsiveness to human need can be reconciled or harmonized in practice (Anthony, 1993).

Case management is a cultural artifact. It is an expression of the larger culture embodied by our contemporary social welfare institution. Its character and its performance are both shaped by the form of this institution and its role within our greater society. This institution does not readily embrace prevention and the proactive offer of support. Service comes to most people after substantial damage has been inflicted by larger systemic forces. There is little opportunity to offer nonservice benefits that will enable people to enjoy a decent standard of living and readily achieve integration into communities of their choosing. Human services respond to crisis and emergency and often adopt a short temporal perspective, probably one poorly matched to the magnitude of the problems these services must address.

"Benefits" within this system are narrowly defined as services since the offer of income is viewed with suspicion if not paranoia—especially if they are designated for people coping with poverty, structural unemployment, or devalued status. The service-driven character of our social welfare institution means that delivery systems must be assembled for the allocation and management of these benefits. This means that formal organizations staffed by professionals become an inherent and defining property of this type of social welfare institution (Meenaghan & Washington, 1980).

As government has moved out of the business of direct service delivery, the provision of services has increasingly become decentralized, specialized, and focused on specific service populations as it is mediated by nonprofit social agencies and increasingly by an emergent for-profit sector (Demone & Gibelman, 1989; Rehfuss, 1989). Obtaining and organizing these services—the principal benefit offered by our social welfare institution—has increasingly become more complex, demanding, and uncertain for potential recipients.

Case management operates within such an institutional matrix. Perhaps we have created it as a way of buffering the considerable complexity and uncertainty inherent in the provision of services so that the success of case management can be appraised by service delivery criteria like access and utilization (Austin,

1993; Belcher, 1993; First, Rife, & Krauss, 1990). Perhaps it represents a desire to achieve a holism that is increasingly elusive in a fragmented world of service created by decentralization, the shifting of authority, and the absence of an accountability linked directly to the consumer. The dilemma of trying to piece together fragments into a unified response to a person often falls to a case manager (Halfon, Berkowitz, & Klee, 1993). But in undertaking this work, case managers operate in a political economy in which stakeholders, organizations, and systems conflict, collaborate, and compete. It is difficult to analyze case management as a form of practice independent of an organizational or systems context in which it is embedded (Austin, 1993).

It is not surprising that the work of case managers is frustrating. It is not surprising that case managers are often consumed by crisis and emergency. And it is not surprising that they feel as though they work with puzzles, trying to fit together complex pieces into a whole, an enterprise made more difficult since the rules are ill defined and the pieces are not engineered to fit together rationally. Or perhaps there are two sets of rules: one for case managers who infuse stewardship into their practice, and one for case managers who take their direction from the perspective of trusteeship.

Despite these criticisms, this is not a book that attempts to debunk case management. From my perspective, if we continue to translate social welfare benefits into the delivery of services provided through a decentralized array of organizations whose specialization creates considerable fragmentation, then case management programs will be a necessity into the near future. If we are committing limited and constrained social welfare resources to the formulation and implementation of case management systems then we should at least try to address those issues that can compromise their effectiveness. Perhaps what we will find, however, is that these issues often arise from deeply held values about who should be helped and how people should be helped—enduring themes concerning the legitimacy of social welfare, and the legitimacy of dependency, in the United States. The implementation effectiveness of case management programs may emerge out of their own achievement of an integrity found in the clarity of their values and the purpose that they embrace.

ORGANIZATION OF THE CHAPTERS

The chapters are organized into five major groupings. The first part, composed of two chapters, examines the role of case management in the human services. The principal theme here is that the manner in which we conceive of the overall role of case management has serious implications for identifying its purposes and goals and its subsequent implementation. Given the proliferation of case management in social welfare, the first chapter attempts to sort out the purpose of case management. The second chapter in this part looks at the idea of street level bureaucracy as an advanced organizer of case management systems. Case management as street level bureaucracy highlights the role of case managers as mediators and buffers between citizens in need and the bureaucratic structures communities have established for meeting needs. Many case managers "internalize" the frustrations, challenges, and obstacles that would otherwise be felt more directly and powerfully by citizens in need operating alone and/or as their own agents.

The second part of the book, composed of four chapters, addresses design and implementation issues. A principal theme in this part is that case management programs need to be explicitly designed, but designers have many options to choose from and many dimensions to consider. Thus one chapter is devoted exclusively to program development. The remaining three chapters address improvement themes relevant to the implementation of case management. I have organized data and observations from several different consultation projects into these chapters. One chapter presents issues identified through the implementation of a case management system as it attempts to become more consumer-driven and community-focused. Another chapter addresses salient improvement themes derived from the implementation of different case management systems. However, these themes are indicators of the many problems these programs face in making relevant and meaningful contributions to human service systems as well as to the lives of consumers. Another chapter in this part addresses one agency's application of Total Quality Management to the improvement of its case management service and the issues raised by this strategy.

The five chapters composing Part III focus on consumerism and the stewardship archetype of case management. Two chapters examine the idea of consumer-driven case management and identify core properties and their application to an actual field setting. Another theme addresses the relationship between a consumer-driven model of case management and the infusion of advocacy practice into case management. A chapter devoted to the application of consumer-driven case management to the social problem of homelessness among families is included, and the salient principles guiding this work are presented as a way of demonstrating the application of core case management ideas to a serious and growing problem. Finally, another chapter looks at the emerging paradigm of recovery within the field of serious mental illness and the implications of this paradigm for case management.

The fourth part of the book incorporates material on the preparation of personnel for case management practice. One chapter examines preservice education of social workers as case managers. It is based on a course I have taught over a five-year period to graduate social work students. Another chapter synthesizes research in the field of homelessness and offers conclusions for the professional development of case managers practicing in this social problem area.

The last part, containing one chapter, looks at the future of case management and examines various scenarios and their implications for the organization of case management.

Most chapters are original ones that I have crafted specifically for this volume. Several are revisions of papers I have prepared for other publications. Several chapters have been coauthored, and I identify these authors at the beginning of the appropriate essay. In addition, I have included brief biographical statements for each author at the beginning of the book. I want to thank these coauthors for their contributions and their collaboration.

PURPOSE AND USE OF THE VOLUME

I intend for this book to serve as a reader or companion text for courses on case management or for core courses in human service practice, especially those focusing on the organization of social welfare and the programmatic structure of contemporary human services. The book does not necessarily have to be read from cover to cover. I hope readers will find several valuable nuggets that capture their attention—ones that will stimulate reflection on their experiences in human service and case management practice. If the book achieves this modest end then I will be satisfied.

PART I

THE ROLE OF
CASE MANAGEMENT IN
HUMAN SERVICES

INTRODUCTION TO PART I

The emergence of case management within multiple areas of human service has given it considerable ubiquity (Donovan & Matson, 1994). This ubiquity within human services and the diversity of case management models and approaches that have emerged reflect the evolution of human service practice. However, the sheer proliferation of case management approaches has created considerable ambiguity concerning the functions, role, and ultimately the purpose of case management. The first chapter attempts to reduce much of the ambiguity surrounding the multiple aims, goals, and models of case management by offering a conceptual schema for organizing these. By offering this conceptual frame of reference, I attempt to get at the multiple roles filled by case management in contemporary human service systems.

Street level bureaucracy, the theme of the second chapter in this part, offers some utility in enriching our understanding of the function of case management in human services by identifying the case manager's role as devoted to connecting people to systems and systems to people. Case managers often engage in screening, eligibility determination, assessment, outreach, linkage to service and benefits, and other activities that, from the perspective of street level bureaucracy, constitute critical policy roles held by lower level actors in public service systems. I do not use the term "lower level" in a pejorative manner but to communicate that case managers are frontline workers, many of whom work on the street, to make human services more accessible or responsive to citizens, on the one hand, or, on the other hand, to control or otherwise reduce the access of citizens to services, to divert them from expensive services, or to decrease economic risk to service systems that may result from overconsumption of services or inappropriate utilization.

11

Case managers, therefore, can be policy actors who have considerable influence on the implementation of human service programs and on the delivery of actual human services to recipients. As street level bureaucrats, they can influence the effectiveness of policy implementation or actually create "implicit" policy through the actions they take to serve citizens in need.

I hope these two chapters taken together communicate the complexity of case management programs and the work of case managers. This part also establishes a foundation for succeeding chapters and, therefore, themes discussed in this first set of chapters will reemerge later in the volume.

CHAPTER 2

SORTING OUT THE PURPOSE OF CASE MANAGEMENT

This chapter is a product of a research and development project I undertook with an agency that sought to become more consumer-driven in its service delivery approach. The agency, which actually represented a large human service system composed of numerous rehabilitation and mental health programs, developed a centralized case management component. The original conception of this case management component was to create a coordinated approach to service delivery for people with the most severe disabilities. However, after a year of implementation, the agency discovered that the case management component was not espousing consumer-driven values but rather was focusing on costs, the rationing of services, and the oversight of people with behavioral challenges who were found to be quite bothersome to the mental health staff.

This chapter is a revision of a workshop I conducted for the staff to clarify the differences between consumer-driven and system-driven case management approaches. The workshop engendered considerable work undertaken by this agency to improve its responsiveness to the people it serves.

The ubiquity of case management in the human services reflects the considerable variation of models, practices, and approaches operating in this area. Most of the discussion of case management focuses on differences in models and practices without really examining the assumptions and properties underlying these different approaches to case management. As emphasized in the introduction, the considerable variety of approaches can be understood from the perspective of who gets served and for what reason these people are offered case management services. Thus, one way of understanding this variation is by looking at the social problem to which case management is linked, and by looking at the people who bear the effects of this social problem. Case management alternatives in aging, developmental disabilities, and mental health may share some commonalities, but they also vary in practice by virtue of the kinds of issues or problems they attempt to address. Mental health case management, for example, may focus on the medical consequences of serious mental illness and on the diversion of people from hospitalization (Degen, Cole, Tamayo, & Dzerovych, 1990; Dietzen & Bond, 1993; Dincin, 1990; Evans, Banks, Huz, & McNulty, 1994), while case management offered to people with developmental disabilities may address goals relating to normalization, independent living, or to supported community living (Bradley, Ashbaugh, & Blaney, 1994).

But when we look closely at the variation in case management models and practices, we can discern a more abstract pattern that begins to differentiate those various approaches into larger archetypes. I use the term *archetype* to focus on these patterns that underlie case management models. These patterns infuse case management with different goals and properties, and they serve to frame practice. They also offer a means to organize by common themes the discrete case management models that have proliferated within human services over the past twenty years.

There are several reasons why these archetypes are useful. First, they help us to reflect on the underlying values of case management practice, and they help us to engage in a dialogue about what we are trying to achieve in human services through the use of case management as practice technology. Second, they can help us to understand more critically the variation in case management models and approaches, and they give some order to a field that is proliferating various models when actually these models probably are variations on common themes found in their archetypal pattern. Third, and perhaps most important, these archetypes help us identify the purpose of case management in the human services. Given all of the variation in this field, the archetypes help us sort out what case management ought to do on behalf of systems or on behalf of people in need.

I identify two principal archetypes within the case management field in the introductory chapter to this book. I refer to one archetype as "system-driven"—or trusteeship—and I refer to the other one as "consumer-driven"—or stewardship. These two archetypes do not suggest nominalistic differences but rather indicate significant, if not profound, differences in form, substance, and function. The aim of this chapter is to outline these two archetypes and the qualities that differentiate them, and then briefly to identify the goal set of each archetype and how various models of case management embody these goals.

It is important, however, to keep in mind that case management is very much an element of our contemporary system of social welfare and the culture that is formed by the values, aims, and assumptions of this institutional matrix. System-driven case management is very compatible with an institutional matrix that defines benefits as services and that prioritizes the delivery of services through organizations and through professionals (Donovan, 1994). Even though consumer-driven case management is offered within an organizational context, as an archetype it suggests alternative ways of offering social welfare benefits, and identifies new types of relationships, new ways of financing human services, and new roles for consumers in controlling human services.

For those of you who feel these archetypes are too abstract, I do apologize, but I ask for your patience. They serve as useful schema, and may be important tools in supporting more informed thinking about case management.

THE SYSTEM-DRIVEN ARCHETYPE

Defining System-Driven Case Management

System-driven case management embodies those values that prioritize a more efficient and effective organizational approach to human service delivery (Sieverts, 1994). The role of case management from the perspective of this archetype is found in its contribution to the realization of better organized human services, ones that are more efficient in their use of resources and more effective from the standpoint of service delivery. We can see this archetype reflected in the use of case management to better coordinate service delivery, to ration access to expensive service alternatives, to substitute less expensive services for more expensive services, to control behaviors of people who can create expense and inefficiencies for a human service system, and to control behaviors of people who are found undesirable or perhaps violate social norms or customs.

The idea of "system control" is at the heart of this archetype. But why is control seen as an important aim of case management? First, in the context of contemporary social welfare systems, social welfare benefits are seen as scarce and limited. The formalization of social welfare as services mediated by organizations and professionals suggests that these resources are scarce and their use must be controlled as much as possible (Sampson, 1994). Demand will always outstrip supply because social problems continue to escalate, and a society that finds few permanent solutions to these problems must continue to manufacture more services, mandate more organizations to provide these services, or expand existing human service organizations.

Yet there is a limit to this proliferation not only because there are limited dollars to invest in problems and their management, but because limited dollars more likely represent an attitudinal limit imposed by public opinion about the extent of help that is permissible and legitimate. (See for example, Gov. Thompson's commentary on welfare in *The National Times,* 1996). In contemporary social welfare, there are limits to formal helping, and human services are often viewed with mistrust by the general citizenry, elected officials, and even by many of the organizations mandated to deliver these services.

A second control feature of this archetype lies in the management of deviance. It is difficult to separate system-driven case management from the idea that an important aim lies in the control or management of people who do not fit into many of our communities. Deinstitutionalization created crises for numerous communities as people who otherwise would have been institutionalized and out of sight moved into neighborhoods. According to Szasz (1994), human service technologies are increasingly used to control deviance through a compassion that really masks a cruel effort on the part of society to manage people who have been marginalized.

Case management may be seen as one of these technologies, and increasingly we see approaches and models of case management implemented in ways that speak more to social control (i.e., protection of the community) than to the support of people who bear the effects of social labeling, social deviance, and social reaction. Case management in this archetype can be linked to coercive strategies designed to make dependency less expensive for the community at large and for specific subsectors of this community. Or, if it cannot make deviance less expensive, then case management can control it so that disruption and disorder are reduced or managed. I have seen a number of case management initiatives developed by business interests or police departments seeking to make sure that people who were perceived to be very different from the norm did not disrupt the peace or commerce.

This control feature does not mean that compassion is eliminated from this archetype. I merely assert that it is not operative as a principal value. The integrity of a system is the primary aim of this archetype—be it a human service system, a human service organization, or a specific community. *The purpose of this archetype, therefore, is found in control: case management here seeks to increase control of people by a system so that costs produced by duplication, utilization, and deviant or unwanted behavior are reduced or at least managed.* The goals of system-driven case management focus principally on the production of benefits for the system, and then secondarily on the production of benefits for the people who are the recipient of services.

The Goal Set of System-Driven Case Management

Five principal goals of system-driven case management can be identified, and all of them reflect the production of benefits for human service systems and/or communities even though there may be some effort to humanize case management. These goals are: coordination, rationing, substitution, behavioral cost control, and deviance management.

Coordination

This goal is expressed in the case management literature by an emphasis placed on making services fit together with the objectives of reducing duplication and increasing the efficiency of service delivery. Although the achievement of the goal of coordination and the objectives sought through this goal are often elusive in practice, the case management literature frequently identifies the importance of service coordination at the client level (Gerhard, Dorgan, & Miles, 1981) and the elimination of duplication at a system level.

However, one can muster a strong rationale favoring the promotion of duplication when it is designed purposefully to respond to people's cultural attachments (such as specialized services designed to respond to ethnicity, sexual orientation, or gender) and to promote access, especially by people who are reluctant to seek services. In addition, people may obtain more responsive and innovative services when there is more competition among providers rather than more coordination, especially at the case level of service delivery. Nonetheless, coordination as a goal is often seen in brokering approaches to case management.

Rationing

This goal is reflected within managed care approaches that establish a utilization approach to case management. Access to services that are deemed to be expensive to the system is managed through a gatekeeping function often incorporating prior approval, assessment, or evaluation by a clinical professional. The case management function is an explicit approach to rationing often incorporated into health care, substance abuse treatment, employee assistance programs, and inpatient psychiatric care. Rationing is adopted to be responsive to the needs of the purchaser or funder of service rather than to the people who bear the effects of the problem.

Rationing can shift costs to the consumer and away from a system, and can shift the burden of care to informal supports and to services outside of a managed care network (Kane & Caplan, 1992). It is sometimes difficult to judge who or what bears the cost of limited access and rationed service delivery.

Substitution

Case management programs can pursue the goal of substituting less expensive supports for more expensive ones. This is very prevalent in case management alternatives that seek to incorporate informal supports, social support alternatives, or family care with the goal of extending case management supports into community or household settings in lieu of the provision of an ongoing program or service staffed by relatively expensive professionals and paraprofessionals. A number of case management alternatives described in the literature offer a rationale for supporting families to provide supportive services and care or for organizing peer supports, social networks, and self-help approaches (Moxley, 1989; Biegel, Tracy, & Corvo, 1994; Seltzer, Ivry, & Litchfield, 1987). And, there has been an effort to substitute family members for case management personnel with professional credentials as a means of reducing costs.

Many of these programmatic descriptions highlight the progressive features of these alternatives, but few discuss the demands and costs that are experienced by family members or other informal support providers who take on case management and direct service responsibilities (Kane, 1988; Brostoff, 1988). In addition, many of these programmatic alternatives do not discuss the possible operation of explicit or subtle coercion of family members or informal support providers to become involved in these roles when they may be reluctant, unable, or unmotivated to undertake case management or direct support activities (Kane, 1988).

Another form of substitution can occur when consumers of services are offered positions as case management staff, ostensibly to make programs more sensitive and responsive to users (Nikkel, Smith, & Edwards, 1992). This form of substitution can create a more consumer-driven alternative (Mowbray, Moxley, Jasper, & Howell, 1995). But it may actually be motivated by the aim of cost reduction or cost control and can be implemented without much support given to consumer case managers or much attention given to their long-term employment or professional mobility.

This form of substitution can create personal and social costs for consumers who may be marginalized by a false professional status that can potentially alienate them from their peers. I underscore the notion of "a false professional status" because several caveats to this form of substitution have been identified. First, consumers may find themselves in positions that are not considered professional despite their personal experience with a problem and a treatment system, and their status may be diminished by their professional colleagues. Second, consumers may find themselves stuck in positions that offer no advancement or movement into career ladders. Third, the impact of these positions and roles on the self-concepts of consumers is infrequently addressed through supervision, staff development, and professional development—a situation that may leave consumers confused about their role and the scope of their competence (Mowbray, Moxley, Thrasher, & Associates, 1996). Finally, organizational staff may not be oriented to this kind of role innovation. They may not be trained to interact with people with whom they may have had previous treatment relationships but who are now colleagues within the same organization.

Behavioral Cost Control

A number of case management alternatives are established to buffer the costs created by people who are high utilizers of a service or who may present behaviors that are considered to be harmful to a community. These alternatives, such as

Assertive Community Treatment (Bond, Miller, Krumwied & Ward, 1988) and clinical case management (Harris, 1990; Harris & Bergman, 1993; Kanter, 1985), often incorporate aggressive outreach components that are designed to locate people in the community and to link with them in order to establish an ongoing relationship. These case management alternatives are not facility-based by design, since the people they target for service do not typically seek out human service professionals, although they may present themselves for service during crises or emergencies, a behavioral pattern that can drive up service costs, treatment costs, and people-processing costs. As part of their mission, these case management alternatives seek to drive down or control the costs created by high utilization behavior by addressing the needs of individuals through innovative arrangements focusing on the provision of community and household support integrated with social services, rehabilitation activities, and medical management. These functions are often incorporated into team configurations whose membership represents critical service functions designed to address the needs of users.

This goal does raise ethical issues pertaining to the system control of people. Assertive outreach in the community may mean that people's privacy rights are violated, and their rights to associate with whom they please may be compromised. The constant monitoring of people, and the intrusion of services into a person's household, raise ethical issues pertaining to coercion and the right to decline treatment. Assertive outreach may make people more visible in the community. This goal and related case management approaches reflect the strain between the system-driven archetype and the consumer-driven archetype. Can assertive approaches to case management embody consumer-driven principles or are they driven by the aims of a system to contain or reduce costs?

Deviance Management

Increasingly case management is seen as an alternative to confinement, as an alternative to incarceration, and as an alternative to hospitalization such as in community commitment. Case management alternatives in the corrections and juvenile justice arenas are designed to increase surveillance of offenders and can incorporate traditional approaches to service coordination, linkage, and brokering as well as novel approaches to supervision involving the use of electronic and computer technologies. Using case management to get people out of jail sooner or to divert people from incarceration can be explicit strategies for reducing system costs or at least making these costs more obscure. Given the degraded state of our corrections system, they also may be more humane alternatives.

However, they can increase the institutional ambiguity surrounding human services by accentuating the mixed loyalties inherent in combining a system control approach with an approach that incorporates the relational aspects of care and support. Deviance management can raise a key question in the mind of a consumer: Whom does this case manager represent? Me or the system? In corrections this may be very straightforward. Case management personnel represent the system of social control. In community commitment, the loyalties of case management personnel are much more ambiguous. Case management personnel are interested in the person's conformity to community norms, but they are interested in the person's needs and in their perspective. It is difficult to combine coercion and support without creating ambiguity or even ambivalence for consumers.

THE CONSUMER-DRIVEN ARCHETYPE

Defining Consumer-Driven Case Management

The pressure for effective and efficient system performance makes it difficult to be responsive to individuals, to their perspectives, and to their social qualities and social characteristics. Sensitivity to cultural factors in human services and to the needs of diverse communities is increasingly important as the United States becomes more differentiated socially and demographically (Rivera & Erlich, 1995). As identified in Chapter 3, "Case Management as Street Level Bureaucracy," the dynamics of organizations and of service situations make the achievement of consumer-driven case management difficult and challenging.

There has been considerable work undertaken to define this archetype, and the models that can be considered consumer-driven ones share certain values. The consumer-driven archetype recognizes the limitations of social welfare arrangements in responding to individuals and humanizing case management practice. There are numerous forces acting to shape the behavior of individuals but few forces acting to shape the performance of social, rehabilitative, and health services to the specifications and expectations of consumers.

Consumers control very little in contemporary social welfare systems, although they may seek control through their behavior, attitudes, and attributions. Services are mediated by organizations and professionals, and these services are not directly accountable to the people who are recipients. Certainly recipients can organize in attempts to exert influence, and enlightened advocates can advance the perspectives and priorities of consumers, but we are a long way from creating systems of human service that are truly informed and driven by what is desired by people who bear the effects of complex social problems.

Nonetheless, the consumer-driven archetype has emerged to counterbalance system control perspectives. *Case management based on this archetype aligns itself with consumers and assists people to organize those supports and services that are most responsive to needs as they define them.* The consumer-driven archetype incorporates five properties that amplify the perspectives and concerns of recipients regarding the purpose and substance of support. First, approaches to case management based on a consumer-driven archetype seek to foster the voice of consumers. Second, they assist consumers to exercise control over the direction and purpose of human services. Third, they seek to promote meaningful choice. Fourth, they value opportunities for consumers to engage in dissent. And fifth, they foster positive reputations among the people they serve. These properties are discussed in more depth in Chapter 8.

This archetype of case management recognizes cost as a very potent force in human services today, but it emphasizes that these costs should not be borne inordinately by consumers and that consumers should not be seen as the principal source of costs either in monetary or behavioral terms. Certain models of case management formulated on this archetype recognize the ethical limitations of system-driven approaches to case management, such as mixed loyalties and conflict of interest, and yet they may not recognize the ethical problems their own approach to practice can create.

The Goal Set of Consumer-Driven Case Management

There are four core goals that compose consumer-driven case management and that define its practice. All four of these goals are framed by a "meta-goal" involving personalization of the consumer and personalization of the service encounter. Personalization in this context refers to the promotion of the personal qualities of the consumer, grounded in an understanding of the person as a cultural and social being who is seeking to exercise control over environmental situations that can be quite demanding and perhaps even hostile. A meta-goal of personalization requires case management to understand the person as an empowered actor (Moxley, 1995a, 1995b) who is using reasonable efforts to accomplish goals or objectives that possess personal meaning. Case management is designed to help the person to gain control over these environmental situations and to achieve what is personally valued and desired. This kind of environmental control is fundamental to the realization of mental health and to personal efficacy. Comparison of the goals listed below to those prioritized by the system-driven archetype reflects the substantive differences between these two case management frameworks.

Responsiveness to Expressed Needs

Most case management alternatives based on a consumer-driven archetype stipulate responsiveness to expressed needs. Unlike system-driven approaches that may adopt a consumer-focused approach in which professionals control the identification of needs, these approaches focus on assisting consumers to identify their own needs and to express what they desire. In rehabilitation case management (Anthony et al., 1988) there is considerable effort in framing aims in terms of the needs that consumers value. The mission of this case management alternative is linked to the field of psychiatric rehabilitation, where emphasis is placed on helping people to define their own conception of success and to achieve personally valued outcomes.

Other approaches to case management seek to understand the person's subjective portrayal of their world and of their situation (Rose, 1992; Rose & Black, 1985). This "subjectification," based on the ideas of Freire (1994, 1968), is a portal through which case management personnel can gain a grounded understanding of a person's life, and of personal experiences—both positive and negative—that can inform and establish the "direction" of case management. This direction is very much informed by what the consumer wants to achieve rather than what a human service system is willing to endorse as a legitimate outcome. And direction itself is framed by the worldview of recipients—people who often confront oppression, victimization, and marginalization in their daily lives. Moxley and Freddolino (1994) identify the importance of basing the aims of case management on the identification of needs and issues faced by people in major life domains.

These alternatives offer strategies for understanding what people want to achieve through the use of case management. But they also have an inherent limitation. It is likely that people will identify basic daily living needs that can be a challenge to fulfill, such as employment and housing. Also, by personalizing these needs, that is, by inquiring, for example, into what people want in housing, consumer-driven approaches to case management risk failing to fulfill these needs after raising the expectations of consumers.

This approach to case management can amplify the inadequacy of many key resources needed and often wanted by people experiencing serious social problems. It highlights the need to link to case management a process of advocacy that assists consumers to bring about what they desire, either working with case management personnel or working in concert with other consumers (Freddolino, Moxley, & Fleishman, 1989).

A Supportive Alliance

Consumer-driven alternatives to case management typically highlight the importance of the relationship between the consumer and the case manager (Moxley & Freddolino, 1994; Rapp, 1992; Rose, 1992). There is the assumption that people bearing the effects of serious social problems like mental illness or domestic violence can experience very alienating conditions that require warm, trust enhancing, and caring responses from human service professionals to offset these negative circumstances (Hodge & Draine, 1993). Typical approaches to "people processing" may reduce the importance of relationship formation and prevent the emergence of an alliance that offers a foundation of support for recipients.

The alliance may be an end in itself since it is seen within the context of consumer-driven models as a way of reducing isolation, increasing social support, offering people a stable source of assistance and affiliation, and improving service satisfaction (Solomon, Draine, & Delaney, 1995). These are seen as relevant achievements that case management offers to people who may often experience oppression and rejection.

Valuing the alliance as a legitimate end reflects a significant difference between system-driven and consumer-driven archetypes. System-driven approaches are likely to be utilitarian in approach and prioritize the achievement of outcomes that are valued by a system such as reducing hospitalization, increasing work, or reducing service utilization. Consumer-driven approaches are likely to be personalized in their approach and value the achievement of collaborative working relationships between case management personnel and recipients found in the extent to which expressed needs are identified, support is increased within the alliance, and the alliance results in the achievement of expressed needs.

Expanding Support

The idea of support is broadly defined within consumer-driven case management alternatives. Freddolino, Moxley, and Fleishman (1989) point out that it is very easy for traditional case management approaches to become encapsulated by the service system that sponsors them, and this can result in the adoption by case management personnel of a very narrow vision of what can be offered in terms of support. Rapp (1992) underscores the importance of broadening the concept of support beyond any one service system to the community at large and of adopting a perspective that defines the community as an amalgam of resources that can be exploited through proactive work undertaken by case management personnel. These perspectives highlight the importance of viewing support as including not only services but supportive relationships, supportive resources, and supportive alliances forged within a community (McKnight, 1989; Kretzman & McKnight, 1993) so as to help people achieve outcomes that are consistent with their preferences, aims, and desires.

The broad range of supports identified within consumer-driven case management alternatives may involve assistive technology, organizational arrangements, innovative self-help approaches, and inclusive arrangements within the community that enable people to take advantage of specific roles and activities (Saleeby, 1992b). Consumer-driven case management alternatives implement a support model in which people are assisted in identifying a personally valued goal and are encouraged to make choices about their lifestyle and living circumstances (e.g., where they want to live). They are then assisted in organizing, implementing, and sustaining supports that are critical to helping them to achieve success in their goal area.

The idea of environmental specificity is incorporated into this support model. Supports are designed and targeted to promote the person's success in a specific environment and specific roles. This archetype of case management, therefore, links personalization to the provision of support and values the tailoring of supports to a person's specific situation (Moxley, 1995a), with the intent of increasing the probability of successful performance. Thus, case management is designed not merely to process people by linking them to services but rather to help people organize supports that result in the fulfillment of their expressed needs and the achievement of a quality of life they find satisfying (Sullivan, 1992).

Personal Influence

Consumer-driven case management alternatives seek to assist people in gaining personal control and influence over the specific situations they face in day-to-day life (Weick, 1992). Thus, this archetype is consistent with practice frameworks that promote mastery, effectance motivation, and self-efficacy (Maluccio, 1981; Saleeby, 1992). These models highlight the importance of the identification of personal wants and desires (i.e., expressed needs) as a strategy for empowering the person and for creating the motivational conditions supportive of self-efficacy and mastery.

These models also place importance on the function of the alliance as a primary support system assisting people in the identification and resolution of barriers that can prevent or frustrate the achievement of their needs and helping sustain people during the difficult process of gaining personal influence over their situations. The expanded notion of support offers specific strategies for helping people to achieve outcomes in real world performance settings. Case management is designed to help people to organize the conditions of personal influence and to sustain the conditions that support effective performance toward personally valued outcomes and objectives.

Critics of this approach to case management may argue that models and approaches based on the consumer-driven archetype are just as coercive as system-driven models. My portrayal of the consumer-driven archetype suggests that people have to perform, and that people are willing to identify what they want to achieve and will undertake the activities to achieve these desired ends. Some individuals may not find this form of self-determination entirely acceptable and may see themselves as merely coerced to perform based ultimately on someone else's values. These alternative values may not prescribe the actual substantive content of the ends but may nonetheless enforce strict expectations that one has to engage in some kind of goal-driven effort.

CONCLUSION

Some of my colleagues in the disability rights movement have suggested that consumer-driven models are indeed new ways of organizing coercion. These colleagues argue that ultimately case management personnel should execute what consumers want and take the necessary action to achieve these outcomes on behalf of consumers, without those consumers feeling obligated to undertake action themselves. From the perspective of these colleagues, this type of action places case management personnel directly in the role of buffer: Their ultimate function is to buffer the consumer from the experience of stress created by an unfair, discriminating, and inequitable social welfare system.

There is probably a third archetype of case management suggested by these criticisms. We can refer to this alternative as a "consumer-controlled" approach to case management. This alternative will be found in situations where case management personnel work directly for consumers, take their direction from consumers, and are directly accountable to consumers because they function as employees or as professional agents who work under contract. Such consumer-controlled alternatives are beginning to emerge as consumers join together to create their own human service organizations or use personal resources to fund case management alternatives, like in the field of head injury rehabilitation.

This third alternative suggests radical change in how we fund, organize, and sustain human services. The system-driven and consumer-driven alternatives coexist within a specific paradigm of human services and social welfare. If consumers become more prominent in human services then perhaps we will see the emergence of more and more consumer-controlled alternatives. Until then case management in human services will be influenced more by system-driven and consumer-driven archetypes, and by the interplay among the many practice models and approaches that reflect the properties of these archetypes.

CHAPTER 3

CASE MANAGEMENT AS STREET LEVEL BUREAUCRACY

This chapter focuses on case management as street level bureaucracy, an idea introduced into the analysis of public service bureaucracies by Lipsky (1980). I use this concept to illustrate some of the issues and challenges faced by human service systems and organizations, and by human service personnel, in trying to use case management to serve people more effectively. Case management as a technology raises important issues about the distribution and allocation of human services and social benefits, and when it is recognized as a form of street level bureaucracy, the issues faced by case management are very similar to those faced by other street level bureaucracies, including welfare, law enforcement, and courts. All of these bureaucracies face serious problems in addressing human needs with limited resources and with limited personnel (Prottas, 1979).

Street level bureaucracies, according to Lipsky, must find ways to cope with the uncertainties inherent in their work, with the absence of strong public consensus about what is the best course of action in a particular social problem area, with moral ambiguity surrounding human services (Hasenfeld, 1983), and with the nature of emotional labor that can so often become taxing, even overwhelming (Hill & Clawson, 1988). Those readers who have worked as case management personnel understand the coping that must be done not only to render "good" or adequate service but also to survive in order to practice another day.

The archetypes identified earlier in this volume do not necessarily control case management practice but more likely serve to inform it. The archetypes suggest patterns of practice and therefore operate on an abstract level as ideals to pursue rather than as strict guidelines or stipulations. The models of case management practice identified within these archetypes are somewhat more concrete representations of practice, but nonetheless they are still abstract. The archetypes and models reflect service ideals, and they are very useful to the conceptualization of a program model and to the orientation of case managers to the nature of practice. These archetypes and related models serve as advanced organizers since they offer cues, concepts, and a frame of reference to practice and lend themselves to the training of case management personnel.

But organizations, programs, personnel, and service recipients have a great deal of discretion when it comes to the implementation of case management practice. Despite idealized forms of case management, the actual character of a case management program may be best seen in its implementation. From a program improvement standpoint—especially when one is interested in using research and evaluation tools to improve case management performance—the departure of a case management program from its idealized form or from its so-called model can be useful in the study of programmatic integrity and validity. For example, we can speak of a discrepancy from a consumer-driven model, and identify ways in which a program can resolve this discrepancy.

However, this prescriptive posture may overlook why there is a discrepancy between the idealized version of the case management model and what is seen in day-to-day practice. Why is it that so many case management programs diverge from the ideals they explicate or promote? Lipsky's notion of street level bureaucracy may offer us some understanding of these discrepancies, and help us to identify those forces or factors emerging in any street level bureaucracy—including case management—that can challenge the programmatic integrity and implementation effectiveness sought by many of us involved in human service and social welfare practice.

CASE MANAGERS AS STREET LEVEL BUREAUCRATS

Defining Street Level Bureaucrat

Street level bureaucrats are those individuals who hold important frontline positions in public and human service organizations that are responsible for interacting with citizens—typically citizens in need—and, as a consequence, are critical to the distribution of something "public," including justice, access, benefits, opportunities, and services. Street level bureaucrats operate at the level of the "street" since it is these individuals with whom citizens are most likely to interact within their initial search for a response to their problem. Street level bureaucrats and the bureaucracies that serve as their hosts are both an expression of social policy. Their existence is mandated, and their roles are formalized, through some kind of social policy mechanism. According to Lipsky (1980), street level bureaucrats are "public service workers who interact directly with citizens in the course of their jobs, and who have substantial discretion over their work. . . (p. 3)."

The history of case management can be interpreted as the history of street level bureaucracies. Case management emerged as a response to the complexity of social problems, and to social policies such as deinstitutionalization, cost containment, service coordination and integration, accountability, and advocacy on the part of groups the members of which often experience discrimination in service encounters. The role of case manager was created to address problems that citizens experienced in their encounters with the very bureaucracies that were ostensibly present to address needs and to deliver benefits. This gives case managers the potential for a strong conflict of interest. They are employed by street level bureaucracies (Ellison et al., 1995). They probably have a mandate to make the very bureaucracies that employ them more responsive to citizens (Williams, 1992). How do case management personnel resolve these potentially conflicting loyalties? It is this kind of dilemma that makes the role of street level bureaucrat ambiguous and potentially stressful.

In a sense, case management emerged out of conflicts that can often arise between social welfare organizations and citizens in need. Much of the case management literature does not argue for radical reorganization of the bureaucracies designed to help people and of those social policies that perpetuate these bureaucracies, but rather argues for incremental or marginal changes to the functioning of these organizations—changes that are designed to make them more accessible, more continuous, more responsive, and more accountable (Abramson, 1986; American Hospital Association, 1992; Applebaum & Christianson, 1988). The case management role perhaps purposively or inadvertently emerged to serve as a buffer either between the organization and the citizen (as in the system-driven form of case management) or between the citizen and the organization (as in the consumer-driven form of case management).

The buffering role of case management is not well developed in the literature, but case managers as street level bureaucrats know well the conflictual nature of their practice and the many problems which they struggle with in order to achieve relevant outcomes. This gives case management a potentially conflictual character—something very consistent with Lipsky's framework of street level bureaucracy (Finch, 1980; Ellison et al., 1995). The work of case management reflects debates about the purpose of human services, the extent to which case management should intrude into the daily lives of citizens, and the "proper"scope of social welfare (Lipsky, 1980).

Despite the controlling features of street level bureaucracies, case managers share with street level bureaucrats a principal characteristic: they have considerable discretion in their work even though their organizations may seek to channel their work in a desired direction (Rossi, 1978). One may think that since case managers are lower level actors who work with people in frontline positions, they have little discretion in their work. Yet, case managers, like other street level bureaucrats, work within loosely coupled systems that need personnel to exercise considerable judgment over who gets served, over the definition of problems, over the distribution of benefits, and over their own motivation to get involved (Brager & Holloway, 1978). Indeed, the actual decisions made by case management personnel, the routines they follow, and the actions they take may actually constitute social policy in action (Neugeboren, 1985). Case managers can shape policy through their discretion and through their encounters with citizens in need in critical arenas like aging, developmental disabilities, mental health care, and health care. They can become active and potent decision makers who help citizens negotiate organizations using creative, inventive, and assertive strategies (Moore, 1987).

Alternatively, case managers have ample opportunity to exclude people from service, to define problems in a manner that fails to lead to eligibility, to prohibit the distribution of benefits, and basically to refuse to serve people who are deemed unworthy. Likewise, they have considerable power to define needs, to create eligibility, and to make services more flexible if they choose to do so (Moore, 1987). This kind of discretion is paramount in systems of human services devoted to responding to the needs of citizens who often possess diminished status. Case management personnel work with people in need—often people whose needs are serious—and if these needs are left unaddressed they can threaten life. Thus, decisions are potentially crucial, and the manner in which case management personnel define and execute their work can have serious ramifications.

I am not necessarily asserting that case management personnel frequently engage in behavior designed to exclude people in need, although this may be a consequence of case management roles embedded in a system-driven archetype. Rather, I identify these as possibilities since few organizations have the resources or management structure to exercise a tight vigilance over case management processes (Hasenfeld, 1983). According to Lipsky, street level bureaucrats can readily change any rule-governed distribution system like a human service just by relaxing the manner in which they implement rules or by tightening up on how rules are implemented.

The Sphere of Work

The sphere of work of case managers as street level bureaucrats is influenced greatly by their power (or their self-perceived power). Many of the case managers I have interacted with over the past five years readily underscore their "powerlessness" in the face of significant work loads, absence of credentials, and considerable distance from sources of authority within their organizations. Yet case managers can readily increase their power through efforts to increase expertise and to acquire know-how that others do not have within the host organization, through a high motivation to get involved and to take responsibility, through the garnering of information that is critical to the organization, and by using their location within the bureaucracy to increase organizational success and effectiveness.

I point out these attributes of the case management position to indicate that case managers are not without power, and that when acting with discretion, they can hold very significant and influential roles within street level bureaucracies (Moore, 1987). The conclusion I make is one consistent with Lipsky's framework: case management personnel as street level bureaucrats have ample opportunity to (1) shape their own roles and practice; (2) influence who gets what benefits, opportunities, services, and supports; (3) influence the performance of their own human service organization; and (4) shape social policy and its implementation. These characteristics of case management roles suggest that case managers can function to shape social policy or at least to influence it at the point of implementation. They are not by necessity passive actors but, if they choose to be, active strategists within bureaucratic contexts (Moore, 1987).

The Conditions of Work

The characteristics of case management work are very consistent with the profile offered by Lipsky of the work undertaken by street level bureaucrats. First, the work itself is very demanding since case management personnel must interact with people in need who often present crises, or unpredictable situations that cannot be readily addressed despite the routines that human service programs attempt to implement in response to uncertainty. The crisis and uncertain nature of case management work can be viewed as an intentional built-in feature. People seek the assistance of case management personnel, and people are directed to these personnel by other street level bureaucrats, because they represent the street level or front-line portal of assistance. Case management personnel often control key systems that have to do with entry into publicly supported human services such as access structures (Applebaum & Austin, 1990), information and linkage (NASW, 1992), eligibility determination, outreach and screening (Davis, 1992), assessment and evaluation (Rothman, 1994), and crisis intervention (First, Greenlee, & Schmitz, 1990).

The work of case managers as street level bureaucrats is very sensitive to resource adequacy and appropriateness. People with serious problems often confront service systems with chronically inadequate or inappropriate resources that lack the kind of robust qualities needed to address the needs and problems presented by recipients (Rothman, 1992). It is likely that demand exceeds supply and that case managers find themselves in a state of overload. Coping with this overload may result in case management systems that merely process people, direct them into inappropriate "routine" services, or create long waiting periods for service. Some case management personnel (and I have witnessed a number of them) may insulate themselves emotionally from the problems people present by disparaging the very people they are mandated to serve, and by focusing more on managing caseloads rather than on changing the systems (or policies) that create service or work problems. Within Lipsky's framework these problems are systemic—they are built into the nature of case management work—because it is difficult to define expectations, and to configure an adequate resource base to serve people with some sense of quality even though the case management literature underscores the important role that case managers should serve in the promotion of quality (Intagliata, 1992; American Hospital Association, 1992).

These factors, all of which define the work situation of case management personnel as street level bureaucrats, are not surprising to those familiar with the nature of social welfare programs and services. Case management represents very difficult work and presents challenges that even the most seasoned and experienced social work and human service professionals are reluctant to embrace, an observation that is consistent with the reluctance of credentialed social workers to engage in case management roles and activities (Moxley & Freddolino, 1994). Four challenges are most salient in case management work: (1) struggling with the service ideal; (2) serving people with diminished status; (3) achieving goals that may conflict in practice; and (4) coping with the demands of case management work.

CHALLENGES TO CASE MANAGEMENT AS STREET LEVEL BUREAUCRACY

Struggling with the Service Ideal

It is probably an understatement to say that much of human service practice is idealized. A considerable portion of undergraduate and graduate education in the human services is devoted to prescriptive perspectives relating to what one "ought to do," and little education is devoted to the realities of practice and to the problems that are inherent in trying to implement idealized perspectives.

The "real" nature of case management can offset the attainment of the ideal, especially when it relates to the achievement of a consumer-driven approach to service. Many of the factors identified above that define the essence of the work of street level bureaucrats offset the implementation of consumer-driven practice, including large caseloads, inadequate resources that combine with the uncertainty of what works, and the unpredictability of the needs presented by recipients (Lipsky, 1980).

At the same time, actual case management practice is often surrounded by moral ambiguity. Case managers may respond to a systemic and community priority of assuring that recipients are employed or at least involved in "gainful activities" when they know that the people they serve may not want to engage in these activities. The idealized vision of case management practice may suggest starting with the consumer, but pressures exerted by the community and its representatives may escalate expectations involving the prescription of outcome and effectiveness.

A struggle with the service ideal may express itself in case management practice in different ways. First, it may emerge as resentment or disillusionment on the part of case management personnel, who cope with this dilemma by changing their expectations of clients, by discrediting recipients, or by losing their motivation to serve people or to extend themselves. Second, it may express itself as a reaction formation among personnel who cling rigidly to official definitions of what is desired or what is an appropriate (or acceptable) outcome. Third, it may be demonstrated as a discrediting of the service ideal and a reluctance to engage in service innovation or improvement strategies designed to move closer to the ideal.

Very talented case managers may soon fall prey to what is described as "burnout" because of the absence of supports that help them address and resolve the discrepancies that exist between service realities and service ideals. Case management programs that want to address this challenge may do so through continuing education about the realities of practice and how to address them through strategies taken from idealized versions of practice; through developmental supervision that helps personnel address the personal consequences of service realities (Bunker & Wijnberg, 1988); and through quality improvement strategies that help personnel examine discrete processes and improve their performance over time.

Serving People with Diminished Status

Recipients of case management services, like recipients of most services offered by street level bureaucrats, are frequently racially, socially, economically, and linguistically different from the providers of those services. This discrepancy between server and served is probably one of the most salient characteristics separating the work of street level bureaucracies from other kinds of service work.

One of the most serious problems created by this challenge is the likelihood that case managers will not see the people they serve as a significant reference group informing their work and guiding their practice (Lipsky, 1980). Street level bureaucrats can take their guidance from the people or positions who oversee their work, from a community ethos, from their own profession, or from their own beliefs. The absence of identifying with consumers or recipients can create substantial social distance expressed in negative attitudes, inaccurate stereotypes, and program policies and procedures built on negative assumptions about service candidates.

I observed an interesting "natural experiment" in which an agency created two entrances to their service system. One was reserved for people with insurance who could pay for psychotherapy, counseling, and family work, while another entrance was reserved for people with serious mental illness who were recipients of case management services. Focus groups and attitudinal surveys conducted revealed that the staff serving the more affluent group readily identified with the problems, concerns, and situations of their recipients, while the other staff did not perceive the people they served in a very positive light, and in fact, saw them as problematic and frustrating. Perhaps it is true that this latter group—people with serious mental illness who were for the most part poor—were more demanding and more problematic than the group receiving traditional mental health services. But what is important here is whether these individuals served as a reference group to guide the work of the staff who were in case management roles. Much of the data suggested that they were not seen as a reference group primarily because they were seen as very different from those who offered case management. And, the agency did little to promote this identification—a potential threat to the adoption by staff of advocacy, quality improvement, and service enhancement activities framed by the needs and perspectives identified by consumers.

Staff may also fear assuming the diminished status of the people they serve. The agency discussed above elevated the status of those people who served affluent clients and reduced the status of those people who served people with serious mental illness who had few personal resources. This diminished status within the agency was expressed in several different ways involving the absence of a career line for case management personnel, less investment in professional development for case management personnel, and negative attitudes held by administrators that served to reduce the importance of the work engaged in by case managers.

This challenge can express itself in several ways. First, staff may lower their expectations of the people they serve, and attribute to them inaccurate and stereotypic qualities like not wanting to have a good home, failing to be motivated, or being preoccupied with only fulfilling the most basic of needs. Second, staff may exhibit a reluctance to identify with the plight of the people they serve, and discount the seriousness of the situations people face in their day-to-day lives. Third, staff may engage in activities, often unconsciously, that increase the social distance between themselves and recipients by dressing differently or expensively, using different language, or setting hours that favor their own lifestyles and not those of the people they serve.

Coming to grips with the perspectives and needs of the people served and gaining an understanding of those forces that serve to diminish the status of recipients may be crucial in making a case management initiative more responsive to the people it serves. This kind of information can offer more accurate stereotypes and help influence the formation of more positive attitudes. In addition, a case management program seeking to be more responsive to the people it serves may look at its staffing characteristics and intentionally change them to be more consistent with the racial, linguistic, ethnic, and socioeconomic characteristics of its recipients. Yet all of these assume that recipients of case management are an important reference group, one whose perspectives need to be considered in framing service delivery.

Merely staffing differently, however, may not address the emergence of social distance between those who offer case management services and those who receive them. The program may need to undertake an intentional strategy of increasing the visibility of recipients as a reference group from which case managers take their cue, an effort that may require innovative interactions between recipients and providers, educational events involving both recipients and providers, and ways of evaluating service delivery from the perspectives of recipients themselves.

Achieving Goals That May Conflict in Practice

Case management as street-level bureaucracy is prone to a goal mix whose elements can often conflict in practice. Case managers often operate within ambiguous environments in which the purpose and commitment to addressing social problems can be discounted by community elites and by the general citizenry. The goal set of case management often reflects the very conflicts created by a clash between the system-driven and consumer-driven archetypes. While the former demands the achievement of efficiency, the latter demands the achievement of outcomes that bring satisfaction to recipients, that is, of consumer responsiveness.

This form of conflict is built into case management practice, and its toll can be great for case management personnel. Lipsky points out that street-level bureaucrats work in jobs with conflicting and ambiguous goals. For case management this means consumer-driven goals may conflict with social engineering goals when, for example, a homeless outreach program attempts to meet those needs identified as important by homeless people, and fails to address the social engineering goals of assuring that people are off the street and in shelters. Or, for case management, this means that consumer-driven goals may conflict with organization-centered goals when the organization places a quota on the number of cases, the processing of cases, mass production, and the routinization of service. This means that consumer-driven goals may conflict with role expectations. For example, mental health case managers may need to organize services outside of the formal mental health system in order to prevent psychiatric problems and crises among the people they serve, but this may conflict with role expectations that case management personnel only focus on medication compliance and medication management.

Goal conflict may express itself in several different ways. It may show up when case management programs are evaluated and data show that case managers are performing according to their role expectations but demonstrating little effectiveness in helping people to resolve problems. Or goal conflict can emerge when the case management program focuses on indicators of effort and not effectiveness. Case management, therefore, becomes the processing of an appropriate number of cases or the delivery of a certain number and type of services. Third, this challenge may emerge when staff reframe their role expectations to become more responsive to the needs of the people they serve, and conflict between administration and case management personnel results from discrepancies in definitions of what is proper and appropriate service delivery.

This challenge reflects the importance of examining the goal set of case management and the importance of looking at goals in conjunction with administrators, staff, funders, and recipients and their advocates. The measurement of goals can drive the culture of any organization (Schein, 1992), and so they deserve considerable dialogue, critique, and development. This stakeholder approach to goal formulation will most likely reflect the conflict that operates in street level bureaucracies, and it highlights the importance of treating recipients as distinctive, important, and legitimate stakeholders and ultimately as a critical reference group whose perspectives are vital to the creation of a viable and effective case management program. Leadership within the case management program, and within the host organization, needs to focus on formulating a goal set that is truly sensitive not only to what people want the program to be, but also to the possibility of the emergence of goal conflict created by discrepancies between what consumers want and what organizations want; between what consumers want and what social engineering desires; and between what consumers want and what role expectations say is legitimate practice. The quest for harmony within the goal set of case management may be a critical (although elusive) feature of program integrity.

Coping with the Demands of Case Management Work

One of the most frustrating aspects of case management work is the strain created between personalized service and bureaucratic routine. According to Lipsky, this strain is rampant in the work of street level bureaucrats. From my observation of case management programs, it is one of the most significant challenges to the realization of consumer-driven practice. This strain is often a product of trying to reconcile idealized practice with the demands created by day-to-day delivery of case management services. As emphasized by Lipsky, coping with the discrepancy between the real and the ideal results in practices that are often negative and that reduce the personalization of public services.

Negative coping practices can take on different forms. They can range from ones that create negative reputations and negative stereotypes of recipients to the preferential selection and cooling out of applicants of service (Rossi, 1978). These, in conjunction with rationing, favoritism, intentional efforts to lower the expectations of recipients, and intentionally frustrating recipients, combine to "help" case management personnel manage the flow of people and the delivery of service, and to bring demand into line with supply (Lipsky, 1980).

Lipsky refers to these practices as informal coping approaches because they are not formally or explicitly sanctioned by the street level bureaucracy—in our case, case management programs. Yet they serve as ways to manipulate the service environment and to help case managers cope with what can be very uncertain situations created by people experiencing the effects of serious social problems. I want to underscore the idea of coping. Case management programs are no different from other street level bureaucracies. There is no potential limit on service and resource demands, and people—recipients, funders, and regulators—often lack the requisite information to understand precisely what the actual limits of a case management service program are in reality. Indeed, I have seen many decision makers and actors external to a case management program make assumptions that programmatic capacity is limitless primarily because they do not think in rational terms about how much service is actually available. Simply speeding up the process can have serious implications for programmatic quality, stability, and legitimacy (Gutek, 1995).

This zone of uncertainty created around a case management initiative may be driving the informal coping strategies used by case management personnel. The uncertainty about the extent of client problems and of consumer demand does not typically lead a program to consider innovative ways of addressing utilization, but more likely results in the erection of barriers that ultimately increase the recipients' costs of utilization. Thus, it is probably ridiculous to act as if people who use publicly supported human services do not really pay for their use, since they often pay through their efforts to deal with the coping barriers that may be informally erected by case management programs and their personnel.

Bringing these negative coping efforts into the consciousness of case management personnel is very difficult and demands sensitive consideration. The coping efforts are typically surrounded by a great deal of denial, and often are reinforced by emotions, attitudes, and stereotypes directed toward administrators higher up in the bureaucracy who may be seen as uncaring, as well as toward recipients, who may be seen as demanding, unrelenting, inconsiderate, and undeserving. Programs that are alert to the possibility of these barriers becoming established features of service delivery may respond by putting into place external evaluation programs that specifically address the process of service delivery and the detection of negative unintended consequences or outcomes. Yet even this act probably requires the case management program and its personnel to value consumer-driven service, and to identify with the people they serve as a principal reference group informing case management practice.

CONCLUSION

The service ideal of consumer-driven practice holds great promise as a framework and advanced organizer of case management. Yet this paper highlights that the achievement of this ideal is fraught with a number of challenges that have the potential of reframing the actual practice of case management. The idea that case management programs, as street level bureaucracies, can control the distribution of services, benefits, and opportunities through formal and informal decisions is an important one that must be attended to by people responsible for the design, implementation, and evaluation of these programs.

This abbreviated analysis of case management programs as street level bureaucracies, and of case management personnel as street level bureaucrats, underscores the importance of the following programmatic needs in formulating more effective case management initiatives:

1. The need to make explicit the actual design of the case management initiative and to base this design on the input and perspectives of multiple stakeholders who deliberate the purpose, goal set, and principal processes of case management.
2. The need to see design as a continuous process of improvement requiring ongoing issue identification, planning, action, and evaluation as well as dialogue among stakeholders about purpose, quality, programmatic features, and effectiveness (Rothman & Thomas, 1994).
3. The need to protect recipients as a principal reference group of the case management program and its personnel, and the need to assure their input and evaluation during the process of case management implementation.
4. The need to identify informal coping processes emerging during implementation that can create negative externalities for recipients and erect bar-

riers to reaching those individuals who can benefit from case management the most.

5. The need to understand from the perspective of case management personnel the challenges involved in offering responsive, consumer-driven case management programs, and the problems that can erode or otherwise degrade the attainment of this ideal (Rapp, 1993).

6. The need to see the realization of consumer-driven case management process as a "work in progress"—one that is very sensitive to its environment and can take on the worst characteristics of street level bureaucracy if left unattended and ungroomed.

7. The need to train case management personnel in a strategic framework that promotes their capacities for inventive and creative problem-solving (Bricker-Jenkins, 1992) within constrained and bureaucratized service environments (Moore, 1987).

These seven needs reflect the complexity of case management programs that are responsive to the people they serve. The needs themselves require sensitive listening to various constituencies, but most of all require or demand a very sensitive ear to the perspectives and concerns articulated by those receiving services and those providing services on the front line. Achieving consumer-driven practice is no easy task. It really does require the joining of idealized conceptions of practice with what occurs in day-to-day practice. Without vigilance it is very easy for case management programs to drift in ways that users and providers may ultimately find problematic.

PART II

DEVELOPING CASE MANAGEMENT PROGRAMS AND IMPROVING THEIR IMPLEMENTATION

INTRODUCTION TO PART II

Much of my consultation work in the field of case management has addressed program development issues, especially ones emanating from the actual design of case management programs to fit the requirements of a local human service system. This work has offered me an opportunity to work with teams of administrators, service providers, and consumers in the design of case management programs and systems. And much of the knowledge and information presented in the following four chapters reflect what I have learned through these opportunities to consult with a diversity of human service organizations in the formulation and implementation of case management designs.

All four chapters relate specifically to the theme of program development and implementation. Content included in Chapter 4 makes use of much of the material offered in the previous chapters. I identify the critical steps a design team moves through in the creation and formulation of a case management program. Embedded within these steps are critical decisions and decision alternatives that will shape the subsequent character of the case management program. These are considered in a systematic manner, and their consequences are weighed in terms of their implications for subsequent implementation of the case management program.

Chapter 5 examines an effort on the part of a community mental health board to transform case management into community support practice. Case management designed to serve people with psychiatric disabilities often is implemented within a framework of community support (Moxley, 1995b; Anthony & Blanch, 1989; Aviram, 1990; Baker & Intagliata, 1984). Indeed, models of community support posit case management as an integral and core element of service (Stroul, 1989; 1993). Based on qualitative data derived from focus groups, challenges in making case management responsive to the needs of consumers within the context of community support are identified. The content offered in this paper serves to further develop the issues identified and discussed in Chapter 6.

Chapter 6 examines improvement themes derived from three consultation projects. These themes cluster in specific areas demonstrating the importance of monitoring case management implementation in relationship to client characteristics (Clark, Landis, & Fisher, 1990), staffing, the ongoing support of staff, and the role definitions and status of staff members, recipients, and supporters of recipients; organizational placement of the case management program (Piette, Fleishman, Mor, & Dill, 1990); the adequacy of community resources available to serve recipients and respond effectively to the needs they present (Cambridge, 1992); and the program theory guiding the delivery of case management services and their impact on recipients. These themes are offered to readers in order to alert them to the possibility that even though the aims of a program are clearly identified, problems can emerge during actual implementation of case management. Indeed, implementation effectiveness is a crucial aspect of making case management work well (Williams, Forster, McCarthy, & Hargreaves, 1994).

Chapter 7 examines the application of Total Quality Management to the improvement of a case management program, the early implementation of which proved to be very problematic within the context of a comprehensive community mental health agency. The chapter outlines an approach to quality improvement that addresses many of the issues identified in the previous two chapters.

These chapters taken together hopefully will increase the fund of knowledge that readers have about case management program design. Readers can project themselves into design roles and attempt to envision the substantive character of the case management program they wish to bring into existence. The very real challenges inherent in making case management work for a specific recipient population do not become apparent until people actually try to design a program and implement it.

CHAPTER 4

A FRAMEWORK FOR THE DEVELOPMENT OF CASE MANAGEMENT PROGRAMS

A version of this chapter appeared as "Outpatient Program Development," Chapter 6 of *Outpatient Case Management* (American Hospital Publishing, 1994), edited by Michelle Regan Donovan and Theodore Matson. Given the many factors influencing case management, the development of case management programs is a complex process that requires systematic thinking by those individuals who compose a design team. This chapter organizes many of the salient variables and places them into a framework to guide the formulation and development of case management programs. The importance of gaining a clear understanding of the purpose of the case management initiative has been a recurring theme in previous chapters. Certainly in the development of effective case management programs, resolving the issue of case management purpose serves as a vital advanced organizer to program development.

The ubiquity of case management in health and human services testifies to its growing popularity as a means of achieving policy and programmatic goals that may, however, conflict in actual practice. In one form, case management is viewed as a tool to forge a more efficient service system by administratively managing the delivery of care, gatekeeping, or rationing. In another form, case management is seen as a means of proactively representing the perspectives of consumers, patients, and clients who can often become stymied by potentially unresponsive service system or who can experience frustration in their attempts to communicate their needs to multiple providers (Freddolino, Moxley, & Fleishman, 1989). Conflicting tendencies exist in this field: Is case management designed to enable systems to better manage people and the resources these systems say these people need or are otherwise mandated to provide? Is it designed to help people to better manage the services, supports, and resources they need or want? Or, does case management need to reconcile these different ends by struggling to accommodate multiple value sets created by differential emphases placed by organizations on efficiency, effectiveness, equity, and the preferences and desires of recipients (Dill, 1987; Netting, 1992)?

FACTORS INFLUENCING CASE MANAGEMENT PURPOSE

Addressing these various purposes of case management has been tackled in human services in a variety of ways and, therefore, diverse approaches to case management have emerged in response to variations in policy mandates, economic issues, philosophical commitments, social problem and health concerns, professional discipline and socialization, and consumer activism, to identify only a few salient factors. The proliferation of case management is visible when we organize human services into their constituent sectors. Implementation of case management occurs in maternal and child health services, aging, developmental disabilities, mental health and psychiatric rehabilitation, head injury rehabilitation, immigration, income maintenance, primary health care, job training, managed health care, and child welfare (Maternal and Child Health Bureau, 1994; Applebaum & Austin, 1990; Arkansas Department of Human Services, 1984; Bachrach, 1989; Baerwald, 1983; Baier, 1987; Brindis, Barth, & Loomis, 1987; Cheung, Stevenson, & Leung, 1991; Cohen & DeGraaf, 1982; Davis, 1992; Dixon, Goll, & Stanton, 1988; Like, 1988).

The diversity is extensive. To lay people and professionals alike, such diversity may appear senseless and duplicative. But this diversity needs to be understood as a product of attempts, however awkward, to offer health and human services within an integrated, cross-system framework that must address the multiple determinants of functioning, including biological, environmental, social, psychological, and cultural factors (Susser, Hopper, & Richman, 1983). In this manner, whether case management is tied to maintaining the health and functioning of people who are well or at risk, or helping people with disabilities enjoy a decent quality of life, the emergence of case management is linked to a modern recognition that health, illness, and disability are best understood within the context of a multivariate and complex model of determinants (Institute of Medicine, 1991). Therefore, delivery systems themselves must respond to this complexity through complex programmatic arrangements.

There are other social, policy, and technological factors that are driving forces influencing the ubiquity of case management. Deinstitutionalization, home-based care, increasing lifespans, the interaction of poor health status with other social problems like poverty, the reality of serious disability and resulting social dependency, the husbanding of precious resources, and cost control are some of these driving forces (Moxley, 1989). An influential driving force is a societal commitment to delivering services outside the boundaries of major institutions and within smaller, community-based facilities, ones consistent with the principles of normalization and community integration. The perceived need for case management can usually be linked to some policy mandate that underscores the high worth attributed to this form of social intervention.

Specific models of case management include clinical case management (Harris & Bachrach, 1988; Harris & Bergman, 1993), rehabilitation case management (Roessler & Rubin, 1982), brokering forms of case management, and case management systems that address the integration of multiple providers into a matrix of interdisciplinary practice. This list of case management models—and the fields or sectors of human services within which they are implemented—does not exhaust the possibilities. Suffice it to say: Case management is in "good currency." It is often seen as a means of connecting people to systems, systems to people, and systems to systems on behalf of people with multiple, complex, and long term service and support needs (Barker, 1987). By virtue of this diversity, it can be seen that case management means many things, and it can mean different things to different people.

Variation in policy mandates, programmatic purposes and functions, models, staffing, and recipient groups creates challenges for meaningful and effective case management program development. It is the purpose of this chapter to highlight and discuss critical variables involved in case management program development and to identify the challenges these factors can create. I do not offer recipes for resolving these challenges. Rather, my purpose is to sensitize readers to a number of the factors that can be considered when conceptualizing, designing, developing, and evaluating case management programs.

GETTING STARTED WITH CASE MANAGEMENT PROGRAM DEVELOPMENT

There are many factors shaping both the form and substance of a case management program. These factors include the actual social or human problem a service seeks to address as well as policy and administrative mandates and stakeholder perspectives. Initiating program development in case management requires designers to take these factors into consideration and to anticipate how they can influence the purpose and design of the case management initiative.

Social and Human Problems

Human service programs must often respond to diverse populations whose human problems are created or influenced by serious social problems. These problems are often complex and reflect interacting conditions. My experience in working with an urban outpatient health service targeting people who were homeless and were coping with mental illness illustrates the necessity of viewing people's problems within a broad social matrix of factors that create and sustain people's problems. Combining physical health services, mental health outreach services, and social services into a complex model of service delivery reflected the very complexity of the social problem this program was designed to address. The resulting case management program needed to be informed about the diverse and multiple needs of this target population and to reflect on how these needs shape its purpose (Moxley & Freddolino, 1991). The program simply did not enjoy the luxury of drawing the line at responding only to the physical or mental health needs of its recipients.

Getting started with case management program development requires human service providers to examine the target population and to identify the social problems and health concerns of the people who will be using case management. Given the covariation among many social problems, needs relating to basic living resources, entitlements, health education, outreach, and on-going medical management may be salient. Thus, it is likely that some form of case management needs assessment conducted on a community basis will be required in order to initiate sound program development. To assure that the case management program will be sensitive to different perspectives, a multi-method approach to needs assessment may be required. Integrating epidemiological analysis, key informant interviews, and the perspectives of potential recipients themselves will enable human service providers to consider both the quantitative and qualitative dimensions of the needs that will inform case management design. Consumer perspectives are especially important because they may prioritize very practical and essential needs relating to survival and community living over clinical needs that appear to providers to be the most salient and important to fulfill (Freddolino, Moxley, & Fleishman, 1988).

In those programmatic situations in which case management will make use of community resources to address the needs of recipients, design teams will want to conduct an asset assessment of the local community in order to identify hidden resources, informal helping resources, and self-help opportunities (McKnight, 1989; Kretzman & McKnight, 1993). The assessment of community assets demonstrates the close linkage that can be realized between a case management initiative and a local community. Thus, the identification of community strengths to meet identified consumer needs can be a significant and necessary aspect of the early stages of case management program development (Rapp & Wintersteen, 1989; Rapp, 1992).

The Policy Space of Case Management

Human service programs are typically influenced by a set of policies that mandate their implementation or, at least, strongly encourage their development (Berk & Rossi, 1990). Such is the situation with case management. For example, Public Law 99-660 identifies the necessity of offering coordinated and integrated service delivery to people with severe and persistent psychiatric problems, while Public Law 99-457 (Peterson, 1989) requires local communities to create interagency structures for the integration of those services for young children with developmental challenges and those for their families using case management approaches at the client level of service.

In conjunction with needs and asset assessments, case management program developers can examine and analyze relevant policies as well as either administrative or regulatory mandates by federal, state, and accreditation bodies. Information obtained from a review of these mandates can help identify the aims of the case management program, especially when considered in conjunction with the social problems, health concerns, and resource needs of the intended target population. Other standards can be factored into this initial inquiry. The social work profession (NASW, 1992; Brennan & Kaplan, 1993), and the American Hospital Association (Rose, 1992), for example, have identified standards, functions, and activities for case management services.

A close examination of the policy space of case management, related administrative mandates, and standards promulgated by professional or provider groups, in conjunction with an understanding of the need for case management within a local community, can reveal the goal mix of case management programs. As emphasized in Chapter 3, these goals can often conflict in practice, creating tension and disappointment for consumers, case management staff, and the host organization.

Eight objectives appear prominent in the literature on case management but do not necessarily exhaust the possibilities, given the diversity and ubiquity of case management services that has emerged in contemporary human services. The existence of these multiple goals suggests that it is difficult to create an encompassing definition of case management that offers unity to this field of human service practice (Bachrach, 1989, 1992a). Clarity of objectives, however, becomes an important design criterion supporting the achievement of an effective and well focused programmatic effort. These goals are:

1. Assuring the coordination and integration of services in order to achieve continuity, often implemented through individualized service plans involving multiple providers and disciplines working collaboratively with the consumer and monitoring the delivery of services across service domains and across time (Bachrach, 1981; Granet & Talbot, 1978; Parker & Secord, 1988).

2. Monitoring the quality of service delivery by examining what is provided, when, and perhaps how (Intagliata, 1982).
3. Exercising social control by reaching out to members of high risk groups whose health or behavioral status may jeopardize themselves or other members of the community; engaging these individuals in a relationship; and monitoring them over time, often with the aim of gaining their compliance with a medical, service, or behavioral regimen (Draine & Solomon, 1994; Durell, Lechtenburg, Corse, & Frances, 1993; Dvoskin & Steadman, 1994).
4. Offering social support to people who may be isolated, stigmatized, or rejected by significant others because of their health status, behavior, or violation of social norms (Baker & Weiss, 1984), and seeking to improve the functioning of people whose performance may be limited due to disability (Stroul, 1989, 1993).
5. Organizing instrumental assistance so that people obtain support to execute the necessary tasks of daily living or have these tasks undertaken for them in the least restrictive setting, often achieved by arranging basic supports like respite care, homemaker services, home health assistance, mobility assistance, or meal and nutritional care (Bogdonoff, Hughes, Weissert, & Paulsen, 1991).
6. Engaging in cost and resource management so that either cost avoidance, cost effectiveness, or efficiency is achieved, typically through utilization management, gatekeeping, and prior authorization activities (Skarnulis, 1989).
7. Serving as an advocate to assure that recipients' needs are identified and fulfilled on a timely basis or to assure that recipients' rights are respected and addressed during the course of service delivery (Moxley & Freddolino, 1990).
8. Buffering the stress people can experience as a consequence of their interactions with the regimented and bureaucratic culture of human services.

The diversity of these goals reflects the challenge inherent in packaging case management and achieving a clear sense of its purpose and subsequent outcomes (Ashley, 1988). Case management programs are often a blend of administrative, management, evaluative, and psychosocial functions organized to address the delivery of services at several levels including the individual recipient, the service system, and the general community. The tension that can be created by the resulting goal mix is exemplified by the dilemmas involved in serving people with multiple, complex, and interacting conditions who require high levels of resource commitment while trying perhaps to ration the range, volume, and intensity of services required by these recipients. Case management mirrors the growing controversies in health care involving dignity, relevance and sensitivity of services, cost control, and quality assurance.

Stakeholder Perspectives

Many groups and individuals have a stake in shaping the purpose and expected outcomes of a case management program or system. Certainly among these many groups are administrators, health and human service disciplines, provider groups, funders, regulators, and recipients and their significant others and advocates. Such pluralism means that each group may expect something different of the case management program, and the involvement of these groups will help shape the subsequent focus of the program. Key decisions in getting started involve the identification of stakeholders and of the extent to which such groups are to be involved in the planning process. Obtaining their input as part of the needs assessment process will assist program developers in capturing the range of perspectives and expectations of these various audiences (Witkin, 1984).

Formulation of an Initial Purpose

A product of this phase of program development is an initial and perhaps rough understanding of the purpose of the case management program. This purpose is an outcome of a consideration of many influences creating a perceived need for case management by the various stakeholders involved in the development of such a program. Getting started in the program development process can involve data collection, policy analysis, stakeholder involvement, environmental scanning, and a reflection on the motivations of the sponsoring organization to add this component. Understanding the community living, human service, and support needs of the intended beneficiaries, and adding to these data the policy and administrative mandates, will assist program developers to begin to shape an initial purpose and working mission of case management within the sponsoring organization and within the community that will serve as the ultimate host of the program.

    The relevance of this mission can be further strengthened by considering the input, desires, and expectations of key stakeholder groups. Yet a critical decision is in the hands of the program developers: given this initial and formative exploration, what will case management achieve, and why is this purpose important to the mission of the organization?

UNDERSTANDING THE CONTEXT OF CASE MANAGEMENT SERVICE DELIVERY

The initial working mission of the case management program can be further refined through an analysis of its actual context. Of concern here is gaining an understanding of the specific situation in which the case management program must operate and within which it will be implemented. Three types of context can be considered, involving the community context in which the program will be operating, the health and human service system within which it will be implemented, and the specific organization that will serve as the host to the program.

Community Context

Case management programs implemented in rural and urban settings face different challenges. Rural communities offer strengths on which a case management program can capitalize (Baker & Intagliata, 1984; DeWeaver & Johnson, 1983). People may be more likely to know one another in a rural community, and case finding, social supports, and norms that support friendly visiting and self-help may be strong. Thus, case management programs seeking to incorporate informal support, self-help, and community involvement and action may be able to make use of these rural attributes.

Alternatively, rural communities can create some significant challenges for case management programs. Transportation systems may be underdeveloped, which means that potential recipients can become easily isolated. In one rural community it was found that the case management system was coping with the absence of public transportation. Thus, the system needed to be designed on an outreach basis so that case managers had a lot of physical mobility. Much of the time of case managers was invested in driving to recipients' homes and assisting these individuals directly with transportation in order to assure their linkage to needed and appropriate health and human services. The impact on case management productivity is obvious. The absence of agency automobiles, vans, or other vehicles meant that case managers had to rely on their own cars and cope with the stress created by the wear and tear on themselves and their autos.

Many rural communities simply do not have a diverse and elaborate network of health and human service providers. Often these communities have a community hospital, several private practitioners, and perhaps a handful of generalist human service agencies. Within this context, implementing a brokering approach to case management—involving the linkage of people to relevant health and human service providers as the principal aim of case management—is very problematic (Rothman, 1992). In addition, achieving interagency coordination of services may be very difficult because of constraints on the availability of providers (Rothman, 1992). I have found that in some rural communities case managers assist recipients and family members to migrate from their home communities to urban areas so recipients can obtain necessary services and supports.

Finally, the closely knit character of many rural communities may mean that attitudes are easily solidified and reinforced. Some communities may have low tolerance for deviance. Strong negative attitudes toward people with serious health, psychiatric, and behavioral problems may exist and, therefore, recipients may be easily stigmatized, may be labeled as poor candidates for service, and may experience high levels of discrimination or outright rejection as a result of their visibility within the community. In one situation, a client with serious mental illness and with a major health problem was "cooled out" by the local hospital and physicians because she was seen as uncooperative, noncompliant, and childish and demanding in her interactions. Health providers withdrew preventive, monitoring, and outreach services, and the recipient began to postpone treatment until a health crisis forced her to contact emergency medical services. Despite her high utilization of expensive health resources, the attitudes of primary health providers reduced their case management effectiveness. Although this case is not unique to rural health systems, it does illustrate the potency of provider attitudes on the provision of coordinated and integrated health services, and it shows how these attitudes can be reinforced within dense community networks.

Urban contexts may offer people with potentially stigmatizing problems more anonymity than rural situations. Tolerance for diversity, deviance, and alternative lifestyles may be higher in urban areas than in rural communities. Case management programs may also enjoy stronger service infrastructures composed of an array of public, private, and nonprofit health and human service providers. And, despite severe cutbacks in transportation resources experienced by many urban centers, they still have public bus systems, connector systems, and paratransit alternatives to support the mobility of recipients.

Yet urban contexts offer other challenges to case management program development. Urban health, mental health, and social service systems are often overloaded, given the concentration of potential recipients within our urban centers and the complexity of problems these individuals pose to service delivery systems. Health problems interacting with homelessness, substance use, mental illness, or family disorganization are not uncommon in our urban centers. Thus, those outpatient health services based in urban centers cannot easily isolate health problems from other social, psychological, and behavioral conditions. Urban case management systems must increasingly address comprehensive needs that often are products of interacting social problems.

Violence and other social control problems may be prevalent in urban centers, and in some cases they are perceived to be at epidemic levels (Devore, 1995). And it is not unusual that case managers have to create interfaces between outpatient health services, police departments, court systems, and jails or correction facilities (Steadman, McCarty, & Morrissey, 1989). Case managers themselves may often deal with risk situations and potential violence as assertive outreach approaches take case managers into neighborhoods where personal safety can be compromised or threatened.

The community context within which the case management program will be embedded must be examined closely. Certainly the salient and hidden strengths of each community must be identified, and the contribution of these strengths to the purpose, aims, and implementation of the case management program can be considered by program developers (Rapp, 1992). In one community, it was found that a committed downtown YMCA facilitated the collaboration between health and mental health providers and businesses to establish an outreach health program for homeless people in the central city business loop. Attention must also be paid to how structural weaknesses existing in the community, such as inadequate mental health services or housing, may influence how the case management program will undertake its work. Inadequacies in a service system may require the case management program to engage in service system development, advocacy, and community development efforts (Moxley, 1989; NASW, 1992; Steinberg & Carter, 1983).

System Context

Case management also may unfold within the context of complex service systems that have been formed through collaborative agreements, consortia arrangements, or the integration of programs or agencies into multi-provider systems. System context may influence the programmatic configuration of case management (Abrahams & Leutz, 1983). Within some health systems, case management programs may be internally driven, while in other health systems, case management may be externally driven. Of course, a mix of internal and external orientations may prevail.

Internal case management may be more directed to administrative oversight of service delivery. The case management program may function truly as a "manager of service" with authority to monitor service delivery and to identify issues pertaining to utilization, quality, cost, and effectiveness (Gottesman, Ishizaki, & MacBride, 1979). In this situation, the case manager may act as an internal correction to the system, working with case-level and aggregate data to control service delivery. Case managers also may fulfill such roles in managed care situations in which utilization management is likely to be a principal aim.

Another form of internal case management may involve offering assistance to recipients as they move through a complex service delivery system (Granet & Talbot, 1978). The case manager in this situation may assure that the identified needs of the consumer are met and that the consumer traverses the necessary services, systems, and departments in a timely manner to fulfill these needs. In one specialized rehabilitation facility addressing the needs of children with developmental disabilities, a case manager is assigned to families as they enter initial assessment to assure that these families move through the interdisciplinary process in an effective and sensitive manner and that the identified needs of children and families are addressed by appropriate disciplines. In this situation the case management function culminates in the collation of essential interdisciplinary data, input, and plans and in the interpretation of this material for the family in planning for the next steps in service delivery. The case manager in this sense manages the client pathway, the movement of the recipients through this pathway, and the troubleshooting of problems, all of which are articulated to achieve service integration (Gerhard, Dorgan, & Miles, 1981; Curtis, 1974, 1979). It also illustrates the importance of assuring recipients of at least one dedicated relationship with a professional during the complex course of service.

Case managers may take external orientations. Some service systems can comprehensively address the health and human service needs of recipients in a so-called seamless manner often sought through capitation arrangements (Myers & Hall, n.d.; Mechanic, 1991, 1994). Yet there may be entitlement and benefit, social support, and other services that the system cannot offer or is unwilling to offer. Thus, the case manager follows along and monitors the status of recipients to assure appropriate connections to necessary services, supports, and benefits. The case manager may also follow the recipient after discharge or between episodes of illness to assure that linkage and engagement continues, that a person does not become isolated, and that essential needs are addressed and fulfilled. Although case managers, in this situation, may be part of a larger system, they may concentrate their attention on the external community situation of the recipient. Under these circumstances the case manager may be more of an organizer of resources, an ongoing supporter of the recipient, and a developer of individualized support systems—a model of case management consistent with the aims of community support.

Finally, some systems may support independently organized and autonomous case management agencies. One function of such agencies is to address comprehensively the case management of specific target populations but not to offer any direct services. Health and human service programs may interface with such agencies in addressing the needs of specific populations such as children in the child welfare system, people with developmental disabilities, and people with serious mental illness. Multiple case management programs may exist in one locale, and it is important for providers to understand the differences in mission and purpose, redundancy, duplication, and potential areas of conflict.

Organizational Context

Examination of the host organization of the case management program offers other contextual considerations for the design of case management. Certainly program developers will want to examine carefully the mission, values, and purposes of the host organization to assure consonance between its culture and the new program. A principle of successful program implementation requires a new program to be consistent with the culture of the host in order to promote acceptance, integration, and use of the new programmatic resource.

The disciplinary orientation of the host organization is an essential consideration in case management program development. In settings that operate along formal disciplinary lines, with distinct roles defined for physicians, nurses, social workers, and other professionals, the issues of who should undertake case management, the credentials of these individuals, and the level of authority of the subsequent roles involve crucial decisions that must be addressed within the discipline-orientation of the host (Levine & Fleming, n.d.). For example, in hospital settings physician authority may prevail and, therefore, case management may be considered solely within the domain of the physician and defined as overall control of the case, with specific activities and functions allocated to other disciplines.

Yet within interdisciplinary settings, case management roles may not be allocated on the basis of discipline. Core credentials may be important. What may be more important, however, is substantive knowledge of a case, the necessary skills to address effectively the unique needs of individual recipients, and the desire to work with specific types of cases or problems (Ducanis & Golin, 1979). Within interdisciplinary settings, a range of disciplines may be involved in case management, and there may be considerable flexibility in the assignment of various disciplines to case management functions and activities.

Still another option involves those settings in which discipline may not be a powerful, overriding issue other than to meet accreditation and regulatory standards. These settings may place some emphasis on deprofessionalization of the case management function, and family members, consumers, and nondegreed staff may all be seen as making legitimate contributions to case management. People with backgrounds as consumers within a system that hosts the case management initiative may bring to case management a commitment, enthusiasm, and purpose that formally credentialed professionals may not exhibit (Solomon & Draine, 1995). Personal experience with a particular social problem, and success in addressing this problem, may serve as legitimate credentials for case management positions (Nikkel, Smith, & Edwards, 1992).

In one outpatient health setting that targeted its primary health services on Asian immigrants as well as migrants from Appalachia, case management was defined as an essential outreach, follow-along, case-finding, and support function. The purpose of case management was to engage high risk recipients and to maintain their ongoing involvement in primary health care. It was staffed by representatives from the target population who worked under the guidance of nurses and social workers.

PROGRAMMATIC DESIGN OF CASE MANAGEMENT

As program developers move on in the planning process they inevitably will arrive at the point at which specific decisions about program design will be necessary. Initial planning activities offer case management program developers an understanding of the needs that will be addressed by the case management program and the potential purpose it can serve. Understanding the contexts of case management sensitizes program developers to the challenges created by the multiple settings in which the program will operate. Specific program design decisions will involve the identification of case management mission, selection of a configuration, identification of functional case management elements, dosage, and staffing. A case management model will be the cumulative outcome of the efforts by program developers to address these various considerations.

Identification of Case Management Mission

Although there are multiple goals of case management, three alternative missions are most salient. An administrative mission—one consistent with the aims of a system-driven archetype—will focus the case management program on the management and control of resources necessary to serve the identified target population. Selection of this mission will probably occur when there is concern about gatekeeping, rationing, or cost containment. Interorganizational coordination of services may be a salient feature of such a case management mission given economic concerns about duplication, overutilization, or inappropriate utilization of services. Of course, such a mission does not preclude concern with assuring quality and relevance of service to recipients, but primary consideration is given to system management of the recipient and to the achievement of appropriate utilization. With this mission, case management is often viewed as a narrow technical function.

An alternative mission is one driven by linkage and support considerations (Moxley, 1989). Here the case management model typically is concerned about assessing—usually comprehensively—the needs of recipients and linking them to necessary services, entitlements, and opportunities. This mission also recognizes the importance of social supports, and so there may be concern with working with families, significant others, and friends to offer enriched supports to recipients. Such a case management mission usually involves multiple providers—perhaps collaborating with primary caregivers—in broad identification of recipient needs and then organizing, brokering, advocating, monitoring, and evaluating the resources necessary to fulfill these needs (Raiff & Shore, 1993). Those case management programs pursuing a mission of linkage and support are often broadly focused and concerned with comprehensiveness of service delivery.

A case management program with a consumer-driven mission prioritizes the wishes, desires, and wants of recipients with little introduction of professionally defined needs (Freddolino, Moxley, & Fleishman, 1989). Case management models with such a mission demand the identification of recipients' needs as they define them, and then case management service provision is designed to assist and support the recipients in achieving these self-defined outcomes. Unlike case management with an administrative mission, consumer-driven programs are not concerned with those outcomes desired by the system but rather those outcomes that are identified and prioritized by consumers themselves. Questions relating to "What do recipients want?" and "How do they want to achieve these ends?" are salient in this form of case management. These case management programs incorporate tools of strengths assessment (DeJong & Miller, 1995), partisan advocacy on the part of case managers, self-advocacy on the part of recipients, creative access to resources through community networks, and an ongoing supportive relationship between case manager and recipient (Rapp & Wintersteen, 1989).

Specification of the case management mission will flow from activities undertaken during the "getting started" phase of program development as well as from the efforts invested in understanding the context of the program. But identifying a salient mission is a critical precursor to further programmatic design of the case management system.

Selection of a Configuration

The configuration of the actual case management program can take several forms, which are based on decisions concerning whether case management will be delivered by individual case managers or by teams. The individual configuration involves the provision of the service by an individual case manager who maintains a caseload of recipients. Many case management programs with a linkage and support mission have such a configuration. The individual case manager will work to link clients to necessary resources, a relevant service when people have specific entitlement and programmatic needs (e.g., the need for homemaker services). However, when people have severe disabilities or problems that require ongoing and intensive vigilance on the part of the case management program, this configuration may be inadequate. Recipients may simply need more flexibility, attention, and assistance.

A team case management configuration offers flexibility in monitoring and response on the part of a program when recipient needs and problems require ongoing attention and vigilance, and the potentiality of crisis is high. One variation of this configuration involves a team of case managers who are managing their own caseloads and meet together on a regular basis (such as weekly or daily) to pool their knowledge of their respective clients. These case managers may cover for one another during on-call periods such as holidays, weekends, and evenings. An assumption of this configuration is that with the added knowledge of individual clients, based on regular team supervision, these case managers are able to act in a more informed and sensitive manner.

Another variation of team case management involves a team caseload in which all members serve as case managers for a group of recipients. These case managers will work together to respond to the needs of these recipients either through specialized or generalist roles. For example, in the Assertive Community Treatment model used to offer intensive case management, clinical, training, and support alternatives to people with serious mental illness who are high service utilizers, a small team of professionals and paraprofessionals work together to maintain their clients in community settings (Bond, Pensec, Dietzen, McCafferty, Giemza, & Sipple, 1991). These team members meet daily to coordinate their objectives, activities, and services.

Within these alternative configurations, of fundamental importance is ensuring that each recipient has at least one enduring relationship with a case manager. Case management programs based on linkage and support or consumer-driven missions recognize the importance of maintaining a dedicated, enduring, and strong relationship between the recipient and the case manager. Yet those case management programs that embody an administrative mission may underestimate the importance of such relationships and, consequently, discount the necessity of ensuring a good, face-to-face working relationship between recipients and case managers.

This is problematic given the high likelihood that case managers work with people who often feel the bite of stigma, discrimination, and isolation. For some people, their only caring relationships may be with individuals who are identified as case managers. And, for other individuals, case managers may be the only individuals who are accountable to recipients within bureaucracies, which can shuffle them around and perhaps neglect their needs. Thus, with any configuration, the case management-recipient relationship is of primary importance (Rapp, 1992).

Functional Elements and Role Definition

Case management functions are typically identified within the context of a sequential problem-solving model of helping (Ballew & Mink, 1986; Rothman, 1994) and thus, assessment, planning, intervention, monitoring, and evaluation are considered important core functions from a conceptual standpoint (Rubin, 1987) and are incorporated into professional standards guiding the execution of case management (NASW, 1992). These functions may be implemented in different ways, depending on the mission of the case management program, so that, for example, programs with administrative missions implement assessment in a gatekeeping fashion while consumer-driven programs engage in assessment through the identification of client wants and strengths.

From a conceptual standpoint, a distinction can be made between direct and indirect intervention approaches (Moxley, 1989). Direct intervention will involve the case manager in working directly with recipients to improve their skills in self-care, service acquisition, self-monitoring, and the troubleshooting of barriers that frustrate needs (Moxley & Freddolino, 1990). In some models, such as clinical case management or rehabilitation case management, direct intervention may take the form of counseling, psychotherapy, guidance, behavioral management, social skills training, and job search skills training.

Alternatively, indirect intervention focuses the attention of the case manager on systems intervention, including perhaps work with service systems, community gatekeepers, and families, with the aim of mustering needed service and social supports for recipients (Moxley, 1989) and identifying and resolving barriers to the fulfillment of needs (Freddolino & Moxley, 1993). Activities like referral, linkage, brokering, advocacy, coordination, and consultation may be implemented in conjunction with service systems, while social network interventions like education, training, and support of significant others may be offered by the case management program. Implementation of the indirect intervention function may vary by programmatic mission. A program with an administrative mission may implement those activities that enable it to control (such as through gatekeeping, prior approval, monitoring, and evaluation) the delivery of services to recipients. A program, the mission of which is linkage and support, may emphasize those activities that result in the promotion and sustenance of social supports, self-help, and mutual assistance.

Actual programmatic experience with these functions may diverge from idealized designs. For example, I once worked with a comprehensive case management program that purports to deliver all major functions. Evaluative data, however, reveal that the bulk of the program's effort is invested in crisis intervention—both directly with its recipients, who are adolescents with serious emotional problems, and indirectly with family members, school officials, and community members. The potential divergence of the actual case management functions from the intended ones illustrates the necessity of employing formative evaluation to examine on an ongoing basis the characteristics and needs of the target population, level of case management effort, actual functional activities, time commitments of case managers, and achievement of specific program objectives (First, Greenlee, & Schmitz, 1990).

Selection and prioritization of case management functions along with the actual configuration of the case management program will be influenced by the needs of the intended beneficiaries as well as by the mission of the program. Case management role definitions also will be important with some functions (such as linkage to income maintenance or housing) assigned to specific case managers perhaps within a team configuration. This form of role specialization contrasts with a generalist approach in which all case managers undertake functions comprehensively with little specialization. The generalist approach may be more consistent with case management programs configured according to individual caseload formats as opposed to formats favoring teams in which some members may serve as service or functional specialists.

Functional elements and role definitions are most importantly related to the know-how to address effectively the social problem facing recipients and case managers. Factors pertaining to early intervention and prevention may be salient in some social problem contexts, while ongoing intensive support may be required by others. Case management programs must analyze the social problems they face and translate these into program theories that incorporate relevant definitions of case management functions and roles.

Dosage of Case Management Service Delivery

Dosage involves how much case management is delivered to the intended beneficiaries measured through the frequency, duration, intensity, or variety of case management activities (Corrigan & Kayton-Weinberg, 1993). Dosage considerations are influenced by the needs of the beneficiaries, the social problem that is the focus of case management, and the covariation of the focal problem with other significant social problems. Case management dosage with people with serious mental illness who have stabilized living situations most likely will be different from the dosage offered to people who have serious mental illness and are homeless or whose lives are not stabilized (Bond, Miller, Krumwied, & Ward, 1988; Rog, Andranovich, & Rosenblum, 1987). In some situations intensive case management is required so that case managers may interact with recipients several times a week and may invest a considerable amount of time during each visit in assisting people to achieve stable living situations or to navigate serious crises (Eggert, Friedman, & Zimmer, 1990).

The sequelae of the problem may be an important consideration in the formulation of case management dosage. Case management contact may increase dramatically during periods of crisis or acute flare-ups of illness. Alternatively, case management contact may be minimal or set at fixed intervals. In much mental health case management, case managers may only see their clients when they have appointments for medical reviews, medication updates, or milestone health visits. These case managers may prioritize monitoring and evaluating their clients' status and perhaps updating needs assessments on a periodic basis.

Thus, the intensity of case management services may vary. Activity may increase during periods of acuity and taper off during stable periods. Transitional points of service delivery may also call for intensification of case management activity, such as during periods of admission, transfer, or discharge.

Another critical dimension influencing dosage is the program's understanding of the specific impairment, illness, or disability that is the focus of case management service. Many illnesses have their own trajectories involving pro-dromal symptoms, acuity, stabilization, and decline. Sensitive case management programs will offer flexible intensities tied to the different service and support contingencies created by the illnesses or problems these programs are designed to address as well as to the preferences of the people they serve.

Certainly dosage is an important variable in case management program development. To ignore it means that program developers have not made explic-it their assumptions concerning the problem they seek to address nor have they most likely identified those principles they wish to embody that will serve as the guideposts to case management intervention. Dosage raises issues pertaining to the quantity of effort of case managers, the degree of prevention infused into the case management strategy, and the timing of actual case management activities.

Staffing of the Case Management Program

Actual staffing of the case management program reflects a group of decisions that are crucial to model development (Levine & Fleming, n.d.). Will the case management program have a strong disciplinary identification? Will it have an interdisciplinary or transdisciplinary orientation? Or, will it be deprofessional-ized? Answers to each of these questions have significant implications for the actual program.

Staffing operationalizes the mission, purpose, and goals of the model case management program. From a disciplinary perspective, a range of professionals fill case management roles, including physicians, nurses, social workers, physi-cal therapists, health educators, and rehabilitation counselors. If one discipline will dominate the staffing of the case management program, specific attention must be paid to the purpose established for these positions, their authority and power, and the respect they can command within the health and human service system or organization. For example, an outpatient health service, offering care to people with debilitating neurological problems, may require nurses with grad-uate degrees to serve in case management roles. Without addressing the authori-ty of this discipline vis-a-vis physicians, role conflict may result, expressed as turf battles, circumvention of the case management system by medical staff, and general discord within the program. Alternatively, the health service may put in place a case management program to decrease unnecessary utilization linked to psychosocial conditions. Graduate-level social workers may be recruited to serve in these roles, but their integration into a medical setting may be attenuated because of conflict created by the collision of medical perspectives with social problem perspectives, and controversy created by different orientations to patient management may ensue (Mizrahi & Abramson, 1985).

Interdisciplinary approaches may be introduced to reduce role conflict, reduce competition among various disciplines, and achieve a synergy among various disciplines within the context of a flexible approach to the staffing of a case management program. Case management staffing may be a blend of various professionals, including medical consultation, nursing, social work, psychology, and counseling (Wodarski, Bundschuh, & Forbus, 1988). These disciplines learn about one another's perspectives, cross-train, and collaborate in a problem-oriented manner. They seek to integrate their various practice methods so that recipient needs are addressed in effective and creative ways. I have seen effective interdisciplinary case management programs that rotate case leadership based on the rule that "the professional who is most appropriate to a specific case takes primary case management responsibility." Appropriateness may be determined by experience, expertise and know-how in the problem area, relationship factors, motivation and commitment, and/or demographic considerations.

Transdisciplinary approaches may emerge when emphasis is placed by the case management program on recruiting professionals with the most appropriate skills and experiences as opposed to those with specific credentials like degrees. Case management from a transdisciplinary perspective recognizes that this approach to practice is not tied to any one discipline but that many different individuals can fill case management roles at various levels of professionalization. Both interdisciplinary and transdisciplinary approaches challenge professionals to build effective teams—ones capable of engaging in creative work, team problem-solving, systems thinking, conflict resolution, communication, and interpersonal support (Senge, 1990).

Expansion of Role Definitions

Researchers, with some success, have explored the expansion of role definitions of consumers, family members, and lay persons by adding case management activities (Solomon & Draine, 1995; Seltzer, Ivry, & Litchfield, 1987). Deprofessionalization can be useful when case management tasks are routine, high levels of clinical judgment are not required, and these case managers are provided good and timely supervision. Consumers as case managers can offer a sensitivity to the problems and issues of recipients through a personalistic approach that credentialed professionals may not be able or willing to offer. In addition, consumers may be more flexible in their execution of case management roles. They may be more amenable than professional staff to serving in community outreach roles, offering friendly visiting, providing support during periods of stress, assisting with transportation, and offering assistance in performing independent living activities.

Case management programs must examine role expansion and innovation very carefully and enter these arrangements with consumers, families, and lay persons with considerable forethought (Mowbray, Moxley, Thrasher & Associates, 1996). These programs must assure that appropriate technical assistance, supervision, training, and supports are available to these individuals so they can obtain the competence to execute necessary tasks in a manner that is consistent with the aims of the case management initiative. In addition, these programs must offer recognition supporting the importance of these roles by assuring that salaries and compensation are equitably established to underscore what are often unique, demanding, and creative contributions made by alternative staff. Case management programs engaging in role innovation practices must also examine opportunity structures for consumers or others who grow and develop as effective staff so they are able to perhaps enter into professional classifications or roles (Mowbray et al., 1996).

The staffing dimension can be given consideration when decisions about programmatic configuration are made by program developers. It is paramount that appropriate staff with the necessary knowledge, skills, and motivations are available to undertake successfully the required functional activities to serve intended beneficiaries well (Moxley & Buzas, 1989). One program with which I have served as a consultant has brought together for elderly persons with complex health conditions an interdisciplinary case management team that is a synthesis of both professional and nonprofessional staffing inputs. Composed of nurses, social workers, and rehabilitation specialists who are assisted by case management associates and volunteer family members, the program is able to offer its recipients a full range of social support, linkage and access services, professional guidance and problem-solving, and assistance with daily living needs. Explicit consideration is given to the support of family members, who are offered considerable information about role expectations and demands, and who are offered supports to help them to fulfill these roles effectively.

COMPOSING A MODEL OF CASE MANAGEMENT

Composing a case management program involves a number of steps and related decisions about initial need, context, and programmatic design. A programmatic model is a product of the successful execution of these steps and the decisions inherent in them. The boundary of the model is formed by a definitive mission, form, and structure. A model is a result of program conceptualization, planning, and development, and these stages are guided by a clear understanding of the needs of the recipient population. Program development proceeds as knowledge of these needs expands; as recognition grows that these needs are products of a complex interplay of health, behavioral, social, and cultural conditions; and as knowledge of the policy space and administrative and regulatory mandates of the program is added and coordinated with essential data gathered from stakeholders.

Formulation of initial program purpose can then proceed, the specificity of which is achieved through an examination of multiple contexts, including community, system, and organizational ones. Using these planning inputs, programmatic design is initiated with specific decisions made by developers regarding mission, configuration, functional elements, role definitions, dosage, and staffing. Definitive rules do not exist for integrating all of these decisions. Effective model design in case management is similar to the formulation of any health and human service intervention. It requires the planning of a program using state-of-the-art knowledge and incorporating a service design based on an identifiable purpose, adequate inputs, feasible procedures, and ethical practices (Thomas, 1984; Rothman & Thomas, 1994).

Evaluation has a vital role in every step of the case management program development process. The initial steps involved in getting started can involve context evaluation of consumer needs, stakeholder perspectives, and policy, administrative, and regulatory requirements, as well as an evaluation of the various environments and settings in which the case management program will operate (Berk & Rossi, 1990; Stufflebeam & Shinkfield, 1986). Evaluation of inputs will have a vital role when decisions are made about actual design of the case management service and necessary facilities, equipment, staffing, and organizational arrangements are under consideration by program developers (Stufflebeam & Shinkfield, 1986). Process evaluation becomes important as the case management program is implemented and program developers are concerned about the integrity of implementation and whether an identifiable case management model is put into action in a manner that is intended by the original design and with the desired attributes (Rossi & Freeman, 1993). Finally, as the program matures, product evaluation will assist planners and administrators to examine whether actual outcomes, effects, and impact are produced by the case management program. All of these forms of evaluation will require program developers to revisit the mission, purpose, and goals of the intended case management program.

IMPLICATIONS FOR EFFECTIVE CASE MANAGEMENT PROGRAMS

An agenda for case management program development is a complex one involving many issues, decisions, and steps unfolding during the course of program development, and perhaps resurfacing repeatedly during this process. The mandate for case management may be clear for many health and human service systems. But how to implement this mandate will require systematic planning, development, and evaluation—perhaps activities with which many health and human service systems are not altogether comfortable.

Given the diversity of case management purposes, approaches, and arrangements, program development is best characterized by choice. Program development really does require planners to examine options and make conscious decisions about these options. Although these choices are easily identified, their consequences create hidden ethical challenges and dilemmas. This environment of choice—and related ethical issues involved in planning case management programs—raises the importance of a pluralistic program development process. It is these considerations that have serious implications for health and human service systems seeking to develop relevant and meaningful case management programs.

Programmatic Choice and Ethical Issues

Many ethical issues raised by case management are tied to the relative novelty of these programs and raise the necessity of informed consent of participants about the strengths, limitations, and intentions of case management service delivery. In a case management program with an administrative mission, participants should be apprised of the aims of rationing and cost containment prior to their actual participation (Kane, 1988). Recipients should be notified about the possibility of "mixed loyalties": Given an emphasis placed on cost control, is the case manager loyal to the organization for which costs are being controlled or to the consumer?

Organizational sponsors of case management must give thought to the potentiality of conflict of interest, a contingency about which all recipients should be informed. Such disclosure is consistent with empowering recipients with as much information as possible so they have (1) a clear definition of case management procedures; (2) knowledge of the risks and benefits involved in case management; (3) an understanding of the possibility of conflict of interest created by the pursuit of multiple aims; and (4) an understanding of recipient rights within the case management system.

A linkage and support case management program is not exempt from ethical issues either. First, recipients may need to understand policies and procedures that guide for the purposes of coordination any disclosure of medical, psychological, behavioral, and personal information to other agencies and providers and that guarantee the preservation of the recipient's privacy. Second, the case management program's aim to organize social supports on behalf of recipients also needs to be disclosed. The recipient needs an understanding of the programmatic expectations placed on people offering support and the potential burdens, demands, and conflicts these can create. Third, significant others should be apprised since the aim of incorporating social supports can create burdens for these individuals that they may not anticipate or can force them to assume responsibility for social support they may not wish to assume.

Using social support procedures may shift the health care burden from provider to family members. It may be a conscious strategy of cost shifting or cost sharing by the sponsor of the case management program. Yet, even if the sponsor is not pursuing these aims, and sees the use and augmentation of social support as a good practice, secondary consumers still should be alerted to this contingency. They should be fully informed about what they are agreeing to undertake and the potential stress and burden involved in serving as primary care-givers.

The issue of "mixed loyalties" can also emerge in the linkage and support model in situations in which case managers are paid directly by families to serve a dependent member (Kane, 1988). Under these circumstances problems can emerge that involve fundamental human rights regarding the expression of sexuality, freedom of choice, and freedom of movement when recipient and payor (i.e., the family) disagree about certain aspects of care, service, and support. Under these circumstances to whom is the case manager ultimately responsible: to family or recipient?

The case management program with a consumer-driven mission may create ethical issues by its commitment to self-determination, empowerment, and autonomy. Yet some individuals may not value these principles. They may not want to carry such responsibility on their own, and they may look to professionals to make critical decisions for them (Rothman, 1989). These individuals may want to delegate their care and support to professionals and decline the opportunity to be autonomous and to pursue self-determination. Of course, precedents for such relationships exist between clients and attorneys and between patients and physicians (Kane, 1988).

Strong norms reinforcing individualism and self-sufficiency embodied by the case management program can result in potential neglect as providers rationalize recipients' desires for dependency as a violation of self-determination, a personal weakness, the absence of motivation, or a lack of commitment and, by virtue of this rationalization, decline to serve these individuals, label them as unresponsive, or stigmatize them. The normative assumptions of the case management program must be examined closely to assure that people's preferences are respected and that there are structures or opportunities to amplify dissent concerning these norms.

A Pluralistic Approach to Program Development

There are no simple solutions to these ethical issues. Suffice it to say that any approach to case management will most likely raise ethical considerations given the fact that these programs are devoted to serving individuals who may experience impairment, stigma, or oppression and often are burdened with multiple expectations and conflicting aims. A case management program, however, can formulate policies and procedures that seek to respond to these issues by clarifying purpose, mission, and aims; clarifying role definitions; and introducing measures protecting the rights of recipients.

A stakeholder approach to the planning of the case management program also can assist the sponsoring organization to form a program with strong legitimacy and the ability to navigate ethical issues as they arise. Case management programs will potentially link their host organization to other human service systems and providers, family members, recipients who may have serious disabilities and their advocates, and community gatekeepers. All of these groups can be involved in the program development process not only to assure that the resulting model will have the requisite inputs but that it also will have relevance to multiple consumers. The sponsoring organization must realize that although the ultimate consumers of case management will be recipients, there are also other groups who may serve as "clients" by sanctioning the program, paying for services, and experiencing directly the outputs of case management efforts. Thus, we again return to the idea that many case management programs will be designed and implemented in a social matrix characterized by multiple expectations about efforts, outcomes, and impact.

A program development steering task force composed of representatives from all vested interest groups can assist the organization in shaping the mission and substantive character of the program. Case management programs that embrace a principal perspective (such as the payor's) as the foundation of programmatic design may reduce or eliminate controversy during planning but, from my experience, conflict will emerge early in implementation as different stakeholder groups attempt to shape the program to meet their own expectations, preferences, and values. Involvement early in program design of groups representing multiple perspectives will most likely create conflict. Yet through the infusion of multiple perspectives the resulting case management program will build a stronger foundation on which to develop a viable approach to service.

CHAPTER 5

CHALLENGES TO MAKING CASE MANAGEMENT VIABLE AS COMMUNITY SUPPORT PRACTICE

David P. Moxley, Orman E. Hall, and D. Larry Branham

This chapter examines the challenges faced by case management that is implemented within the context of the community support model. Three of these challenges are discussed, involving (1) service organization as a potential bias; (2) a consumer-centered frame of reference as a limiting factor; and (3) the potential encapsulation and containment of recipients. These challenges were identified through focus group interviews with consumers, case management staff, and family members who were involved in a project undertaken by the Fairfield County Alcohol, Drug Addiction and Mental Health Services Board, located in Lancaster, Ohio, to improve services to people with serious mental illness. The board initiated the introduction of team-based and collaborative case management to improve the responsiveness of mental health services to adults with serious mental illness residing within the county, and to strengthen the local community support system within the county.

With the encouragement of the Ohio Department of Mental Health, and bolstered by an Innovations Grant awarded to the county board by the department during 1991, the new case management effort was initiated. The county board originally sought three program innovations. First, it wanted to address the human resource component of case management by strengthening the professional standing and recognition of staff fulfilling case management roles. Second, it wanted to demonstrate the feasibility and effectiveness of matching case management services and resources to the needs of specific subgroups of consumers created by their service histories, functional characteristics, and clinical profiles. Third, it sought to expand the community support opportunities available within the county through the mobilization of consumers to engage in mutual support and self-help, something that was recognized as important to the quality of life of consumers as well as to the enrichment of the programmatic framework within which case management was to operate.

The initiation of case management within the county was not without difficulties, although substantive gains were made in the establishment of case management, community support, and consumerism during the period of the project. However, the data suggest the substantive nature of problems that can emerge when local mental health systems implement case management as part of a community support system. The intention of this chapter is to identify the challenges that emerged during the course of the project, and to reflect on their implications for advancing the evolution of community support systems and case management for people with serious mental illness.

The material for this chapter comes from the experiences of the three authors who were involved either in the administration, development, and evaluation of the case management program; a review of key documents prepared for the purposes of reporting on the status of the project to the county board, and to the Ohio Department of Mental Health; and the completion of three different focus groups with various stakeholder groups (case management staff, consumers, and family members) involved in the implementation of the case management effort.

Case management has been recognized as a vital element of the community support system model since its inception and introduction as a reform sponsored by the National Institute of Mental Health during the mid- to late 1970s (NIMH, 1980; Turner & TenHoor, 1978). The model identifies the importance of the organization and delivery of comprehensive services, supports, and opportunities to people with serious mental illness, and does not necessarily limit this array to only mental health services. Living in the community requires a diversity of supports that involve, according to the community support model, in addition to traditional mental health services, outreach, crisis services, health and dental care, housing, income support, peer and family support, rehabilitation services, and protection and advocacy opportunities (Stroul, 1989; 1993).

Case management, according to this model, is essential to the effective organization and delivery of an array of services to consumers (Tessler & Goldman, 1982). The principal responsibilities of case management include the assessment of needs and the assurance that consumers obtain all services necessary to fulfill these needs; the coordination of all services consumers obtain to ensure that they are compatible and consistent with the overall goals identified by and for consumers; and the monitoring of services to ensure that they are appropriate to the changing needs and status of consumers (Stroul, 1993).

To be effective, case management must be community-based and community-oriented, according to the community support model. Stroul (1989) notes that "case managers must work in the community with clients, families, and agencies to manage, coordinate, and unify the many components of the CSS" (p. 86). They must reach out to consumers in an "aggressive manner" and move around the community, linking with various people to assure that people with serious mental illness are identified and are offered services that are consistent with their needs.

Case managers hold pivotal roles in the conceptual model of the community support system. Case managers serve as a principal mechanism for achieving the multiple aims of community support systems, including their concerns for responsiveness to needs and relevance of service. They embody the model's concern for flexibility, coordination, integration, and comprehensiveness. Within the actual conceptual model of community support, case management serves a wraparound function to ensure that all of the necessary services, supports, and opportunities "wrap around" the consumer in an individualized, sensitive, relevant, and accountable manner (Stroul, 1993).

The importance and significance of case management as a foundational element of effective systems serving people with serious mental illness is recognized at the federal level within Public Law 99-660, a policy product that reflects the work of consumer advocates endorsing the need to organize and sustain responsive, individualized packages of services. Case management has been a principal policy initiative within many state departments of mental health, including the Ohio Department of Mental Health (Hyde, 1989). Ohio's early work during the 1980s to bring the community support system model to the state, and to diffuse it within county-level mental health systems, helped to promote the visibility and importance of case management as a preferred form of service technology. These efforts within the state expanded as the Mental Health Act of 1988 identified the necessity to establish a community-support form of case management within all of Ohio's local mental health systems. More recently, as a consequence of Ohio's efforts to implement public managed care, case management is shifting to a focus on the provision and organization of community support.

Yet the actual attributes of this form of case management, and the assumptions made by the community support system model, can place significant and unintentional limitations on the implementation of case management within service systems and community contexts. The purpose of this chapter is to identify these attributes and their assumptions, and identify the implementation problems that can arise, using data obtained from one project that sought to implement and institutionalize community support system case management within one local mental health system in Ohio.

CHALLENGES TO CASE MANAGEMENT WITHIN THE COMMUNITY SUPPORT SYSTEM MODEL

The form of case management identified within the community support model is different from many other forms of case management, especially those that are driven more by systems ends of cost containment and the management of utilization. The Community Support System (CSS) form of case management can be characterized by at least three attributes that give it a distinctive yet potentially troublesome character as an approach to practice. These are: service organization as a principal aim of case management; a consumer-centered frame of reference; and the potential for structural encapsulation and containment of recipients.

Service Organization as a Potentially Negative Bias

A principal aim—if not the principal aim—of CSS case management is to organize an array of effective service responses to the management of serious mental illness. The conception of disability implicit to the community support model is based on role functioning deficits, and presupposes that many consumers will require a range of services to be successful in the community, some of which are controlled by mental health systems, and others that are not controlled by these systems but that are nonetheless needed by consumers, like health care or vocational rehabilitation. The purpose of these services is to increase the level of support available to consumers, a form of support that is designed ideally to reduce role functioning deficits through the buffering of stress, the management of symptoms, the promotion of skill acquisition, and the provision of entitlements linked to housing, income, and medical care, for example.

A potential problem with the community support model lies in its conception of serious mental illness. The model, a product of deinstitutionalization as well as the gross dissatisfaction many policy makers voiced about the process of deinstitutionalization and its negative consequences for people with serious mental illness, views mental illness as a lifelong catastrophe that severely and substantially disrupts functioning in multiple spheres such as in the interpersonal, self-care, economic, independent living, cognitive, and/or emotional domains. Basic assumptions the model makes about serious mental illness may include chronicity, dependency, and the need for lifetime management.

Emerging conceptions of mental illness emphasize the possibility of recovery. They link this hopeful outcome to the realization of quality of life defined by consumers themselves, and to the achievement of a standard of living that is seen by consumers as at least adequate to a dignified lifestyle within a community. Anthony (1994) sees recovery as a subjective notion produced by the careful orchestration of supports defined and prioritized by consumers as vital to their well-being. These supports may fall in areas that are encompassed by the essential components of the community support model (e.g., employment, housing) but are more consistent with a mission of psychiatric rehabilitation: helping consumers to achieve success in roles and environments of their own choosing with a minimum of ongoing professional assistance (Farkas & Anthony, 1989). A commitment to recovery may release community support systems from the assumption of chronicity.

The service focus of the CSS model, and the form of case management emerging out of this model, assumes that a community has the necessary services available to support consumers, or, if this is not so, that the community has the willingness and capacity to create services needed by people with serious mental illness. The success of CSS case management is somewhat dependent on the successful realization of this assumption. This means that a potential strategic challenge for case management systems within this model lies in the development of a matrix of services within a community that can be measured by (1) increasing the number and diversification of services in each key component area of the idealized CSS model; and (2) enhancing the motivation and expertise of service providers to support people with serious mental illness.

If the case management system or sponsoring agent does not have the capacity to encourage the development of, or to actually create, needed services, then a significant weakness will exist within the case management system. It is not surprising, therefore, that the effectiveness of those forms of case management that make use of brokering or coordination strategies to respond to consumer needs is dependent on the "richness" of services available within a particular geographic area (Rothman, 1992). The effectiveness of case management within the context of the community support model is contingent on the continuous expansion, development, and refinement of this system, a significant and perhaps arduous program development challenge that cannot be ignored by most case management systems, especially those that are salient components of community support systems.

We cannot think about the performance of case management constructively without really understanding critically the capacity of a service domain within a specific community to serve and support people with serious mental illness. If the service system is deficient, we postulate that the burden of meeting consumer needs will be shifted from the service system to the case management system, and case managers will experience heightened stress from such a shift

(Senge, 1990). Case managers can be shifted from their roles as brokers, organizers, and coordinators of service to roles more characteristic of direct service provision—including the direct provision of daily living supports. As case and need identification continues, a case management program in the context of a weak community support system can become overwhelmed by the sheer number of clients requiring service. Thus, the successful execution of CSS case management is linked to the adequacy of the service context (Moore, 1992), to the ability and competence of this context to evolve over time, and to a willingness by system and community leaders to enhance the range of available supports. The weight of community support cannot be placed entirely or even substantially on the shoulders of case management.

A Consumer-Centered Frame of Reference as a Limiting Factor

A basic philosophical and operational principle of the community support model is found in the commitment of this model to a consumer-centered approach to service delivery. According to Stroul (1993), "services should be based on and responsive to the needs of the client rather than the needs of the system or the needs of providers" (p. 77). This desired attribute of the community support system gives two orientations to the CSS form of case management: an orientation to the consumer, and an orientation to the system of services that ostensibly must be responsive to the needs of consumers.

A consumer-centered frame of reference is somewhat different from a consumer-driven one. In the latter, the organizing principles of the service system and of case management focus on fostering the consumer's control, choice, dissent, and reputation (see Chapter 8 for an explanation of these qualities). Consumer-centered approaches to practice aim to identify needs, principally through the perspectives of enlightened professionals who are seeking to organize a system of services that will meet these needs. Consumer-centered approaches to practice place the case managers or other providers in critical roles as the identifiers and definers of these needs, with input sought from consumers.

The service orientation of the community support model with its explicit bias toward the organization and delivery of comprehensive services may possess a serious design limitation by virtue of its consumer-centered frame of reference. CSS case management may define needs as service needs. The realization that needs are often subjectively tied to the perspectives of people who feel or experience these needs, with a service defined as one means (perhaps among many) of fulfilling these subjectively and personally defined needs, may be overlooked or otherwise ignored by the case management component. Thus, while a person may articulate a desire for a home to a CSS case manager, the consumer-centered approach to service delivery may frame this as a need for a supervised housing alternative. But from the perspective of the consumer, the housing alternative offered to meet "a need for a home" may fail to incorporate the very qualities and values that make it a home for this person.

Certainly our labeling of a consumer-centered frame of reference as a limitation may be seen as unfair by advocates of the community support model, especially since we have not identified the other salient principles of the model (such as its commitment to empowerment, normalization, and racial and culture appropriateness), but the assumptions of the model do tend to be based on the ideas that consumers want services and will cooperate with the professionals and organizations controlling the community support system. Perhaps consumers do not want services, or perhaps they do not want to translate the fulfillment of their needs into services. Concepts other than needs and services can be incorporated into the community support model to make it more consumer-driven and less consumer-centered. Certainly the notion of want or desire based on the subjective perspectives and experiences of consumers can move a system away from services as its principal orientation, and in the direction of establishing other types of support systems, perhaps ones organized by and for consumers.

The realization of a consumer-centered community support system also presupposes that the CSS case management component is placed into a context that shares consumer-centered values. These values may be expressed through accessibility and timeliness; appropriateness and sensitivity to cultural and racial attributes; and responsiveness to the consumer as a real consumer. The CSS case management program cannot easily escape the value orientations of the service providers on which it is dependent since it will directly feel in very real terms whether this system is trying to respond to consumers in a competent and accountable manner, whether this system is found by consumers to be frustrating, or whether it is actually trying to evade responsibility for serving people with serious mental illness.

It appears that the CSS form of case management assumes that consumer-centered practice must be operationalized both within the actual case management component as well as within the larger community support service system. This is indeed a challenge since it gives a duality to the case management role. The CSS form of case management cannot escape this duality: the necessity to operationalize consumer-centered practice in face-to-face interactions with consumers; and the necessity to push a system of services, the programs offered by this system, and the personnel who staff it in the direction of consumer-centered practice despite forces that may work against the diffusion and acceptance of core CSS values. Perhaps a shortcoming of this assumption is that neither consumers nor service providers may want to move in this direction. Community support systems and their case managers may increasingly feel conflict with consumers and with service providers. It is this conflict that may place serious limitations on the actual development of a community support system and the ability of case management to fulfill the role and functional requirements of the idealized model of community support.

The Potential Encapsulation and Containment of Recipients

The community support system model advocates the mobilization of a community to support people with serious mental illness in becoming contributing members of the community, although the actual definition of this community and its attributes is not entirely clear. Certainly this is the desire of many mature community support systems, those that have moved and developed beyond the organization of service providers to a comprehensive system of service delivery. Community as a construct has not been well developed within this approach to service, but some thought, especially through federal CSP initiatives, has been given to the role of support offered through geographic communities, communities of identity (especially the contributions of consumers to self-help and mutual support, and the contributions of family members to the support of consumers), and communities of interest based on neighborhood life, safety, economic development, and the inclusion of people with serious mental illness in those collective infrastructures available to all citizens within a community.

Community support systems may inadvertently assume that their mission is merely to organize and develop formal human services and, as a consequence, operationalize practices that insulate people with serious mental illness from the community and encapsulate them within professional networks of support (Moxley, 1983). This possible encapsulation creates a number of issues for both recipients and CSS case managers. CSS case management may get entangled in this assumption and may unconsciously embrace the conception that system involvement is permanent; that it substitutes for naturally occurring interactions and relationships within the community; and that there is no hope for recovery or exit from the system, only the provision of continuous support. Certainly efforts to develop effective and comprehensive support systems come from a concern to compensate for the potential neglect of people with serious mental illness, a concern that is well founded given the recurring theme of neglect in the history of society's response or lack of response to the problem of serious mental illness (Isaac & Armat, 1990; Johnson, 1990). But this assumption can limit the viability of a community support system within a specific community, the form of case management the system promotes, and the conception of community the system endorses.

The fate of community support systems is tied to communities. The systems will experience directly the ability or inability, the willingness or unwillingness, of a community to promote the quality of life and to support an adequate standard of living for all of its citizens, including people with serious mental illness. Communities will also make a determination as to whether and to what degree people with serious mental illness are worthy of support. A community support system is not only dependent on a service infrastructure, it is also dependent on those institutional systems, collective resources, and qualities that are critical to the community's well-being. Community context and structure are especially relevant to a CSS form of case management if it is seeking to move beyond service adequacy to address the quality of life and standard of living of people with serious mental illness. Without an external perspective to the enhancement of the larger community as a supportive context, the creation of the community support system and the development of its comprehensiveness may become the principal if not the only ends—and, as a consequence, community integration of participants will not be realized. This can result in goal displacement: the purpose of CSS case management is to provide more and more support, rather than assisting people to establish new statuses and roles in their community (Mayer, 1973), and to attain new platforms of independent living, ones based on the preferences and self-defined ends of users of the community support system.

CONCLUSION

To truly operationalize the spirit and substance of community support, CSS case managers have to move beyond service activities, and to promote utilization of community resources and institutional systems in collaboration with members of the community who do not immediately identify with the plight or situations of people with serious mental illness. This means that case managers will interact with institutional gatekeepers who influence the use of community utilities available to every citizen, such as employment opportunities, transportation, housing, education, training, child care, and legal services (Lappe & DuBois, 1994).

Internal or External Orientation of the Community Support System

A duality introduced into CSS case management is found in the extent to which the case management system is internally oriented or driven in the development and organization of those services that are most fundamental to addressing the management of the medical and disability dimensions of serious mental illness, versus the extent to which the case management system is externally oriented or driven in the opening up of community opportunity structures, ones that are fundamental to the realization of enhanced quality of life and standard of living. Many community support systems are working to better organize their service systems through the augmentation and integration of mental health, social service, rehabilitation, and health care components. This effort reflects the service bias of many community support systems, and perhaps we can identify these community support systems as first generation systems.

Second generation systems demonstrate a heightened concern for community infrastructure development and normalization, and are sensitive to the necessity to create presence within, access to, participation in, and use of those principal community institutions or resources that can advance the quality of life and standard of living of people with serious mental illness. An emerging shift in the purpose of psychiatric rehabilitation illustrates the focus and priorities of these generational distinctions exemplified by CSS case management. First generation case management systems will focus on the management of illness and the reduction of disability through the marshalling and organization of services, frequently medically oriented ones. Service routines are evident in these case management systems: the attention of case managers is focused almost exclusively on crisis intervention, linkage of recipients to entitlements, and the stabilization of housing.

Second generation case management systems will focus on recovery, on the improvement of the status and roles of consumers, and on the achievement of recovery through the objective improvement of standard of living and the subjective improvement of quality of life. Long-term visions will orchestrate the work of case managers so that the service routines identified above do not become ends in themselves but means to address community involvement, the achievement of housing preferences, the exploration of work, and the involvement in self-help and mutual support.

Strategic Challenges Facing Case Management in Community Support Systems

Both generational exemplars are confronted with strategic challenges. For the first generation CSS case management system, perhaps a principal challenge is to expand its vision beyond service systems and into the general community. For the second generation CSS case management system, perhaps a principal challenge is to expand partnerships and collaborative initiatives with generic community institutions so that, for example, a community college becomes more responsive to the training aspirations of adults with serious mental illness; a child care center enhances its abilities to assist mothers coping with serious mental illness to support the development of their toddlers; or employers are able to help people with serious mental illness to build meaningful career paths. In other words, second generation community support systems work to expand and open up generic opportunity structures with the aims of making these structures sensitive to the needs of people with serious mental illness, and of increasing the competence of these structures to facilitate the involvement and development of participants coping with psychiatric issues.

Strategies for the second generation case management system may be geared directly and assertively to the diffusion of the responsibility for support into the larger community, a variation on the theme of those case management models that endorse the identification and use of broad-based community resources within a consumer-driven framework (Rapp & Wintersteen, 1989; Moxley & Freddolino, 1990). The aim of these models is to promote the recovery of consumers. Without this orientation to community, then the improvement of quality of life and standard of living may be elusive ends.

The absence of this orientation may mean that many community support systems, and their case management components, may be limited by their very assumptions about serious mental illness, its duration, and its consequences. They may also be limited by their assumptions about what constitutes a community; the role that critical community attributes (like cultural, economic, demographic, political, and institutional ones) serve in fostering or undermining support systems; and their understanding of what constitutes "community" and "support," two constructs critical to the underpinnings of community support as a model of human services.

CHAPTER 6

IMPROVEMENT THEMES IN THE IMPLEMENTATION OF CASE MANAGEMENT IN COMMUNITY SUPPORT SYSTEMS

The themes included in this chapter were identified through field research undertaken with three different case management initiatives. All three case management programs were permanent parts of mental health systems. The case management programs emerged during the late 1980s and early 1990s as part of mental health systems reforms within communities seeking to improve service delivery to people with serious mental illness. Yet this was the only characteristic they shared in common. Each case management program was implemented in different contexts and in different communities.

One program was implemented within the context of a multi-program mental health organization. This agency saw case management as an opportunity to expand its community service delivery through outreach, advocacy, and service development initiatives. Another program was implemented within a county mental health system seeking to install a community support model of service delivery to people with serious mental illness. This system initiated case management as a strategy of creating customized service responses through the modified use of wraparound ideas and practices. The final program was sponsored by another county mental health system that made substantial progress during the decade of the '80s in serving people with serious mental illness. Case management became a principal strategy of organizing a countywide community support system and a major means of supporting people in independent living. At the time of my consultation and field research work, this system was looking at ways of infusing vocational development and rehabilitation practices into case management.

A multi-modal approach to field research was undertaken to

organize, identify, and label the themes contained in this chapter. This approach included key informant interviewing, focus groups, direct observation of case management practices, program reviews, and the examination of official documents. The themes are stated as generalizations concerning improvement. They are identified as generalizations because all three programs grappled with these improvement issues.

The improvement of case management programs and systems is a complex enterprise primarily because case management itself is a complex undertaking. Most approaches to case management do not embody typical human service practice, much of which involves office-based interventions in which professionals or those designated as helpers interact with people in need within the context of agencies. In this typical practice, often involving psychotherapeutic or counseling approaches, people in need interact with helpers in very controlled circumstances, and the helper can partition the needs presented by these individuals seeking help into their requisite emotional, cognitive, or behavioral domains. Often the environmental dimension can be factored out of this form of practice, and helpers do not really have to address fully the resource situations of the people they serve, or confront the dramatic problems that can occur in real life settings and in daily living situations.

Many case management initiatives simply cannot escape these realities since these programs have been designed to reach out to people in need, to offer services in community contexts, and to arrange supports with the aim of helping people to cope with the demands, emergencies, crises, and inadequacies of daily living. It is not unusual for case managers who really do implement this environmental and community-based approach to practice to describe their work as not only demanding but also exceedingly stressful. The stress is not abated by colleagues whose office-based practice is venerated as real professional work while the work of case management may be discounted as less sophisticated, quasi-professional activity.

It is important to underscore the demanding nature of case management practice. since as we get into the improvement themes that I identify as operating in three different case management initiatives it may be easy to discount these programs as disorganized and ill planned. All three case management initiatives from which improvement themes are identified are very good. All three were developed in attempts to improve service organization and delivery as well as community and personal support of people with serious mental illness. And all three were developed within well-meaning host organizations or systems that value good practice in mental health. Nonetheless, those of us who understand the realities of case management practice know firsthand how many case management initiatives can drift in the wrong direction or, more importantly, can fail to anticipate the problems that can emerge from complex undertakings.

Suffice it to say at this juncture: Case management is not typical human service practice. It is not necessarily office-based or even facility-based practice. As noted in the first part of this book, it is very diverse and can be very sophisticated. Whatever form case management comes in, its effective implementation deserves vigilant oversight and continuous improvement.

TEN IMPROVEMENT THEMES

The ten improvement themes are outcomes of improvement-oriented evaluation undertaken by the author with these three case management initiatives. An improvement-oriented approach to evaluation follows a systems strategy of evaluating a human service object along four dimensions: context, input, process, and product. The resulting CIPP evaluation model enables users to identify issues primarily for the purposes of formative improvement of the identified object. (Stufflebeam & Shinkfield, 1986) In this case, I worked with the three case management initiatives to identify areas (i.e., themes) in which they can improve using the perspectives of multiple stakeholders who experience the effects of case management service delivery—either as recipients or users, providers, administrators, or a principal audience such as family members. The themes are organized by the constituent elements of the CIPP evaluation model.

Context Themes

Context involves the case management initiative's general task and/or the policy environment in which it is embedded. The context of the case management initiative involves the linkages the program has to other organizational entities and to other programs within the system in which it transacts business. In addition, context can include the characteristics and needs of the people who are the intended beneficiaries of the case management initiative. Three improvement themes that were relevant to all three case management initiatives involved (1) model conflict between case management and the host's model of service delivery; (2) confusion created by multiple models of case management; and (3) resource inadequacies.

Conflict with a Human Service System's Model of Service Delivery

The manner in which a case management model is configured and the compatibility of this configuration with other programs and aspects of a human service system can create a number of improvement issues pertaining to implementation effectiveness of the case management initiative. The case management initiative that became part of a multi-program mental health organization was conceptualized as a community approach to practice in which case management personnel undertook proactive outreach to people with very serious problems—people who often came to the center in emergency or crisis.

People experiencing housing crises and people who experienced chronic homelessness were among these individuals. This proactive outreach resulted in dramatic increases of referrals of people with very severe situations and problems that, in turn, created a great deal of controversy about the appropriateness of case management services within the more established programs of the agency. Many of the personnel within these established programs did not see these referrals as appropriate to the established missions of the traditional counseling, crisis intervention, and family service programs of the agency, and this, in turn, created serious issues pertaining to the overarching mission of the organization and the integration among program elements. Case management for this organization was conceptualized as a model of community practice designed to implement outreach, support system development, and service advocacy. Yet, without a shared conception of this purpose in the agency, many of the other programs were ill prepared to collaborate or to engage in teamwork. Case management in this situation only amplified the already existing inadequacies of the agency in serving so-called hard-to-reach populations within their immediate service area.

Both case management initiatives implemented within county mental health systems experienced model conflict from an intersystem perspective. As both of these systems became more effective in serving people with serious mental illness within their established community support systems, they became more interested in creating linkages between their case management components and vocational rehabilitation systems. Both of these mental health systems designed their case management systems based on a strengths orientation, and sought to respond to their clients' desires to become involved in employment and career development. Case managers were well trained to identify the preferences and goals of their clients, and then to organize and implement advocacy to fulfill these desires.

The vocational rehabilitation systems within these local communities did not share these orientations, and indeed saw a strengths orientation as unrealistic, destructive, and inappropriate. Vocational rehabilitation systems wanted people to accept the work opportunities offered by these systems and to comply with the vocational rehabilitation routines, which often meant only testing people and then placing them in sheltered settings or in community enclaves. What is salient here is that both systems (i.e., mental health and vocational rehabilitation) experienced high levels of discord and conflict because of basic disagreements concerning how the rehabilitation process should be implemented. This discord and conflict resulted in a standoff in which little if any good intersystem collaboration transpired, and opportunities for service integration were lost.

Failure to address the theme of model compatibility may jeopardize both the effectiveness of case management and human service delivery, and the realization of desired client-level effects and outcomes. The theme really does identify the need to be vigilant about the context in which case management unfolds and to pursue a unified approach to service delivery, if this is even possible. For all three case management initiatives, this theme suggests that case management is very much part of organizational, community, and human service contexts that cannot be ignored. Achievement of a "system" requires improvement of the fit between case management and its host contexts, and, in turn, requires a system dialogue about what case management is designed to achieve operationally and in the lives of its consumers (Senge, 1990).

Multiple Models of Case Management May Create Confusion

The three case management initiatives discussed in this chapter were developed and implemented by mental health systems searching for more effective ways of creating community support systems for people with serious mental illness. Yet, within all three field situations, several different approaches to case management were found to be operating within local communities, typically undertaken by organizations not within these mental health systems but that offered services and supports needed or wanted by people with serious mental illness. The variations of these case management programs and their sponsors underscore the ubiquity of case management identified in the first part of the book. These include case management initiatives undertaken by the Private Industrial Council, whose form of case management focused on the organization of supports designed to help people take advantage of employment and training opportunities (e.g., child care and transportation); vocational rehabilitation, whose form of case management focused on brokering and purchasing relevant vocational development and rehabilitation opportunities; AIDS consortia, whose approach to case management addressed advocacy and community support of people coping with the medical and social consequences of this disease; and managed health care, whose approach to case management focused on utilization management and gatekeeping.

The lives of many people with serious mental illness within these three different communities and mental health service systems were touched by these case management programs, depending on the problems they experienced and the constellation of needs they possessed as a result of these problems. What became obvious in this variation was that most of these case management approaches did not focus on utilization management and the reduction of service involvement—although this appeared to be an explicit aim of the managed health care approach to case management. Most of them addressed the problem of how to organize complex supports into manageable support systems for their users— ones that would support people's functioning (Anthony et al., 1988). This finding underscores how much of what we call case management really does involve the orchestration of community supports that are relevant to community and independent living. Indeed, case management actually involves basic social work processes (Rose, 1992; Rothman, 1994), and may highlight the need to reframe what we mean by case management in many service contexts in order to differentiate it from case management within managed care systems. Much of what we mean by case management may be community practice undertaken to help people take advantage of needed support systems, create systems of support, and strengthen support systems.

Thus, this theme highlights the importance of considering the variation in what is called case management that can exist within a local community. For these three case management initiatives, it was not unusual for them to "bump up" against other case managers and other case management programs. People with serious mental illness seeking assistance may actually be involved in several different case management initiatives, reflecting just how difficult it is to achieve any semblance of a unified approach to human service delivery within local communities. Centralization of care under one umbrella and use of a unified financing mechanism may be limited if it is undertaken solely from the standpoint of medical management as opposed to a social support perspective.

Despite the specter of control and rationing managed care may create as potential threats to consumer-driven practice, the argument for a unified source of managed service delivery may not be discounted given the proliferation of case management initiatives within any one community context. However, it does raise issues about what exactly a system is seeking to manage. Improvement here may require the creation of an organizational or systemwide dialogue concerning what supports are needed in order to achieve the ends of case management practice that is focused on the promotion of community support and the achievement of rehabilitation outcomes valued by recipients.

Resource Problems Operating as a Serious Limiting Factor

The previous improvement issue does underscore a consistent finding among all three case management initiatives. They are very sensitive to the resource contexts in which they operate, and this creates serious issues for the organization and provision of support (Rothman, 1992). Case management systems most likely will be as effective as their resource contexts—especially in problem areas that require people to be very dependent on community resources to meet basic independent living needs. This is a very serious issue faced by the three case management initiatives. Deficiencies in basic resource domains like housing, training and education, health care, employment, informal social supports, and transportation will be felt directly by case management initiatives whose missions are to create community support systems. These deficiencies will likely set the stage for crises and emergencies, so that case management personnel find themselves addressing issues pertaining to social isolation, housing loss, housing inadequacies, and unemployment since it is these issues that dramatically reflect structural inadequacies in many local communities.

Many of the case management initiatives I have observed—including two of the three I discuss in this chapter—became encapsulated within vicious cycles of crisis and emergency. Despite having a great deal of data and information on the structural and resource inadequacies within their local communities, these programs are usually not designed to feed this information into any relevant decision-making forum. The absence of a strong community perspective, and even a community organization capacity, handicaps case management (Kretzman & McKnight, 1993). It is difficult, I have found, for case management programs to contribute to a dialogue about how to rectify these systemic problems, or to address root causes from an advocacy standpoint. Thus, it is not unusual for case management personnel to say they undertake advocacy when people are in "trouble" by resolving this trouble through the arrangement of access to a time-limited option (such as a shelter situation). It is very unusual for case management personnel to articulate longer-run strategies using the abundant information they obtain about community issues and resource problems for the purposes of resource development and system improvement, even though this is indicative of good practice (Steinberg & Carter, 1983).

Can improvement actually occur in relationship to this theme? Case management initiatives may need to recognize that improvement will not occur in the short run although progress can be made through the development of discrete resource alternatives. One of the initiatives I observed made explicit use of the information and data collected by case management personnel but nonetheless was unable to influence the program development strategy of its host organization. The agency did not see this kind of work as a legitimate part of case management nor did it see the development of alternative resources as the legitimate work of administrators.

If case management continues to focus on the organization of community support for people who may feel powerful negative effects when these supports are weak or simply nonexistent, then who can ignore these resource inadequacies? Is a case management system based on emergency and crisis a desired end? These are crucial questions pertaining to improvement—not only the improvement of case management, but the improvement of service systems and the lives of recipients.

Input Themes

Input involves the resources that are essential to effective program and service delivery. Input includes physical facilities, equipment, personnel, and other tangible supplies needed to bring the case management initiative into operational reality and to maintain it as an effective human service program. Three input themes were identified that cut across the case management initiatives. The first theme deals with the threats to model integrity when case managers do not have adequate tools or resources available to engage in productive and effective community support. The second theme addresses the professional status of case management personnel. The third theme identifies the need to expand what we mean by professional identity in case management programs.

The Integrity of the Case Management Model

All three case management initiatives held high performance expectations of their case management personnel. But in all three situations, the case management initiatives did not give explicit attention to the tools their personnel needed in order to engage in effective community support practice (Rapp, 1993). This was particularly true in the implementation of effective outreach procedures and activities. Case managers needed specific resources to make community outreach possible, including such things as flextime, the availability of agency-supported automobiles, the availability of consumer transportation, and the availability of computer and telecommunications capacities.

The integrity of all three of these initiatives was based on being in the community, networking with community institutions and organizations, conducting outreach to consumers in their homes or in locations remote from the sponsoring agency, and undertaking intervention activities in community locations. It was puzzling to find that these three programs, despite their commitment to community support practice and to the mobility of their case management personnel, did not establish explicit frameworks guiding what case managers needed to do and what tools they needed to be equipped with in order to perform effectively. In one situation, case managers had to rely on their own automobiles, which created an inordinate amount of stress for personnel as cars depreciated and car repairs mounted. These same case managers operated without mobile telephones and without laptop computers, both of which would have increased their service delivery efficiency. The sponsoring organization's response to these deficiencies was that the resources did not exist to "embellish" the program. Some organizational leaders dismissed these tools as exotic.

Case management personnel found the inconsistencies between expectations and the availability of appropriate tools to be distressing. Some case managers resolved this distress by scheduling increasing amounts of time at the agency and expecting clients to come to the facility for appointments. Community support practice in this case was not very different from typical facility-based practice. Of course, those people who were most mobile and able to come to the facility were seen most often, while those people who did not have either the mobility or inclination to seek services at the facility (often those people who needed specific supports) were seen less often or not at all.

The integrity of case management within the community support framework was compromised at the multi-program mental health agency by the absence of the necessary tools to engage in the desired form of practice. Case management personnel were quite frustrated by the inability to undertake more proactive work. Appeals to agency administration went unheard since the organization was unwilling to address the issue of worker and consumer transportation resources.

The improvement issue here is very specific and concrete. What are the resources needed to engage in a form of practice characterized by mobility, outreach, and networking, all of which contribute to a community presence by case management personnel? Each case management initiative must anticipate worker needs in order to realize with integrity the desired model. Thus, merely specifying the form of case management practice that is desired is not enough. Integrity is a function of being explicit about what is desired and of operationalizing the personnel supports needed to achieve in actual practice the model that is desired.

Good Case Management Practice

Good case management is sophisticated work. Examination of the expectations of case management practice within the three initiatives reveals that much is expected of incumbents from the standpoint of professionalism, including professional accountability, development, and performance. But despite the value placed on community support practice, case management within these initiatives remained an entry level position attractive to young, relatively inexperienced workers seeking their first position in human services. In some ways the characteristics of these workers were an asset. The programs did not have to address ingrained negative stereotypes often prevalent among longer-term workers. In addition, the workers demonstrated high levels of flexibility, a willingness to learn very difficult and challenging tasks, and a willingness to work under very demanding circumstances. The characteristics of the workers, the reluctance of the sponsoring organizations to put in place incentives and rewards for the desired form of practice undertaken by case management personnel, the absence of a broad range of supports elevating the effectiveness of the case management roles themselves, and the stigma assigned to people with serious mental illness (who were often characterized as unattractive candidates for service) served to discount not only the importance of these positions but the professionalism assigned to them within the sponsoring organizations.

A comparison of role demands created by case management to those created by typical counseling or psychotherapeutic positions revealed within these initiatives the sophsticated and demanding nature of case management work. A comparison of these positions within each of the initiatives revealed that case management required more flexibility in activities, time, and behavior; considerable use of judgment in relationship to risk-laden community living situations, interaction with social control agencies like the police, involvement in addressing rights, and status violations; and considerable use of creative thinking and problem-solving with consumers, families, neighbors, and service personnel. Case management personnel often spent more time than personnel in traditional roles in collaboration and teamwork, and in negotiating and mediating very difficult situations in the community.

Numerous improvement issues cluster within this thematic area. First, it is important for case management initiatives to frame this form of practice as professional work of the highest order and to venerate the work of community support as an essential aspect of the sponsoring organization's role and function within the community (Moxley & Taranto, 1994). Second, underscoring this importance through a vigorous human resource development program, and establishing a set of incentives for continuing in these roles, can bolster the standing of this form of practice and of the personnel who engage in it. Third, it is important for case management initiatives to examine reward and support systems for case management roles that differentiate these roles from other types and forms of human service practice. This is not merely to identify the importance of this practice, but to underscore that case management within community support systems requires its own spectrum of personnel supports.

Experimentation in the Personnel Area

All three case management initiatives adopted a narrow definition of what they meant by professionalism through its equation with professional credentials. Placing formal sociological definitions of professional aside, there has been considerable expansion and diversification of what is meant by "professional" within the field of psychiatric rehabilitation and community support. Anthony and his colleagues differentiate between credentialed and functional professionals, and identify important contributions that can be made by both categories of personnel in psychiatric rehabilitation. Credentialed professionals, people who obtain training and education within sanctioned disciplines, are different from those professionals who are trained and educated—often on the job and through specialized nondegree programs—to execute effectively specialized roles and functions within human service programs. Functional professionals can engage in roles like peer support specialist, supported employment coach, or housing specialist.

The failure to interpret "professional" broadly placed functional and contextual limitations on these case management initiatives. Not only did these programs fail to promote the professional contributions of case managers within the context of their sponsoring organizations, they failed to expand the availability of roles for new incumbents who could bring different resources, skills, and experiences to these positions. The field of psychiatric rehabilitation recognizes the array of roles that consumers themselves fill in systems of community support (Mowbray, Moxley, Jasper, & Howell, 1995). Variations in roles of "consumers as providers" include consumers as program staff, as peer support providers, as self-help leaders, and as initiators of new innovations in critical domains of community living such as housing.

Improvement of case management can benefit from experimentation in the area of role innovation by offering consumers new opportunities as providers of case management services. Yet such improvement must be undertaken systematically with an eye to promoting the professional development of these new role incumbents, supporting their effectiveness within sponsoring organizations and systems, and preparing "old line" professionals to accept and collaborate with consumers in new roles. Such role innovation can foster within community support systems the expansion of resources, the flexing of roles, the matching of various needs and people to case management personnel, and the opening of new opportunity structures for people who have been largely confined to roles as recipients.

Process Themes

Process involves specific program activities and behaviors that must be implemented in order to achieve the goals and aims of the case management initiative. In addition, process relates to the sequencing of these activities and behaviors, and their programming into explicit and expected routines of service delivery. Two process themes were most salient across the three case management initiatives. These involve: (1) the need to identify and explicitly define basic intervention processes; and (2) the need to configure case management as a crisis service if much of the time of case managers is devoted to crisis intervention.

Increasing the Implementation Effectiveness of Case Management

Continuous quality improvement identifies the importance of addressing the quality of the processes that create products or outcomes. Yet in all three of the case management initiatives, these programs tended to ignore basic processes in favor of a philosophical orientation to practice. Thus, a considerable amount of time was invested in helping workers come to grips with the "correct" philosophy. Leaders of these initiatives believed that workers who embraced the desired philosophy would ultimately perform in the correct way.

This was not the case. Even workers with the correct philosophy did not necessarily perform in effective ways. There was no assurance that they would perform in this manner because none of the initiatives made it a priority to train their staff to the desired standard using the desired performance. Two problems calling for vigorous improvement stand out within these initiatives. They failed to make explicit the standards of program performance, and they failed to make explicit the procedures by which these standards were to be achieved, criteria essential to good human service intervention (Thomas, 1984). Certainly these programs identified salient characteristics of desired practice, such as achieving a strengths and community orientation, but these characteristics were not rigorously translated into standards and processes. Using Thomas's criteria of a "good" human service intervention, these intiatives failed on two counts: they failed to operationalize what was meant by "objective capability"—that is, what the initiative should ultimately achieve in practice—and they failed to make explicit their procedures for achieving what is desired.

Dramatic improvement can be a product of selecting the right things to improve, and then attacking these vigorously. The philosophical orientations of these three initiatives did establish the context within which improvement can begin. But they then needed to move to the next step of identifying key intervention processes, standards guiding what these processes need to achieve, and an understanding of how processes and standards contribute to desired performance expectations and results.

According to Continuous Quality Improvement, the aim of overall programmatic improvement lies in making best practices or at least good practices routine daily practice. This offers case management initiatives a practical aim: What best practices should these programs embody, and how are these practices converted to standard routines or protocols? For the case management initiatives, which focused on community support, standards lie in making routine key processes in the areas of case identification, outreach, strengths and community assessment, relationship building and enhancement, crisis prevention and intervention, consumer-driven planning, support system development, advocacy, data and information system management, community barrier analysis, and evaluation of practice and environmental intervention. Weak or nonexistent standards can threaten effective implementation and can prevent the realization of essential programmatic outcomes (McGrew & Bond, 1995).

Absence of explicit standards and processes in these areas means that the staff-training component—essential to the realization of any high quality initiative—is weak if not nonexistent. Linking ongoing, vigorous training to effective protocols of practice may be a fundamental strategy for the improvement of case management service delivery. These protocols are a substantial component of a case management program's technology, and they represent the "know-how" of the program. Making this know-how a real aspect of human resource development suggests another necesssary improvement task: making explicit to case management staff what is expected of them from the perspective of performance.

Designing the Case Management Initiative to Manage Crises

Despite the considerable conceptualization invested in sorting out case management—what it is, what it should do, whom it should serve—discussions with practicing case managers suggest that a considerable amount of their time is invested in the management of emergencies and crises. Perhaps this orientation to crisis and the work that comes out of it is related to the manner in which we have structured social welfare in the United States and in many local communities. Social welfare services and supports can only really kick in legitimately when there are crises. People should not really expect proactive service delivery, and people should rely on other sources of help until their situations really do become insufferable.

Case managers as street level bureaucrats operate in constrained resource situations. The people they work with often represent the most needy within a community and the most sensitive to changes or alterations in the resource base of a community. Basic living resources are not available in abundance. Indeed their availability is somewhat marginal—slight changes in policies can alter resource availability dramatically and leave people destitute. Case management in many circumstances may be "practice on the margin," and the margins are quite slim. No wonder case management personnel often find the people they serve to be in crisis quite often. No wonder case management personnel often find their work to be characterized by crisis.

There may be another explanation of why case management personnel deal with crisis so much. Organizations may shift the burden of effort from organizational programs to the case management service, seeing case management as a program that can handle almost any service contingency. Thus, it is not unusual that case management programs in developmental disabilities link case management services to habilitation programs; mental health agencies link case management services to specialized residential settings; and child welfare agencies link case management services to treatment programs. When these programs cannot maintain a person, the burden for finding solutions can be shifted to case management.

Preoccupation with crises was a salient attribute of the three case management initiatives. Little time was available, from the perspective of the case management personnel of these initiatives, to invest in "high quality, routine practice." Their reality tended to be crisis laden and crisis driven. During an interview, one case manager repeatedly interrupted me when I asked about consumer-driven practice by saying, "Don't you mean crisis-driven practice?"

My inclusion of this particular improvement theme is somewhat tongue in cheek. We should not have the expectation that case management initiatives must become crisis intervention programs even though right now they most likely undertake a significant level of crisis service. An improvement orientation and ethos demands the identification of root causes and the testing out of action plans designed to make an appreciable impact on these root causes. Each crisis tells its own story. Each can offer data concerning improvement and the movement away from a crisis orientation. As identified above, a critical protocol undergirding good practice in case management may involve the use of procedures designed to prevent or reduce crises. Perhaps by solving the crisis problem, case management programs can indeed become more proactive in fostering community support.

Product Themes

Products involve the specific things attained by the case management initiative, either intentionally or unintentionally. Products can be confined to aspects of achievement, or they can involve outcome and ultimately impact. The two themes identified within the product component involve the definition of desired performance, and moving from an achievement orientation to an impact orientation.

What Case Management Staff Need to Know and Understand

A recurrent theme thoughout this chapter involves the need to clarify case management performance expectations. Considering that this theme operated with equal saliency in each of the three case management initiatives, and is interrelated with almost any other theme, it represents a fundamental issue that must be resolved in order to develop and implement good case management practice. Its placement within the section on product themes underscores the importance of this thematic issue to identifying the intended outcomes and impact of the case management initiative. Given staff confusion about what constituted desired case management performance within these initiatives, it is not surprising to find that these staff were confused about the ultimate product of their practice.

A number of factors appeared to influence the absence of well thought out performance expectations. One of these factors is the weak linkage between case management and "whole system" thinking. In other words, the real purpose of community support within these three initiatives and within their host systems was not well articulated. One system on the verge of running down and closing a state hospital allowed this aim to frame and give energy to case management and community support, only to find to the chagrin of the system's leaders that people were not living in good situations despite staying outside the hospital. Another initiative—the one based within the multi-program mental health agency—had difficulty giving an explicit purpose to case management, most likely because it failed to think through the purpose and operation of its community support system. Dissatisfaction with the case management initiative in the third system was perhaps more an outcome of success than failure. This system had reached a hiatus in the development of its community support system, and it was seeking to move to a new generation of community support: from a medical orientation to serious mental illness to a rehabilitation one—a move that the case management initiative did not really grasp in either conceptual or operational terms.

Understanding what the whole system of community support looks like, and is intended to look like, can offer case management a platform on which to design its key processes and model. Without this whole system orientation—one that attempts to make each key component a contributing part, and one that attempts to integrate these parts—case management may focus on its own ends. Unfortunately, from the perspective of street level bureaucracy, these ends may be nominalistically defined: as getting people more and more services or entitlements without helping them to achieve personally valued outcomes in substantive life domains.

This theme highlights the importance of focusing on the performance model of case management as an important aspect of product. The performance model may be expressed at the level of the worker and may attempt to model those processes that case management personnel need to be implementing in order to realize the purpose of case management and its contribution to community support.

Case Management Programs Must Expand Their Vision beyond Achievement and Outcome

All three case management initiatives could readily identify the achievements and outcomes they sought. Most of these end statements were framed from the perspective of what the community support system desired, and what it sought to achieve in service to people with serious mental illness. Statements of achievement were dominated by outreach to specific populations, the involvement of certain types of people in clinical care, the reduction of the use of expensive treatment alternatives, the prevention of recidivism, and the implementation of community-based treatment alternatives for high risk populations.

Many of these achievements reflected the status of the community support systems within their local communities and the preoccupation of these systems with the provision of mental health care. Case management initiatives were identified as salient means for the achievement of what was desired from a systems standpoint, yet little detail was provided about how case management and its personnel were to achieve these desired ends.

Lists of outcome statements were readily identified, with these outcomes framed by the involvement of case management in the control of costly symptoms and behavioral constellations. Few outcomes focused on what changes case management was to make in the improvement of the community support system, framed especially from the perspective of the people who use case management and supportive services.

Absent from these three initiatives were true statements of impact about how the lives of people with serious mental illness were to be materially and substantially changed through their involvement in case management. Impact on people's lives expressed through changes in standard of living and quality of life were not well articulated; there was little use of the words of those people served, nor incorporation of the values, directions, and perspectives they saw as important. The ends of case management were not directly linked to the improvement of the status of the people who were coping with a very serious social problem, the consequences of which can be quite negative.

The ultimate test we should put to case management systems operating within community support systems lies in the impact they help to bring about, with impact understood as the improvement of a person's life circumstances. This may require case management within community support to adopt a broader practice framework: to incorporate community practice into its designs. Despite the innovation with which these three case management initiatives were struggling, they all practiced within a medical paradigm of serious mental illness that shifted the locus of care and intervention from the institution into the community.

A paradigm of community practice focuses the attention of case management personnel on resource arrangements that make an appreciable improvement in standard of living and quality of life. This shift requires these initiatives to begin to examine their intended impact, and to begin to understand the kind of changes, if any, recipients want to see in their own lives. Making this form of impact a relevant aspect of case management as an element of community support practice shifts the archetype of case management from a system-driven variant to one that is more compatible with a consumer-driven one.

CONCLUSION

These improvement themes underscore the complexity inherent in the development of effective case management programs, especially those relating to the improvement of the community support available to people with disabilities. These case management alternatives do not have a discrete functional objective like the improvement of quality of care or the management of utilization. Alternatively, they can be described as programmatic forms with very complex goal sets and, as a consequence, an improvement orientation must address multiple dimensions, including context, input, process, and product. Each of these dimensions embodies a number of issues that, if left unaddressed, can compromise the performance of case management, case managers, and community support systems.

These dimensions and the issues they involve challenge the leadership of case management initiatives—as well as the organizations and hosts of these initiatives—to give considerable thought to the desired (and perhaps undesired) performance of case management systems and programs. Without making performance explicit there is a high probability that case management programs will simply fail to perform, or worse, will enable a system of human services to shift the burden of ineffective programs and services to the case management system. By making performance explicit, system leaders can identify what is expected— a state of affairs that can be evaluated and subsequently changed either in the spirit of improvement or in the spirit of accountability.

CHAPTER 7

APPLICATION OF TOTAL QUALITY MANAGEMENT TO THE IMPROVEMENT OF A CASE MANAGEMENT PROGRAM

Sandra L. Taranto and David P. Moxley

Total Quality Management is a fairly new approach to the improvement of products and services. It is being widely adopted by organizations in the public, private, and nonprofit sectors. The movement recognizes the importance of establishing an approach to service designed to exceed the needs of consumers, the continuous improvement of quality, ownership of quality improvement efforts by all organizational members, teamwork, systematic evaluation, and the development of human resources. In this chapter we outline the initial efforts of the case management program at Community Care Services, a comprehensive community mental health center located in Taylor, Michigan, to establish a platform supporting the continuous improvement of case management services. Sandra Taranto has been a key manager involved in this initiative, and David Moxley has served as a consultant to the case management team.

The chapter focuses on the early parts of this process, especially the parts devoted to helping case management personnel to appreciate their roles and to gain a basic understanding of case management models and approaches. The case management initiative was initially driven by fiscal concerns, but it ultimately resulted in the adoption of case management ideas and practices designed to improve the delivery of services to people with serious mental illness or serious mental health problems. This chapter addresses the need to support case managers in their quest for a viable identity. The content illustrates the importance of paying considerable attention to human resource development within case management programs.

Case management and Total Quality Management share a lot in common. Case management, as a distinctive approach to the delivery of human services, offers a human service professional an opportunity to interact closely and intensively with recipients of an organization's services (Rose, 1992). Many case managers gain a holistic and broad understanding of the lives of the people they serve since the manner in which they practice offers them ample opportunities to assess and to understand the development and community living situations of their clients, and the issues that these people must address in their daily lives. Case managers often obtain a keen understanding of the range of services their clients are receiving, and the supports they need but are not getting.

Case managers confront daily in their practice the challenge of fulfilling the needs of their "customers." And, consistent with basic ideas of Total Quality Management, they must understand how to meet these needs, as well as the limitations in service processes, products, and effectiveness that can frustrate or prevent the fulfillment of these needs. Case managers can be frontline representatives of continuous improvement efforts. Through broad and diverse consumer-focused assessment, planning, monitoring, and evaluation efforts they can gain a rich understanding of the strengths and limitations of a service system, and the critical areas in which the system must improve in order to meet the expectations or needs of its users.

Yet despite their efforts to obtain and organize rich portrayals of the needs and situations of consumers, case managers are too often ignored by their own sponsoring organizations or systems as frontline resources in the quest for the continuous improvement approaches that are increasingly being implemented and institutionalized in human services. There are many reasons for this state of affairs. Case managers often hold line staff positions, and their voices are not amplified so that senior administrators hear what they have to say (Dill, 1987). Case managers themselves experience diminished status not only because case management is often interpreted by human service organizations as quasi-professional work, but also because many of the people served by case managers are devalued within their communities and within organizations that are ostensibly devoted to serving them.

Nonetheless, case management has increasingly won the attention of local, state, and federal policy makers. It is seen ideally as a relevant frontline strategy for helping people with serious problems or disabilities to organize and implement individually designed packages of human services, social supports, and societal opportunities that, taken together, are thought to help improve the functioning of recipients.

Case management can be viewed as Total Quality Management in action. In its ideal, consumer-driven form, case management is committed to identifying needs from the perspectives of the direct recipients (Anthony et al., 1988). It is committed to assuring the quality and improvement of the services, supports, and opportunities that are determined to be important by recipients (Rapp, 1992). Achieving effective teamwork based on good communication is fundamental to the success of case management since effective delivery of case management requires personnel to collaborate with other providers within the sponsoring organization, across service systems, and across the community to ensure that effective team-based support systems are in place for all recipients. Finally, engaging in ongoing monitoring of services and appraising their performance and effectiveness are fundamental case management ideas (Moxley, 1989).

The implementation of case management, nonetheless, is difficult. Poor implementation effectiveness is known too well by case managers themselves and their recipients. Numerous challenges to implementation exist, including those pertaining to the power and influence of case managers, underdeveloped and poorly integrated service systems (Mechanic, 1987), poorly developed basic social and community resources (like housing and employment) that are accessible to every citizen (Rothman, 1992), and discriminatory practices within our communities that prevent recipients of these programs from achieving an appreciable level of social integration.

If we are to invest precious resources in the implementation of case management services and programs, we must be very concerned about their implementation effectiveness and, likewise, cognizant of the many challenges that can prevent or frustrate the implementation of effective case management initiatives. Total Quality Management is one tool that can be used to develop and improve the implementation effectiveness of case management over time. It is a method of operating and a management philosophy that utilizes team processes and tools to search out and select opportunities for improvement (Kennedy, 1991). These opportunities are measured by consumer satisfaction, and the entire process is driven by consumer-identified needs. The relevance of Total Quality Management to human services is reflected by the influence of consumerism and a shift from a product to a marketing orientation (Cohen & Brand, 1993). Using Total Quality Management to improve case management can reinforce the basic ideals of case management services, especially those relating to an outcome orientation, improvement of service systems, teamwork, and responsiveness to consumers.

PURPOSE AND CONTENT OF THE CHAPTER

This chapter reflects our attempts, working in conjunction with the personnel of a case management program, to improve the implementation effectiveness and performance of the program through the use of the core ideas, principles, and practices of Total Quality Management (Creech, 1994). These efforts were driven by widespread dissatisfaction with the purpose, focus, and performance of the emerging case management program within Community Care Services (CCS). Thus, we first review the problem this agency faced and the obstacles that emerged to frustrate case management implementation. We then review the relevance of Total Quality Management, the factors motivating the agency to employ Total Quality Management as an organizational improvement strategy, and the early process we used to initiate improvement of case management. Finally, we offer conclusions about the continuation of the process and about how to make case management a salient component of an organization's efforts to implement Total Quality Management.

FACTORS COMPROMISING IMPLEMENTATION EFFECTIVENESS

Organizational Response to Changing Mental Health Policy

Until approximately five years ago, Community Care Services designed the majority of its services around a clinical model of mental health services. The agency had achieved broad spatial decentralization within its service area through the establishment of area subunits. However, most of these units were focused on the delivery of office-based clinical services designed principally for people with acute mental health problems. The culture of the agency formed around this technology, and personnel with the correct type of clinical credentials, who practiced from this traditional perspective, enjoyed the highest standing within the agency.

The agency implemented its case management program in 1991, during a period of fiscal challenge and uncertainty for the organization. Personnel in the clinical core of the agency were threatened by job loss if the agency did not adapt to new mental health policy conditions requiring the movement to a more community-focused and outreach-oriented approach to service delivery. Regional policy changes within the mental health system were demanding that Community Care Services, and many other mental health agencies, begin to focus on the diversion of people from psychiatric hospitalization, the reduction of length of stay within state facilities, the prevention of hospitalization, and the timely access of consumers to rehabilitation and clinical care. These policy changes demanded that Community Care Services emphasize community support and the creation of service alternatives designed to implement community support of people with the most problematic mental health backgrounds.

Despite this substantive change in mental health policy, it was first interpreted by the agency as a financial threat. Clinical personnel were shifted into case management roles to preserve their employment and to reduce the immediate financial threat to the organization. The pressure to implement case management reduced its legitimacy within the agency, and personnel who were shifted adopted negative attitudes toward case management. Personnel who continued in clinical roles were not educated about the role changes required by case management and the substantive policy reasons behind them.

Thus there was no preparation for this change. There was no opportunity to educate the organization as a whole for the nature of the policy change that was occurring or the implications of this change for the entire system of services sponsored by Community Care Services. These conditions produced a very confusing and perhaps negative context in which case management was to be implemented.

Novelty of Case Management

In addition to hasty implementation, case management was a relative novelty to the mental health board that endorsed and sponsored its implementation, for the agencies that were to adopt this new technology, for the personnel who were to use it, and for recipients. Certainly this change signaled a coming shift in the configuration of the local mental health system (to a managed service system, and to more of a community support approach), but this broader change in configuration, and the purpose and role of case management within it, was not well articulated, clarified, or operationalized. For CCS, this change was substantial, but the origins, purposes, models, state-of-the-art practices, and functions of case management were not fully appreciated or understood internally. Thus, all staff, including the new case management personnel, felt considerable ambiguity about what case management was as a service technology and what it should achieve.

There was little correspondence between the agency's understanding of case management and the understanding of case management possessed by the local mental health board. The new agency case managers were angered by how many professionals within the system trivialized their role and placed it into a deprofessionalized context. This unclarity only served to stir the emotions of the new agency case management staff, many of whom were experienced and well-trained mental health professionals. It reinforced their initial doubt and misunderstanding, and only served to reinforce their negative attitudes toward the actual change that was occurring.

What soon became apparent was that there were multiple understandings and expectations held about case management by different stakeholders. The absence of any consistent, operational understanding of case management that cut across the agency as a whole (or across the mental health system as a whole) jeopardized the legitimacy of case management and the effectiveness of its initial implementation. In addition, there was little consensus within the agency concerning how case management should perform, the value it should produce for consumers or for the service system, and the emerging mental health policy concerning community support.

The Consequences of the Absence of Mission

The CCS case management component had no clear nor explicit mission during the early period of its implementation. The absence of a clear programmatic mission was a product of the failure to build consensus within the system, and within the agency, concerning the aims, form, and substance of case management. The absence of a mission signaled the absence of a clear case management model adopted by the agency. A poorly defined mission is one condition leading to poor quality.

In addition, a poorly defined mission allowed case management personnel and subunit supervisors to use their own ideas about how case management should be implemented and how it should perform. This only gave a haphazard and inconsistent character to whatever implementation effort was being undertaken by the agency. The absence of a clear mission weakened the formation of a unified identity among agency case managers, prevented the agency from achieving an actual system of case management within the service core of the organization, and weakened substantially the formation of a team among case managers and between case managers and other service personnel within the agency.

A Summary of Implementation Obstacles

Thus within the agency, there was no strong educational initiative to prepare the agency for the introduction of case management, and there was a failure to offer a clear rationale guiding the change and the need for this new service technology. People were abruptly reassigned to these new duties without an explicit and careful process identifying the type of personnel, and the specific people, who could make the most relevant contribution to case management. The absence of an explicit model, and of a plan guiding implementation, weakened the subsequent standing of case management within the actual team that was formed and within the larger organizational service system. The absence of explicit guidelines to supervisors assured the idiosyncratic implementation of case management across the subunits of this decentralized organization.

Implementation effectiveness is achieved when credibility of a change is established, supported in part through a thoughtful and well articulated process of change in the mission of the sponsoring organization. Implementation effectiveness is strengthened when key people are engaged in a change effort and responsibility for oversight is assigned to these individuals, rather than dispersing it into decentralized enclaves of the organization. Implementation effectiveness also requires that the purposive design of new positions is explicit and the relationship of new roles to other established positions within a human service organization is addressed. For example, failure to consider the correspondence of the new case management roles to those of established clinical roles set the stage for conflict between the incumbents of the new positions and the incumbents of the more traditional therapeutic roles.

However, the problems experienced by CCS in the implementation of case management were not necessarily of its own making. The oversight agency originally saw case management as an opportunity for changing the mental health system both fiscally and programmatically, and did not offer a framework within which service effectiveness potentially offered by the case management program could be understood. The oversight agency did place some serious design limitations on the actual case management positions, most notably by requiring the splitting of therapeutic roles from case management ones. This was done without offering a strong service rationale for this split or offering other models in which such role integration could be achieved successfully and with the realization of greater benefits to certain subgroups of consumers (Harris & Bachrach, 1988). Most problematic, however, was the failure of the oversight system to identify clear expectations concerning performance, outcomes, and impact of case management.

These issues, problems, and challenges suggest relevant foci to quality improvement of case management. It is critical to begin improvement efforts with an explicit programmatic design, a plan for the organization of the case management program within the sponsoring agency, and an explicit design of case management roles. Certainly this design work must also be placed into a larger context of organizational policy and programmatic change, so that the context created by administrative systems, other programs, and other personnel is hospitable to at least accepting if not endorsing the introduction of the case management program.

This agency is not unique in the problematic implementation of case management. The introduction of case management within many systems has not enjoyed the benefits garnered from explicit programmatic design or explicit organizational preparation through policy change, education, awareness building, and the identification of the consequences for other agency programs and personnel. The endorsement of Total Quality Management by CCS in 1993 offered the case management program a strategic opportunity to return to some of these key tasks, and to examine quality by addressing basic programmatic design, fostering a mutual understanding of case management within the program, and specifying an initial agenda guiding quality improvement undertaken by case management personnel themselves.

RELEVANCE OF TOTAL QUALITY MANAGEMENT TO THE IMPROVEMENT OF CASE MANAGEMENT IMPLEMENTATION

The policy forces motivating CCS to embrace Total Quality Management were similar to those supporting the movement of the agency to case management. By 1991 CCS became increasingly aware of skyrocketing costs, liability risks, and competitive pressures created by managed care. To survive, the agency needed to learn to work smarter, more quickly, and more effectively in the delivery of services to mental health consumers, many of whom began to present needs that were products of communities experiencing vast social, economic, and physical changes. A strategic planning process was implemented during 1991 that involved the agency board, staff, and volunteers. The process led to the adoption of statements of beliefs and mission that served as the foundation of the agency's five-year plan. A principal product of this planning effort was the acceptance of Total Quality Management as an important tool in the overall improvement of agency services.

In the fall of 1993 and winter of 1994, administrative and management staff participated in an intensive Total Quality Management training process. A steering committee was developed to guide the ongoing implementation and management of the agency's process of Total Quality Management (Rago & Reid, 1991). Training of line staff was initiated in the spring of 1994. Pilot teams were developed, whose missions were to identify an area for needed improvement and to use the process of Total Quality Management to develop a plan for improvement, make recommendations for improvement, and/or initiate implementation of their plans. Specific departments within the agency identified their own improvement plans, which focused on fulfilling customer needs.

The case management group had been meeting while the strategic planning process and Total Quality Management training were proceeding, and much of its work paralleled the process of continuous improvement. Total Quality Management provided the case management group with the opportunity to formalize their own process of improvement, legitimize it through the use of a common language based on Total Quality Management training, and ultimately to present administration with a document that identified concrete and critical issues, ones that influenced, both positively and negatively, the delivery of quality case management services. The group utilized Total Quality Management to define the mission of case management, and also the mission of the case management group as a Total Quality Management team.

Use of Total Quality Management thinking offered the case management team an opportunity to identify specific issues that were operating through the earlier hasty implementation of case management. Team members realized that they possessed considerable data regarding the serious problems faced by recipients in their daily lives, and that these data were invaluable to the agency in the creation of new programmatic or service initiatives designed to fulfill these needs and/or resolve the problems faced by consumers. The presentation of the document to senior administrators of the agency helped support the success of Total Quality Management within CCS. Linking Total Quality Management to case management illustrates how an innovation in managerial technology can complement innovations in service technology to make continuous improvement a principal objective of a human service organization.

PROCESS OF CASE MANAGEMENT IMPROVEMENT WITHIN THE AGENCY

Building a Team Understanding of Case Management

Case management from the perspective of CCS administration focuses on linking, coordinating, and monitoring, and encompasses many of the characteristics of a brokerage model. The case management team needed to undertake an intentional effort to educate itself about alternative case management models, and the strengths and limitations of these models. Self-education by the case management team covered basic theories of case management and prevailing models; the linkage of these models to certain human service functions, populations, and outcomes; and the need to define an agency model that respected community context, service system characteristics, and needs of consumers.

This self-education resulted in the adoption by the case management team of a model of practice that was not consistent with the more traditional conception of case management held by senior administrators of the agency or the model held by the local mental health board. The case management team adopted a more comprehensive and rehabilitative approach to practice. The group recognized the necessity to adopt roles as mobilizers and organizers of supports that reduce the impact of disability. Supports, from the perspective of the team, are mobilized to develop self-help and self-care capacities, to empower others to resolve their own difficulties, and to meet their own goals or desires. Case managers identified with an advocacy approach to practice, and endorsed the use of a strengths perspective rather than a clinical or diagnostic approach that is prevalent within the clinical core of the agency.

The case management team struggled with undertaking self-education in a rational manner, while still harboring anger emanating out of perceived injustices, and skepticism regarding whether anything of substance could actually change. This is not unique to case management, nor even to the hasty implementation in which this case management initiative occurred. It is very characteristic of quality improvement efforts undertaken within any sector of our society (Harrington,

1995; Sashkin & Kiser, 1993). There is a tension created by a struggle to begin improvement, and a struggle with self-doubt created by past disappointments.

A basic idea of Total Quality Management lies in the domain of human resource development. Teams have to take time to educate themselves concerning the nature of their work, state-of-the-art practices in their work area, and model practices designed to improve basic processes. Failure to offer case managers the opportunity to engage in this process of human resource development shortchanges if not undermines the actual process of Total Quality Management.

Creating a Group Identity as Case Managers and as a Case Management Team

The process of self-education offered the opportunity for members of the case management group to build cohesion as a team. The decentralized organizational structure separated case managers into discrete units, and divided them by specialized functions and specific geographic locations. Creating a work group so essential to the achievement of an identity as a team was challenged by the actual organizational structure of CCS. Self-education enabled case managers to come together on a regular basis to reflect on their identity as a case management program within the larger agency, and what this program should produce in the lives of the people served, as well as for the larger system of services sponsored by the agency. Self-education was largely invested in defining the value of case management to principal customers—to users and to the service system (Egan, 1993).

With the encouragement of agency executives, the team emerged within the agency as a practice group with a specific purpose found in refining the operation of case management as an agency program. The actual team was recognized by central administration as a principal practice group within the agency that could model how a program could be improved in a highly decentralized human service organization. Thus, the case management team searched for two missions. First, it sought to establish its mission as an agency-sanctioned practice group. Second, it sought to establish its mission as a case management system within the agency. Both missions are vital to the success of Total Quality Management.

The mission of the case management practice group was framed from the perspective of continuous improvement. It now reads as follows:

> It is the mission of the Case Management Practice Group to engage in a proactive process of professional development and the improvement of case management service delivery through the identification of salient issues facing case management, the consumers the agency serves, and the community the agency seeks to serve, and the meaningful resolution of these issues through the application of state of the art knowledge, team problem-solving, and team collaboration with other programs and leaders of the agency.

The work of the case management practice group is framed by two missions: one devoted to the improvement of case management; and, as illustrated in the next section, one devoted to clarifying the contribution case management makes to a system of consumer-driven services.

Formulating a Frame of Reference Guiding Case Management, and Specification of a Programmatic Mission

Given the orientation of case managers to outreach and to the organization of community-based service delivery for their clients, they gain critical information from describing firsthand the resource and environmental problems faced by consumers of mental health services. Data regarding resources and environmental problems were related to the quality of service delivery by CCS and by other agencies, and identified the need to integrate these data into the parallel TQM process occurring within the organization. The case management team looked at its own processes, data collection activities, and data utilization efforts. Opportunities to integrate data into program development initiatives of CCS were identified as important areas of service system improvement in order to improve the daily living circumstances of the agency's consumers.

The team's examination of itself in relationship to CCS required that case managers address how they could make significant and substantial contributions to the attainment of the agency's vision and mission, an activity that required the team to forge a psychological connection between itself and their larger organizational host. In the words of the case management team itself:

> We feel that case management can make significant and substantial contributions to agency vision and mission. The mission of the agency is being reconsidered and reformulated in light of the need to address the integration of community supports and individual coping. The mission of the agency is to promote the functioning of people and case management contributes to this aspect of the mission by addressing the environmental resource dimension of human functioning. The mission of the agency seeks to improve people's quality of life as it is expressed physically, emotionally, spiritually, socially, and vocationally. Case management contributes to this aspect of the mission by linking people to specific resources that support their quality of life. The mission of the agency seeks to integrate formal and informal support systems. Certainly case management struggles to help people make use of their natural support systems. Finally, the mission of the agency is expressed in outcome terms by helping people to achieve concrete life outcomes, something case management does on a daily basis through its advocacy, linkage, and resource development activities.

A consideration of the agency's mission and the contribution of case management to this mission produced the vision and mission guiding case management at Community Care Services. These two products offered the team specific anchors to an identity that was once shifting and ill defined. The vision formulated by the team is the following:

> We envision case management to be recognized by consumers, the community, agency staff, and administration as client advocates with sensitivity to an individual's culture and lifestyle. The expertise of case management lies in providing access to those resources which are defined as a need or even a want by our consumers. We will focus on access to physical health care, vocational development, employment, housing, and community support. Case management programmatically organized within the agency will involve a cross-section of professionally credentialed personnel collaborating with technically trained staff and consumers to offer a mixture of peer support, formal services, and social network supports.

The vision enabled the case management team to formulate its mission, one that is consistent with the overall direction of the agency, and its efforts to improve the quality of the service it delivers. The case management team established its mission as:

> The promotion of the functioning of the people served to the best of their ability—physically, emotionally, spiritually, socially, and vocationally by connecting natural and formal support systems. Our success is measured by the achievement of concrete, pragmatic life outcomes resulting in consumers becoming as independent and self-sufficient as possible.

The team established for case management within the agency an explicit framework of practices and values guiding these practices. They saw the value of capacity building to be the heart of their work, and they recognized the importance of building capacities of community and individuals. Case managers recognized the importance of being prepared and skilled in assisting individuals and their communities to develop self-help and self-care capacities. They identified the importance of empowering individuals to resolve their own difficulties and meet their own needs. This meant for them that case managers must invest considerable energy in offering consumers, and their significant others, basic information about entitlements, technical assistance in how to meet identified needs, problem-solving and training in self-advocacy, and representation services when individual resources or capacities did not meet the demands of the environment.

This activity represented a critical step in Total Quality Management. It defined for the case management team its linkage to the larger organization, and identified for the team its distinctive contribution to the clients of the agency. This work helped to link the team as a technical function (i.e., as a case management function) and as an improvement structure (i.e., as a practice group) to the larger Total Quality Management process sanctioned by the agency. The formulation of vision and mission won support for the team from senior administrators who saw its work as constructive, as consistent with the overall ongoing Total Quality Management process sponsored by the agency, and as a direct contribution to supporting the success of TQM within the agency.

This activity also demonstrates how crucial the formulation of focus and direction is to any quality improvement initiative. A team has to define where it wants to go, must define an envisioned platform of performance to which it can compare discrete improvement projects, and must determine whether the actual opportunity for improvement is consistent with where the team wants to end up. By defining its vision, mission, and values, and the relationship of these to the agency's mission, the case management team formulated a frame of reference for planning and evaluating its improvement activities. This frame of reference establishes the basic identity of the team.

Identifying an Improvement Agenda

Any quality improvement effort is challenged by what to select as worthy and meritorious projects (Elliott, 1994). For any organization there is a universe of issues at all levels of the agency to be addressed. Implementation of Total Quality Management calls for the careful consideration of these issues and for the critical selection of a handful of initiatives that will make a significant if not substantial impact on the quality of agency performance. Indeed, effective implementation of Total Quality Management requires the establishment of a carefully considered agenda of change undertaken by a team making use of continuous improvement principles.

The Case Management Practice Group worked intentionally to create an agenda designed along the dimensions of merit and worth. The team's analysis of the poor and hasty implementation of case management at the agency showed that the technical qualities of case management were weak, and the organizational acceptance of this innovation was low. Issues pertaining to the technical quality and competence of case management involved merit, that is, the extent to which case management could engage in those technical processes that would produce desired outcomes for clients and the agency. Those issues pertaining to organizational acceptance of case management involved worth, that is, the extent to which case management was seen as valuable to the work of the agency. The question of worth really pertains to the extent to which case management is positioned internally to produce value for the agency, and pertains to the extent to which organizational members see its products as valuable.

The Case Management Practice Group, therefore, pursued two quality improvement goals. The first goal, which pertains to technical merit, involved the continuous improvement of those technical processes that would enhance the quality of case management performance in the achievement of outcomes valued by users of the system. The second goal, which pertains to worth, involved the improvement of the awareness and understanding of agency personnel about case management mission, functions, and activities. These two goals framed the agenda of discrete improvement projects undertaken by the Case Management Practice Group. All projects were screened to determine whether they contributed to the improvement of the technical aspects of case management or to the improvement of the position of case management within the agency's system of services.

Establishing Discrete Improvement Projects

Presently, the improvement agenda of the Case Management Practice Group includes three projects that involve the improvement of the technical merit of case management service delivery and two projects that involve the improvement of the value of case management to the agency. One of the principal technical improvement projects involves the strengthening of the orientation of case management personnel. This project seeks to improve the initial preparation of new case management staff to their roles, to the agency, and to the service system within and external to the agency. The project seeks to increase not only the knowledge and understanding that new case management staff have of case management, but also to improve the process of transitioning new staff into a complex and demanding role.

A second technical improvement project involves the development and implementation of ongoing case management team training. The objective of this project is to increase the use of state-of-the-art practices that are consistent with the mission and vision of the case management program. This project has involved case management staff in the identification of training needs, appraisal of the relevance of agency-sponsored training events, and identification of external training opportunities. The practice group seeks to identify core training competencies and to identify how these will be addressed through a case management training system.

The third technical improvement project focuses on the formulation of case management practice policy that promotes the internalization of state-of-the-art consumer-driven practices within the case management system and within the agency. The team has defined practice policy as statements of objectives and the means to achieve these objectives that are designed to support clients in the achievement of valued outcomes. Initial work in this area has resulted in the formulation of practice policies in the areas of wraparound funds under the control of case managers that can be used to promote a flexible response to client needs during emergencies; the expansion of transportation resources designed to support consumer outreach and the community mobility of case managers and consumers; and the management of caseloads to assure timely and responsive services to consumers.

The agency training and awareness project has been selected to improve the understanding of agency personnel of the mission and aims of case management, and of how the various subunits of the agency can make use of case management to achieve valued service and support outcomes. Another project on the agenda of the practice group will examine client-level needs data, with the objective of identifying the development of an agency-sponsored resource designed to meet the identified client need. This project reflects the commitment of case management to the improvement of support systems available to the clients served by Community Care Services. Both of these projects reflect the "worth" dimension of the practice group's improvement agenda.

CONCLUSION: NEXT STEPS IN THE PROCESS OF TOTAL QUALITY MANAGEMENT

Total Quality Management is an ongoing process, and a sincere commitment to the improvement of case management practice is itself never ending. For the Case Management Practice Group, building an improvement agenda, and selecting and implementing discrete projects for improvement, is an ongoing process that reflects a primary principle of Total Quality Management. To assure that desired outcomes are achieved through this process, the Case Management Practice Group will have to become vigilant in monitoring and evaluating its progress. Progress made in discrete project areas requires the formulation of indicators of quality that can be verified on a continuing basis as a means to prevent backsliding.

Linking monitoring and evaluating to action plans within discrete project areas is the logical next step of the actual quality improvement process. Within each one of the discrete project areas described above, the Case Management Practice Group will have to formulate specific action plans and to identify discrete or composite indicators of success that can be monitored over time. These plans must demonstrate how improvements will actually be made in a specific area, and must show how to determine the impact the improvements make in the realization of the case management system's mission and vision. Examples of action planning include:

1. The improvement of the skill base of case management personnel.
2. The improvement of the professional role of case managers within the agency.

3. The integration of the case management role with other helping roles within the agency and community.
4. The improvement of the resource base so that consumer needs can be addressed more proactively.
5. The establishment of core case management standards that can be applied flexibly in a context experiencing considerable diversification of case management roles, programs, and activities.

Translating these action plans requires the Case Management Practice Group to be empirical in its orientation to the improvement of processes and outcomes. This is somewhat foreign to workers who have often experienced orientations to organizational and systems change that can only be described as ambiguous and crisis-oriented. Nonetheless, the practice group, like other groups of human service professionals, must learn competencies fundamental to the improvement of service and support processes. Yet, without a clear understanding of case management purpose and outcomes, this approach to change itself becomes opportunistic. As noted in other chapters, sorting out the purpose of case management, and establishing a clear vision about its contribution to a service system, become important tasks in making case management an effective human service alternative. In addition, execution of these tasks is essential to a program of continuous improvement and Total Quality Management.

PART III

CONSUMERISM AND CASE MANAGEMENT

INTRODUCTION TO PART III

As indicated in earlier chapters, some forms of case management, and various programmatic models, have emerged out of a context of consumerism and social action. This part looks at the relationship between consumerism and case management by first addressing in Chapter 8 the properties of what is often referred to in the literature as consumer-driven case management. Specific properties of consumer-driven case management are offered, and these set the stage for a consideration of issues related to consumerism introduced and examined in later chapters. Chapter 9 relates directly to the content of Chapter 8. It discusses how consumer-driven properties are applied to the problem area of psychiatric rehabilitation. Chapter 10 offers a framework of case management practice based on advocacy, and the framework itself embodies many of the properties outlined in Chapter 8.

Chapter 11 is devoted to the examination of case management practice with families who are homeless. This content is built on the properties of consumer-driven case management practice and offers specific principles for the provision of case management to families who struggle with homelessness. This social problem was specifically selected to exemplify the application of consumer-driven concepts and ideas because it is not only serious but complex, and it illustrates the intersection of multiple social issues that converge on very vulnerable families. It is a problem that requires a commitment to a preventive posture on the part of case management programs in order to ensure that families do not experience homelessness as a recurring, chronic situation, which is too often the outcome in real life.

The final chapter in this part looks at serious mental illness and recovery and the role of case management in promoting long-term, positive life outcomes for people struggling with psychiatric disabilities. This chapter looks at the concept of recovery that is only now emerging within the context of proactive systems of community and personal rehabilitation. Case management as an important element of the recovery process is examined as part of a matrix of supports that combine consumerism with rehabilitation.

All five chapters contribute to enhancing readers' understanding of the impact of consumerism on case management systems and how this philosophical orientation can be translated into specific programmatic approaches and practice strategies. Thus, I hope that these chapters contribute to a more organized and focused perspective on consumer-driven service delivery, one that is differentiated from case management approaches seeking to implement a systems-driven archetype.

CHAPTER 8

PROPERTIES OF CONSUMER-DRIVEN FORMS OF CASE MANAGEMENT

David P. Moxley and Michael Daeschlein

The authors share an interest in the creation of consumer-driven forms of human service delivery. Michael has devoted his professional career to strengthening the voice of the consumer within the field of developmental disabilities. He has been very concerned with the idea of support and its application to employment, habilitation, and community living options for people who have developmental disabilities, as well as its application to helping consumers gain more control over the direction of their lives.

In this collaboration we define and elaborate the core properties of consumer-driven case management. We identify five key ideas that serve as the basis of any consumer-driven system of human service delivery. We then identify and discuss the forces that are moving us in the direction of increased consumerism and consumer-driven human services, and the forces that are barriers to the realization of this innovation in the human services.

There is growing interest in consumer-driven case management as an approach to human services. Much of this interest is stimulated by expanding consumer movements in which the people who bear the effects of a problem are increasingly becoming more vocal and assertive about the needs they want to fulfill, the aspirations they want to realize, and the concerns they want to address (Shapiro, 1993). Consumer-driven case management finds one expression in programmatic forms that are staffed by consumers themselves. These programmatic forms seek to incorporate flexible supports, self-help approaches, and a sensitivity to the perspectives and desires of consumers themselves—approaches to practice that are best achieved, say consumer advocates, by people who themselves have direct and personal experience with a particular set of issues.

Other programmatic forms, those staffed by functional and/or credentialed human service professionals, may adopt a consumer-driven approach to case management as a strategy of achieving more responsiveness to consumers, and as a strategy of humanizing not only the process of case management itself but also the delivery of the actual human services to which case management offers access. The idea of consumer-driven case management communicates a desire to offer users control over the process and outcomes of human service delivery, a quality that is often missing from the American approach to social welfare (Osburne & Gaebler, 1992).

We can contrast consumer-driven forms of service delivery with consumer-centered ones. The latter commit themselves to the broad-based identification of consumer needs and to the creation of innovative support systems that assist consumers to fulfill these needs. Consumer-centered approaches may underscore the necessity of consumer involvement and input, client satisfaction, and systematic needs assessments. Yet it is our assertion that consumer-centered forms do not really focus on changing the role and status of consumers within human service delivery systems. Consumer-driven approaches are concerned with consumer status, and with heightening and strengthening this status.

Consumer-driven case management has emerged in a context of consumerism, advocacy, and a growing understanding that people who struggle with a particular social problem, and its specific social and personal consequences, are in the best position to determine the purpose, direction, and substance of case management service delivery. Yet even though there is growing interest in consumer-driven forms, there is a real need to expand our appreciation of this model of case management and to elaborate the key variables composing it.

Despite the endorsement of this form of case management by advocates in such diverse arenas as developmental disabilities, aging, serious mental illness, and Acquired Immune Deficiency Syndrome, the general properties of consumer-driven case management have not been fully delineated so as to contribute to a general approach to this type of case management practice. It is the purpose of this paper to identify these core properties, and to offer an understanding of those forces within the culture of the American social welfare institution that support or limit the emergence of consumer-driven case management as a programmatic alternative in human services.

PROPERTIES OF CONSUMER-DRIVEN CASE MANAGEMENT

The concept of "property" refers to a trait that is characteristic of an object or involves the qualities that describe the substance of a particular object. If consumer-driven case management is a distinct and definable human service object, one should be able to identify those key properties that give it distinctiveness.

Contrasted to systems-driven case management, in which there is concern for the role of case management in preserving the integrity, efficiency, and performance of the human service system, consumer-driven case management finds its distinctiveness in defining, organizing, and implementing human services from the perspective of the person we may refer to as the user or the consumer.

Perspective is important to the realization of consumer-driven case management, since the elimination of the consumer's perspective is often characterized by users as a paternalistic tactic that heightens the loss of consumers' control over their own destiny. Indeed, critics of contemporary human services often focus on the absence of the consumer's perspective, resulting in systems of service that are not readily amenable to the exercise of self-determination on the part of users, or in systems of service that do not address those concerns or needs that users themselves choose.

Although the literature in the area of consumer-driven case management practice is somewhat fragmented, there is a growing body of knowledge and practice theory in this area (Ashbaugh, Bradley, & Blaney, 1994; Wieck, 1989). Combining this literature with perspectives from the disability rights movement (Percy, 1989; Morris, 1991; Shapiro, 1993; Oliver, 1990), various consumer movements within human services (Williams & Shoultz, 1982), and critiques of majoritarian culture by members of minority groups (Aronowitz & Giroux, 1991; Smart, 1993; Brown, 1994), five ideas animate consumer-driven practice and give it meaning when linked to case management. It is these five ideas that establish the properties of consumer-driven case management. They are the achievement of voice; the incorporation of control; the exercise of choice; the legitimization of dissent; and the protection of reputation. Implementation of these ideas creates new roles for consumers within human services, strengthens or otherwise improves their status, and suggests that involvement in human services of an active consumer increases sensitivity to need, promotes effective service delivery, improves outcomes, and increases the accountability of human service professionals.

Thus, when trying to understand whether—or the extent to which—a service system possesses consumer-driven properties, one has to observe closely a person fulfilling the role of consumer or recipient. We can then ask five basic questions:

- Does the person possess an active voice; is this voice encouraged, heard and taken seriously; and does this voice determine the purpose and direction of human services?
- Does the person exercise control over outcomes and the strategies used to achieve these outcomes?
- Is there a valuing of meaningful choices from among real substantive alternatives?

- Can the person readily and safely engage in dissent, and does dissent result in the freedom to rectify what has created dissatisfaction?
- Does the system protect the reputation of the people it serves, and, perhaps more importantly, even venerate people, their histories, and the barriers they have experienced in their life journeys?

When we are able to answer these critical questions in the affirmative, we witness the emergence of forms of case management that recognize and value an active, critical consumer, and that legitimize and reward this posture. Consumer-driven case management institutionalizes these five ideas, and creates a programmatic culture that recognizes the fundamental importance of the consumer's perspective and its activation within the service delivery process.

THE FOSTERING OF VOICE
Voice and the Identification of Need

The first idea is related to the achievement of voice. This idea turns our attention to the often observed situation of recipients of human services as having little voice—there are few opportunities that strengthen and amplify the voice of consumers so that their perspective contributes to the development of human services; or, preferably, so that the voice of the consumer is so dominant it actually determines the direction and substance of human service delivery. Without voice, consumers are indeed disadvantaged when it comes to asserting what is needed and how these needs will be fulfilled. Without voice, consumers will find perhaps other means of communicating the absence of their perspective, ways that may only lead to pejorative labels bestowed upon them by what some activists may describe as "their handlers."

A study by Freddolino, Moxley, and Fleishman (1988) indicates how important it is to amplify the voice of consumers. As part of a field-tested advocacy study, these investigators obtained the perspectives of consumers who have been labeled as seriously mentally ill on what they needed in order to live in community settings. Not surprisingly, participants identified needs clustering in the areas of income and benefits, housing, legal assistance, employment, and health care. Substantive concerns within these areas suggest the importance of fulfilling basic living needs as a strategy of improving the quality of life and standard of living of people labeled as seriously mentally ill. Yet it was apparent that the mental health system did not work with consumers to identify these needs and to focus on their quality of life. Without voice, the "real needs" of consumers may be overlooked or merely ignored.

Voice and Power

Amplification of the voice of users is a recognition of the power imbalances likely to exist between professional staff members and those served in a consumer-driven system. There is a recognition by the case management program of the inherent power imbalance between people who receive services and representatives of the service provider organization. Such power imbalances can become especially significant when people experience stigma and discrimination because of the social consequences of their need for support, or when people do not have the resources to support their own choices and, as a consequence, must become dependent on an agency or organization to meet even the most basic daily living needs.

These power imbalances may be invoked purposely by the organization and its staff to manage the actual demands placed on it by users, thereby increasing the social distance between those serving and those served. The exercise of power by human service professionals may be an intentional tactic designed to manage and shape the behavior, attitudes, and perceived needs of recipients. Unfortunately, the exercise of such tactics may result in learned helplessness on the part of consumers, or in hostile, acting out behaviors. The absence of voice, therefore, may come at a very high cost to consumers.

Those case management programs seeking to define themselves by consumer-driven practices can begin by understanding the importance of identifying needs directly from the perspective of consumers themselves, and by committing themselves to creating those options, opportunities, and benefits that seek to fulfill these needs in a manner that consumers see as meaningful and relevant. Human service systems, however, may hestitate to perform in this manner, since they may argue that consumers will be too demanding or even unreasonable. Yet, our experience underscores the practicality and pragmatism of most consumers. They often want to fulfill those needs (e.g., employment and vocational development) that will give them the tools to be successful and autonomous. But too often case management programs predetermine needs, and create routines to implement services and supports designed to fulfill the needs that professionals and funders see as important or meaningful (e.g., defining job readiness).

Alternatively, a consumer-driven case management program will acknowledge its inability to predefine what is actually needed by recipients without fully understanding their perspectives. Professional expertise within a consumer-driven option involves the skills of working with consumers in achieving an active voice, and then facilitating a process of clarifying goals, identifying options, and executing plans to amplify this voice.

Consumer-driven practice really does require close collaboration between professionals and consumers in achieving an understanding of the life situations of consumers, and of how consumers want to change or otherwise improve their situations. Indicators of this capacity to collaborate may be seen in structural elaboration of the case management program achieved by the incorporation of consumer perspectives into the governance of the program, the involvement of consumers as direct service staff and as advocates, and the linkage of the program to external consumer groups and social movements within the community.

Voice and the Multiple Effects of a Problem

Voice is meaningless unless it is actually translated into concrete options for service, support, and benefits so that consumers see the connection between the identification of their priorities and the responsiveness of the case management program to their perspectives. These concrete options emanate from an empowered voice of the user when the case management program understands the complexity of the social problem experienced by consumers. Problem definition within consumer-driven alternatives does not focus on the symptomatic or behavioral state of the individual, but is expanded dramatically to address the multiple social and cultural effects linked to the problem.

The multiple dimensions of a problem can be appreciated when we reflect on how serious mental illness—or, for example, Acquired Immune Deficiency Syndrome—is more than an illness. They have profound social and personal consequences for people who experience these problems. These can include stigma, discrimination, abuse and neglect, isolation, rights violations, diminished quality of services, inadequate intensity of support, and inadequate benefits and opportunities (Hillyer, 1993; Lane, 1992; Eisenberg, Griggens, & Duval, 1982; Gliedman & Roth, 1980). As a case management program begins to amplify the voice of the users, and as it struggles with translating what is desired into concrete realities, the program itself cannot escape the adoption of a broader conception of its role and purpose within a community.

Indeed, it is probable that a consumer-driven case management program is more likely to recognize the imperative of consumer advocacy than if it simply confines its attention to a narrowly defined conception of the problem and to a narrowly defined conception of its role within a service system. It is difficult for a case management program that seriously listens to the perspectives of users to avoid a broad programmatic mission—one that is especially sensitive and concerned with the improvement of the quality of life of users and the diminution of threats to this quality of life.

Mechanisms and tools to amplify voice will dominate the quality improvement agenda of the case management program seeking to be more consumer-driven. These may include regular forums held by consumers for consumers; interviews with consumers, the purpose of which is to understand their needs; and focus group interviews with consumers who have particular perspectives on the social problem. Consumer-driven information systems are another indicator that a program has made a commitment to the realization of consumer-driven case management and has created capacities to identify what consumers want for themselves, as opposed to what professionals want for them. However, as we have emphasized above, while it is one thing to identify these perspectives, it is another to respond to them through concrete options.

Interactions between individual consumers and staff members are used as a means of identifying what is wanted, desired, or needed from the perspectives of recipients. These perspectives may then contribute to a formative database of needs that amplify the inadequacies of the case management program and other sources of community support. Group strategies for understanding consumer perspectives are used to amplify voice, especially as voice is connected to the social position and social attachments of users. Thus, for example, race, ethnicity, socioeconomic issues, gender, geographic location, and sexual orientation become important factors in understanding how needs and desires are linked to subgroups of users, and how the perception of what is needed may vary among the subgroups composing the collective users of the case management program. Interactions with users—whether with individuals or groups, or whether in the context of informal and formal forums—become important avenues for the amplification of the voice of users.

Voice and the Social Characteristics of Consumers

The recognition that voice is very much attached to the social characteristics of groups, and that need is linked to the very histories people have with social structures (Kozol, 1995)—including human service agencies—and the reactions of these structures to their "problems" may suggest that the concept of "voice"alone is too limiting in trying to understand need. Indeed, consumer-driven case management programs recognize the importance of moving beyond understanding the "voice" of consumers as a monolithic perspective, to understanding the voices of all users based on a conscious appreciation of the diverse backgrounds of people served by the program.

The competence of a consumer-driven case management program is found, in part, in pluralism, and in its ability not only to respond meaningfully to the majoritarian perspective of users, but also to the perspectives set forth by members of minority communities. Competence of a consumer-driven case management program also is found in its ability to achieve a broad conception of need—a conception that is constructed from the perspectives that recipients have of the effects of the issues they face in their daily lives. And the competence of a consumer-driven case management program lies in its responsiveness to those effects of the problem that recipients see as most important to address.

Equity, therefore, is an animating value of a consumer-driven case management alternative. *This form of case management seeks to improve the concrete living situations of consumers, and to collaborate with consumers in changing the social circumstances that diminish their standing as fully enfranchised citizens. The incorporation of the voice of consumers—and the various voices of subgroups—into the actual design and delivery of case management becomes a vital strategy supporting the realization of equity.*

THE INCORPORATION OF CONTROL

Within typical human service delivery it is rare for consumers to have control over the service and supports that are ostensibly designed to offer them help and assistance. Systems-driven case management by design is intended to benefit the human service system in such areas as the control of access and utilization, coordination of service delivery, containment of costs, postponement of assistance, and testing of the sincerity and motivation of consumers. Consumer-driven case management by its very purpose and nature seeks to embody policies and practices promoting the control of the consumer over actual service delivery and its outcomes.

The infusion of control over the case management and service delivery process not only heightens the status of the consumer, but also places the consumer in a role that fosters decision-making, reflection on preferences, the anticipation of consequences, and the appraisal of benefits. The fostering of these qualities may be very influential in offsetting the potential encapsulation of consumers in service systems that by design can reduce their power and can result in their depersonalization (Lipsky, 1980).

Control is achieved when a consumer knows the outcomes available, can specify the outcomes to be achieved, can influence dramatically the manner in which services and supports are offered and configured, and can establish and enforce consequences for inadequate or inappropriate performance on the part of providers (Meenaghan, 1974; Meenaghan & Mascari, 1971). These aspects of control reinforce the fundamental role that self-direction and self-control serve in fostering positive human development. They underscore the critical connection between control over daily lives, and the manner in which control and mastery reinforce self-esteem and personal well-being. They also indicate how far a journey we must travel in contemporary human services to realize the attainment of systems that establish the consumer as the controlling agent in the delivery of human services and in the achievement of consumer-valued outcomes.

Control over Outcomes

Determining what is to be achieved is not a trivial aspect of human service delivery, especially when we consider the critical linkage between the articulation of needs and aspirations by consumers and the fulfillment of these needs as tangible end states. Thus, one can appreciate the intimate connection between voice and control as two interrelated building blocks of a foundation of consumer-driven practice. Too often human service delivery is preoccupied by means rather than ends. Several systems in child welfare and mental health that we have observed actually define outcome as the provision of a specified number of visits or of contacts between consumer and helper.

The contemporary environment of human services, with its emphasis on managed service delivery, favors the specification, articulation, and appraisal of outcomes, although this outcome orientation is likely to be undertaken from the perspective of the funder. This is antithetical to a consumer-driven system of case management, which will work closely with consumers to help them articulate measurable outcomes that capture personal meaningfulness and relevance. While a consumer-centered system is concerned with the meeting of needs, a consumer-driven system is concerned with creating outcomes that make an impact on the life of the consumer, with this impact defined by the consumer and not by the system of human services. We may assert that consumer-driven forms of case management are driven by vision. The vision is articulated by the consumer, and is used to direct the planning of supports and opportunities to make this vision come to life in the real world of the consumer.

When we are trying to determine the extent to which a system is consumer-driven we can look to the outcomes that human service delivery seeks to achieve with the users of the system. We will be especially concerned with the extent to which outcomes (1) are articulated using the voice of consumers and the needs and aspirations they identify, describe, and prioritize; (2) are truly linked to what consumers want to achieve, and not to what a human service system says it is willing or able to achieve; (3) are relevant to the daily life of consumers, and communicate the impact or changes consumers want to achieve in their daily lives; (4) are truly end statements that communicate a change that is independent of service provision and service delivery; and (5) will bring satisfaction to the user when they are accomplished, especially when assessed by the extent to which the accomplishment of outcomes improves the quality of life, standard of living, or life satisfaction of consumers. Outcomes therefore are linked to the perspective of the user, and their worth must be judged by the perspective of the consumer. The consumers' appraisal of their satisfaction with outcome is an important aspect of their control over case management.

Another tactic useful in determining the extent to which a system of human service delivery is consumer-driven is to look at what the system measures. Measurement systems are fundamental to understanding organizational culture since they offer a concrete portrayal of what a system is trying to achieve and what it values (Schein, 1992). Systems seeking to embody consumer-driven culture will prioritize measures that capture the perspectives, concerns, and values of users. Case management programs that are systems-driven will incorporate measures valuing benefits to the system of human services.

Control over the Process of Service Delivery

The actual process of service delivery, and how it unfolds in time, space, and functions, communicates to consumers messages about their worth as human beings and as people who want or need the support of others. How services are actually provided plays an important role in determining whether a system of case management is consumer-driven. One aspect of how services are provided lies in a recognition that systems of human service are discrete entities that accommodate to their own needs for order, certainty, routine, and stability, often at the expense of the well-being of consumers. As discrete entities, many human service systems become specialized in their work, and as a consequence prioritize a certain set of outcomes or certain routines.

We only need to look at many community mental health systems to recognize the limitations of focusing on the symptomatic and medical status of people with serious mental illness, while overlooking issues and concerns raised by consumers concerning their quality of life and standard of living. Case management and mental health personnel will only look at what the system prioritizes, and will confine their attention to the resources, services, and options the system offers within the framework of its priorities. It is not surprising that those community mental health systems that are illness-focused have not been able to offer high quality housing, employment, and community integration alternatives to address long-term quality of life concerns of consumers.

A consumer-driven case management system, even if it is based in a specific human service delivery system, will recognize the importance of moving beyond its organizational and systemic auspices to fulfill the needs of consumers, and to achieve outcomes valued by consumers. Services and opportunities available through a consumer-driven case management system are not by necessity defined by their locus—in other words, they do not have to be offered, let's say, within a mental health system—but rather by the functional outcome the service or support intends to achieve. Consumer-driven case management systems will make use of innovative and creative inputs offered by mental health, rehabilitation, education, employment, and other sectors of our communities. Consumer-driven case management will identify more with the consumers it serves than with the system in which it is placed, making consumers a principal reference group of case management staff. Service provision will be characterized by flexibility, innovation, and movement beyond the host human service system into the community in search of resources, opportunities, benefits, and alternative services that are relevant and meaningful to the outcomes identified by consumers.

Thus, the community focus of the consumer-driven case management program will be a salient characteristic of its service provision. Indeed, a consumer-driven case management program may be so oriented to the community as a resource system within which to address the needs of the people it serves that its efforts to organize services illuminate serious structural and resource adequacy problems within the community. As noted above, a consumer-driven case management program will strive to identify and address these problems.

The pace and order of service delivery are other distinguishing qualities of consumer-driven case management. There is respect for individual pace, and consumers can determine their own movement through a service delivery process that is itself flexible and personalized for and by them. Services correspond to the varying needs of consumers rather than standard schedules, time limits, and the requirements of artificial programmatic frameworks such as continua (Taylor, 1987). Pace is seen as a variable reflecting consumer preference, and its variability across consumers recognizes that habilitation, rehabilitation, and case management are not predictable processes that can be standardized but vary considerably by complexity, severity, and uniqueness of the needs and concerns presented by users. At the same time, the case management system offers a vigilance that prevents participants from stagnating because they are overlooked, do not have adequate information, or are not receiving the necessary depth of attention to achieve those outcomes they see as meaningful.

Assistance from a consumer-driven case management system is easily triggered by consumers. Personnel prioritize friendly and courteous contacts with users that are respectful of their privacy and their wishes for autonomy. Assertive outreach approaches, those characteristic of consumer-centered practice, are not adopted. Good practice is seen as friendly outreach characterized by the warm and unconditional offer of help in a way that is meaningful to the consumer, with the expectations that this help can be accepted or declined by the user. A consistent offer of help that is respectful of a person's preferences and values concerning utilization signals to the user that the case management option is available but that it is up to the person to trigger its use. This practice ensures that the case management system cannot shirk its responsibility for contacting recipients, and it also ensures that the right of individuals to decline or decrease involvement stands as an important alternative.

The service delivery process adopted by consumer-driven case management alternatives embodies some important principles underscoring the necessity of reinforcing personal control exercised by consumers. First, decision-making itself must be executed in conjunction with individuals rather than without them. Working in the best interests of the person must be avoided, since the best decisions are those made by an informed and respected consumer. To quote a saying emblazoned on a poster: "Nothing about me without me" (Mouth, 1995).

Second, there is an expectation of lifelong growth and change. A discrete outcome may be short-lived (e.g., finding a job), but nonetheless it stands as an important learning experience. At the same time, a consumer-driven case management program does not adopt "individualized power curves" that demand or expect continuous change by consumers.

A consumer-driven program recognizes that all of us reach plateaus, and that all of us require periods of rest, diversion, and relaxation. People—not mechanical devices like habilitation standards, quarterly objectives, and annual plans—drive a consumer-driven program. In addition, the standards for the opportunities and supports available to users of consumer-driven services are the standards the community holds for typical citizens. That is, a diminished life is not somehow acceptable because it is the life of a person with a label. Would typical members of our community work for the compensation and benefits commonly provided by a sheltered workshop? Would they give up the privacy and self-determination commonly lost by residents of a large congregate facility? Would they limit their recreational activities to only those available to van loads of residents?

If not, these options should not be among those provided to users of consumer-directed services. At the same time, personnel of consumer-driven programs do not impose their personal values on the indiviudals they serve. The case manager, for example, who values an office workplace and regular business hours would not impose these, through judgmental behavior or decreased support, on an individual attracted to a factory environment and late work shifts. Therefore, a consumer-driven program recognizes that common community standards must be extended to all, while the unique values of individuals must also be respected.

Control over Performance

Ultimately for a system of case management to make consumerism a viable way of offering services, consumers themselves must exercise control over the performance of the case management system and over the network of providers who offer services and supports. In most human service systems, the people who are served experience very little control over the consequences of the performance of the professionals staffing these systems. Indeed, it is a fundamental characteristic of the structure of American social welfare that social benefits are delivered to people through mediating structures like organizations, agencies, and professionals. The resources that enable people to design their own supports and services are not given directly to them at a level that is adequate to meet expressed need.

How can a consumer-driven case management program offer the people served control over performance? First, these programs commit to the identification of consumer defined outcomes based on needs the resolution of which are seen as important and critical by consumers. Second, providers will be directly accountable to consumers for achieving these outcomes, and when these outcomes are not achieved, consumers can readily dismiss the provider and make arrangements for services and supports from alternative sources. Third, consumers are not necessarily channeled into service providers who are part of a "problem network" of organizations. For example, merely because people are labeled as seriously mentally ill, it does not mean that services or supports must be confined to the mental health system. Indeed, depending on the outcomes identified and prioritized by consumers, the best service provider may be an organizational entity or support system within the community and outside of the formal mental health system. Consumers seeking high quality educational outcomes may seek these through community colleges or a technical training program; consumers seeking cultural development may join an amateur theater group or enroll in an art school for instruction; consumers desiring job supports may obtain these directly from a potential employer.

From our perspective, accountability linked directly to the consumer is a defining property of consumer-driven service delivery. Such accountability will incorporate several qualities. Accountability to consumers requires a true outcome orientation and defines performance of providers and the case management system as fundamental to this outcome. The consumer is not confined to a system of service that is unresponsive or that performs poorly. Consumers have the option of transferring the benefit to another provider who is willing and able to assist recipients to achieve what they desire for themselves. And the case management program incorporates the appraisal of outcome and performance within its information, administrative, and advocacy systems. As a consequence of these qualities, the examination of performance becomes a basic foundation of the culture of case management service. Consumer and case manager collaborate in the determination of whether providers perform in a manner that is consistent with the desires of the consumer. A consumer-driven case management program will have the capacities to implement and sustain this kind of culture based on beliefs of empowerment, self-determination, and the value of consumer perspective.

THE PROMOTION OF MEANINGFUL CHOICE

Many human service programs portray themselves as possessing the capacities to offer meaningful choice to the people they serve. An aspect of this portrayal lies in the offer to consumers of the opportunity to develop individualized goals and objectives. Yet the true offer of choice is not realized by many human service systems and the case management programs that are designed to organize the services and supports offered by these systems. The realization of meaningful choice may mask a serious deficiency in many human service systems. Too often choice is nominalistic. It involves only a limited array of options that are not really designed to capture the values of the chooser. Or worse, the consumers do not have opportunities to identify their own values, thereby ensuring a client role characterized by dependency, low expectations, low status, and other evidence of a disempowered person.

A consumer-driven program of case management recognizes the difficulty inherent in offering a range of alternatives and information tied to these alternatives that promote meaningful choice on the part of consumers. A consumer-driven program does not shirk its commitment to choice but rather sees the diversification of alternatives valued by consumers to be a very critical aspect of system performance. This recognition raises a number of qualities a consumer-driven case management program must incorporate, including diversifying resources that may be in short supply and/or structurally limited, planning support systems that are sensitive to the consequences of choice, and reframing risk and failure.

The Diversification of Resources

Consumer-driven case management programs confront very real structural problems in their communities that can place significant limitations on the availability of resources that are valued or seen as meaningful by consumers. This is very much apparent in the areas of housing and work, two sectors of our communities in which options are increasingly in short supply or merely not available to everyone (Rifkin, 1995). Increasingly, programs in aging, homelessness, developmental disabilities, and serious mental illness are trying to promote the development of consumer-driven housing and employment options based on the identification of consumer values and preferences. Yet even though these values and preferences are identified, it does not mean that they can be fulfilled within communities that may ration the availability of good housing and good employment opportunities. One only has to examine supported employment programs to understand the "food and filth" bias of the employment opportunities made available to workers. In addition, resolving the crisis of homelessness in many of our communities may be elusive until we recognize that there are many structural limitations to the production of housing and to the achievement of decent housing that is clean, safe, and accessible to transportation and to essential community resources needed for independent living.

Most case management programs that focus on meeting the needs of people who experience high levels of social rejection and stigma feel the structural limitations on the availability of basic life-sustaining resources. These programs will bump up against these limitations when trying to fulfill the employment, income, housing, nutritional, and transportation needs of the people they serve. Consumer-driven case management programs will probably feel these limitations more acutely and dramatically because the mission of these programs requires them to be driven by the preferences, values, and desires or aspirations of the people they serve. They will feel these limitations more acutely than traditional case management programs because they are sensitive to the barriers and issues experienced by the people they serve.

Because of these limitations, a contradiction may emerge within consumer-driven programs. Structural limitations in the availability of community resources may accentuate the conflict within consumer-driven case management programs, as consumers and their advocates become critical of the efforts and effectiveness of these programs in addressing structural limitations and in being able to achieve the kinds of outcomes identified by consumers. Some consumer-driven programs may experience periods of crisis as people question the authenticity, commitment, and legitimacy of the case management services.

There is really no easy way for consumer-driven programs to address what amounts to a flawed social system and a flawed system of social welfare. Consumer-driven programs will feel the discrimination, stigma, and rights violations experienced by their consumers because they attempt to align themselves with the people they serve. Feelings related to these negative outcomes such as helplessness, frustration, and anger can readily emerge within the program.

Yet consumer-driven case management programs work to highlight and amplify the structural limitations and contradictions inherent in serving people whose status is too often diminished. These programs will create partnerships with the people they serve, their advocates, and their movements to undertake activities to increase the range of resources available to the people they serve. This means that a critical aspect of the work of consumer-driven case management lies in advocacy, perhaps in what has been identified as systems advocacy: the ability to improve social system performance or a community resource on behalf of a particular group.

Unfortunately, a heightened advocacy role may prove to be problematic when a consumer-driven case management program argues that the needs of the people it serves are more worthy than the needs of another group. People who have developmental disabilities may be portrayed as more "needy" than people with serious mental illness. People with serious mental illness may be portrayed as more needy than people coping with the effects of AIDS. Consumer-driven programs may need to give considerable thought to their advocacy agenda, and to how their advocacy work can legitimize the needs of a range of groups within the community so that advocacy does not come down to increasing intergroup competition over a limited range of resources. A commitment to this kind of strategy may enable consumer-driven case management programs to link with other advocacy initiatives—ones that can enhance horizontal resource structures within our communities and accrue benefits to a range of people and groups, like those relating to the enhancement of health care, housing, employment, vocational development, and transportation.

Such a community development posture on the part of a consumer-driven case management program can give it a distinctive character within its community. And it can differentiate consumer-driven options from other more illness-specific or system-driven approaches to case management.

The Availability of Robust Support Systems

When we value choice, we cannot escape the possibility that people will chose in ways that are not consistent with the choice human service personnel would make on behalf of the people they serve. Nonetheless, simply because choices made by the people served can contravene those made by professionals does not mean that the case management program does not offer supports designed to help people to be successful. Indeed, a characteristic of consumer-driven case management systems may lie in the extent to which consumers are making bona fide choices about their lives—their direction, and their actualization. Consumer-driven case management systems encourage these choices. They do not invest energy in trying to circumvent these choices. Rather, gaining an understanding of the consequences of the choices made by people served, and the requirements that these choices entail for the creation and implementation of robust support systems, can pay off in very relevant knowledge useful to program improvement.

The effectiveness of consumer-driven case management programs may lie in their ability to connect consumer choices with effective support systems. "Robust" is used as a term to communicate the characteristics needed to realize a strong, relevant, and responsive system of support. Robust human services possess vigor, vitality, and a sturdy character, so they can respond effectively to the demands created by the choices of the people served by the case management program. The creation of robust support systems may be an essential defining quality of a consumer-driven case management program. The competencies to create these systems based on the values, preferences, and aims of the people they serve are essential to good consumer-driven practice.

The following characteristics may constitute criteria for evaluating the extent to which a support system is robust:

1. The system is intentionally designed to help people realize their choice and to be successful in the situation they have chosen. If a person has chosen to work in an employment situation that creates some degree of stress, the support system is designed to help the person manage this stress successfully. The system, as a consequence, is driven by the functional outcome selected by the person served.
2. The person served is not expected to achieve the outcome alone, even though the outcome is chosen by the person. The responsibility for the

achievement of the outcome is vested in the person and in the support system. Accountability is shared, and the system has a strong commitment to the realization of the outcome.

3. The support system is animated by the practicality of its purpose. Members recognize the importance of working with the person on pragmatic achievements, and therefore members are available to undertake activities that range from the mundane to the exotic.

4. The system is flexible and can respond to problems or issues experienced by people who are served within the general community, within the immediate environment of their choice, and in relationship to any changes of life circumstances. Thus, if a person is living alone in an apartment, the system can come to the assistance of the person through the provision of tangible resources to address even nonhousing issues because it is recognized that these issues can disrupt or challenge the housing outcome the person seeks to achieve.

5. The system is characterized by a high degree of collaboration that is non-hierarchical. While confidentiality is valued, with the permission of the consumer, members of the system can readily communicate with one another about the status of the supports needed by the person to be successful. This communication is not frustrated by status, credentials, or turf. Communication sounds different from the typical discussion of the consumer as a case or problem; instead it sounds like a discussion of a colleague by a group with whom the colleague shares respect, trust, support, and mutuality.

6. Support roles within the system are defined from a standpoint of inclusion and by necessity. A system assures that all necessary supports are available and that they have the information and skills to respond to the person. The system is inclusive of the range of supports that are found useful by the person, and professionals, family members, and peers are all seen as legitimate and potential providers of these supports.

7. Supports can be easily triggered by the person, and it is well understood how these supports are activated. Likewise, the person can easily stop the support or deactivate it.

8. The support system is accountable to the person, and its mission is to help the person to achieve success in the area they have chosen. However, the person can make other choices that may require the system to alter its configuration and its way of working with the person. The system sees this change as good, and it does not stigmatize the person for making a different choice. The culture of the support system recognizes that experience with a choice is an end in and of itself, and that increased experience can set the stage for more informed and more self-satisfying choices on the part of the person served.

Reframing Risk and Failure

To endorse choice, consumer-driven case management programs recognize that there is an element of risk that the person and the system assumes. In the field of developmental disabilities, the "dignity of risk" has long been recognized as an animating idea of normalization (Wolfensberger, 1972). To live in the community, to live alone, to undertake stress-producing work, to pursue higher education, and to bond with another person in a romantic relationship all create risk. Yet there is a certain human dignity in the assumption of this risk, and as people embrace this risk they are defining themselves increasingly as autonomous and self-directed people. The assumption of risk and the threats and opportunities it presents may be essential to human development. Indeed, many models charting the human lifespan identify those junctures in which choice and risk combine to create the energy of human development.

Simultaneously, risk is not framed as a paralyzing and overwhelming quality. Alternatively, it is something that is understood as a threat but is seen from the perspective of prudence as a quality that can be reduced through a robust support system and by the acquisition of skills on the part of the person served. Risk, from the perspective of a consumer-driven case management program, is something to be recognized and respected. It is something that is not to be avoided or feared. And it is something that is not discouraged. Perhaps the most vital expectation communicated by consumer-driven case management programs is the strong possibility that choice creates risk but that such risk can be addressed through a collaborative partnership between a person and a good support system.

Additionally, our consideration of risk should not be limited to the possible negative outcomes for the person taking action. There are also risks with safely complying with the directions or advice of program staff, such as the risk of not learning from one's choices and, therefore, not developing self-awareness; or the risk of becoming disempowered and dependent upon professional guidance.

Finally, failure is reframed by the consumer-driven case management program as something that can be experienced by someone when they act on their choices. Events are not seen as one-time opportunities—something too often found in some programs that say to consumers, "You have only one opportunity to do things right." Something is learned from every event. Consumer-driven case management programs realize that it may take several different trials for a person to be satisfied or feel successful. A cycle of getting a job and then leaving it only after a few weeks will not be framed as a failure but will be seen as a signal to gain a better understanding of what is needed, what is desired, and what will be accomplished. A consumer-driven case management progam is not preoccupied with the success or failure of a single episode. Rather such a program is committed to a longitudinal perspective found in helping a person to progress as they define it over an appreciable period of time.

THE EXPECTATION OF DISSENT

Consumer-driven case management programs value opportunities for dissent among the people they serve. Voice, control, and choice all underscore the importance of dissent—the willingness of consumers to disagree, to challenge, to withhold approval, or to refuse to conform. Consumer-driven case management programs recognize the importance of dissent to the strengthening of the role of the consumer, and to the realization of empowered consumers who are learning more and more about what they want to achieve and how they want to go about achieving those outcomes they value.

Valuing dissent among consumers means that consumer-driven case management programs recognize the structural problems that can force many users to comply with arrangements they may not want or value. Indeed, in some service delivery systems such compliance and "going along" may be treated as signs of health. Such a prescriptive position is not shared by consumer-driven programs in which choice and control are valued to such an extent that the expectation of dissent is heightened within these programmatic forms.

Contemporary human service systems committed to quality are increasingly embracing indicators of consumer satisfaction as measures of system performance. To use these measures effectively and with the greatest impact, these systems will probably have to recognize that dissatisfaction and disapproval may be the energy that will animate the greatest system changes. Consumer-driven programs do not insulate themselves from the expression of dissatisfaction by consumers. These expressions may be normalized as indicators of the emergence of perspective and voice on the part of the people served.

Perhaps one of the most influential practices implemented by consumer-driven case management programs lies in the satisfaction review that offers consumers an opportunity to reflect on what they are pleased with and what they are not pleased with. This review, when undertaken with sensitivity and with seriousness by consumers and case management personnel, can establish a new norm directing how services are offered and how they are perceived by the users. By prioritizing the perceptions of users and by taking action based on these perceptions, a consumer-driven case management program can underscore the importance of the role of the consumer in the improvement of the quality of services. Taking people seriously, and acting on their perceptions, may be essential aspects of the process human service providers have labeled empowerment.

There are certainly numerous factors and forces that can compromise the willingness of consumers to express their dissatisfaction. These factors and forces may operate both in consumer-driven programs and programs following other models of service delivery. However, consumer-driven programs look for the operation of these forces and factors, and they seek to drive them out. Whether by creating consumer-driven forums in which issues and concerns can be identified, developing information and evaluation systems capturing the perspectives and attitudes of consumers, or building in actions to improve programs based on these perspectives and attitudes, consumer-driven case management programs are relentless in the improvement of their systems at the direction of their principal beneficiaries—those people who are served by the program.

Dissent must also be appreciated in terms of its role in the actual case management process. Consumer-driven case management programs seek to place consumers in decision-making roles in which they can control services and the performance of providers. The value of dissent allows consumers to "vote with their feet" by reflecting on whether a provider is performing in a desirable manner and whether the consumer wants to remain with the provider. Dissent permeates case management planning, service organization, monitoring, and evaluation. Consumer-driven case managers receive considerable information from consumers so that the merit of provider performance can be judged:

> Accountability of provider performance and the benefits of the plan will be judged by consumers on an array of criteria including the acceptability of professional effort and the meaningfulness of functional outcome. In other words, from the perspective of consumers, did these efforts contribute to their movement along a personalized pathway of recovery? (Moxley, 1994b, p. 11)

Dissent requires increased freedom for consumers within human service delivery systems. This freedom requires more voice, more control, and more choice. Voice, control, and choice are imperative in order to make dissent and the accountability it implies a reality within human service delivery systems. Case management programs that value dissent will seek opportunities for consumers to act on their evaluation of the people who come to serve and support them. Consumer-driven case management programs will structure dissent into the roles of consumers, into the expectations of case management personnel, and into the manner in which providers are monitored, evaluated, and rewarded. Assuming that the benefits and services that are available to consumers are adequate to meet their needs, these criteria offer a strategy for structuring empowerment within case management programs.

THE FOSTERING OF POSITIVE REPUTATION

Consumer-driven case management programs protect and strengthen the reputations of the people they serve. People do not become diagnoses, and there is a keen understanding among case management personnel that diagnostic impressions can become negative stereotypes and can be used to degrade the reputation of people served. It is not uncommon to hear disparaging remarks made by human service personnel about people who are seen as difficult or whose needs require creative and flexible effort by staff members. Labels like "borderline personality" or "schizophrenic" can be used to communicate more meaning than what is intended by the actual diagnostic labels. Consumer-driven case management programs take labels seriously, and understand that respect and dignity afforded users are mainstay values that should not be compromised under any circumstances.

Consumer-driven case management programs also protect the reputation of consumers in their relationships with others. Nothing is done to diminish a consumer in the eyes of friends, family, or other community members. A case manager, for example, would not provide support if it could come from a more typical source such as from a family member who is motivated and interested in offering it. Or, the case manager would not portray the person as incompetent and lacking in strengths or assets. To do so could cast the person as highly dependent or incompetent and could weaken the relationship between the consumer and family member.

Consumer-driven alternatives respect the wholeness and complexity of a person's life, and these programs recognize the fact that the consumer/organization relationship is but one part of the person's life and personal history (Poertner & Ronnau, 1992). Thus consumer-driven practice recognizes that:

- A person's history with a service system is not all of one's history. People are much more than consumers or recipients of human and case management services.
- A person's life is much greater than the scope of interest of a service organization or even of a comprehensive system of services. It is difficult for even the most well intended service organization to fully grasp and understand the richness and texture of a person's history.
- A person must determine the extent to which his or her life is the object of an organization's concern, and the degree of dignity and respect a person is afforded will influence the quality of the relationship the person decides to establish or maintain with the service organization.

The adoption of these "first principles" establishes a framework for the fostering of a positive reputation of the people served by consumer-driven case management programs. Humility on the part of service providers is a check against the arrogance of labeling people as good or bad. Humility recognizes that it is difficult for anyone to fully understand the wholeness and complexity of someone's personal history.

Behavior that is often labeled as problematic can also be seen through the lens of this particular property. A consumer-driven case management alternative makes a *presumption of reasonableness* with regard to all of an individual's behavior. That is, the individual's behavior is reasonable, given the circumstances surrounding the behavior. These circumstances may include (1) one's history with service providers or employers, or community members, and the treatment the person has experienced through their interactions with these individuals; (2) one's level of skills that are relevant to the behavior; (3) one's genuine understanding of expectations and alternatives that are operating in a particular situation; and (4) one's history of consequences and outcomes regarding the behavior or similar behavior.

The general implication of this presumption of reasonableness is that the staff seek to understand the circumstances that make the behavior reasonable and understandable. Personnel of a consumer-driven program know that the people they serve have experienced often unreasonable circumstances that have resulted in negative consequences for them. Motivation is understood as a product of a set of circumstances and not merely a product of a person acting in a vacuum or in response to a single stimulus. For example, individuals participating in a sheltered workshop may be viewed as unmotivated because they are lazy or not interested in working. Lack of motivation may be a reasonable response to a set of circumstances characterized by low wages, devalued work, demeaning treatment, and little hope for advancement. An entirely unreasonable professional—someone who has not embraced a consumer-driven mindset—will respond to these circumstances by demanding the demonstration of improved motivation as a prerequisite for helping the person access other, more valued options. A reasonable response lies in helping the person to try options that bring more personal satisfaction and are more likely to support the desired level of performance.

Consumer-driven case management programs purposively embody principles of practice that support and protect the reputations of the people served by the program. The lives of consumers must be understood in the context of circumstances that call for sensitivity to what Coles (1989) refers to as the life stories of people. This kind of understanding, sensitivity, and commitment establishes a higher platform of practice than what is often found in typical human service and case management programs. A commitment to the purposeful development of the reputations of consumers will likely result in more sophisticated and meaningful practice. To fail to value the reputations of the people served may cause case management programs to degrade into victim blaming, a state of affairs that can dramatically compromise the movement of case management toward consumer-driven practice.

CONCLUSION

These five properties—voice, control, choice, dissent, and reputation—define consumer-driven case management, from our perspective. They also offer this model of case management a distinctive role in human services. These properties link case management closer to the development of people, rather than to the functioning of human service systems or human service organizations. Through this linkage to human development, case management programs that seek to embody consumer-driven properties will struggle with what Mary Catherine Bateson has called "composing a life." We reach higher planes of development as our voices are amplified, as we make choices that are animated by the values that are important to us personally, and as we gain increased control over our personal lives and the supports we need to achieve those outcomes we have identified as important. We reach higher planes of development as people listen closely to what we want for ourselves, and as they become our partners in helping us to achieve these desires. We reach higher planes of development when people treat us as reasonable actors whose behavior unfolds within a set of forceful circumstances that can dramatically influence us—for better or worse.

"Helping people to compose their lives" may sound to some people like a tall order, or it may strike some people as arrogance. Case management programs, however, are in the business of helping people to struggle with serious life circumstances. Client-focused programs may interpret this business as cataloging specific needs and figuring out how these needs will be met through an array of services. Consumer-driven programs may interpret this business as helping people to make vital life decisions, and to move in directions they see as desirable through the orchestration of supports that are valued and that make sense to them. Thus, the voice of the person becomes so important because there is a certain danger in the voice of a system or organization overpowering the voices of the individuals who are served—especially when dissent is not seen as a legitimate option. Control becomes so important because there is a certain danger in the exercise of bureaucratic and organizational control over individuals who are served. Choice becomes so important because there is a certain danger in the unilateral choices made by professionals supplanting those made by individuals who are served. And reputation becomes so important because it is so easy for human service organizations to misinterpret what people are trying to achieve for themselves.

The value of consumer-driven case management lies in its promise of protecting the centrality of the person in the process of human service delivery. It offers the promise that systems must increasingly become personalized and humanized through the provision of flexible, responsive supports, services, and opportunities if they are to be driven by the aims, desires, and preferences of consumers. Why? Because the business of "good" human services is to help people live rewarding lives (Galbraith, 1996). This is a very challenging agenda. But then consumer-driven case management is not typical practice.

CHAPTER 9

A MODEL OF CONSUMER-DRIVEN CASE MANAGEMENT IN PSYCHIATRIC REHABILITATION

David P. Moxley and Paul P. Freddolino

A version of this chapter was published in *Psychosocial Rehabilitation Journal* (October, 1990) as "A model of advocacy for promoting client self-determination in psychosocial rehabilitation." It is included here since it brings to life several of the ideas concerning the properties of consumer-driven case management presented in the previous chapter. The original focus of the paper is retained—that is, its advocacy orientation—since we believe that it is difficult to pull away consumer-driven case management from the idea and practice of advocacy. The content of the paper presents the Client Support and Representation model, a field-tested approach to case management, advocacy, and problem-solving developed for people identified as seriously mentally ill. Although the model addresses the needs of people with serious mental illness, it is very applicable to people experiencing diminished status. This approach to case management and advocacy, therefore, can find applicability within the fields of developmental disabilities, aging, poverty, and long-term illness. The original preparation of this paper was supported by research funded by the National Institute of Mental Health Grant Number 1RO1MH37051.

The provision of psychiatric rehabilitation services is guided by two fundamental principles, both of which are important to working effectively with people coping with disabilities as a result of serious mental illness. First, people are viewed as motivated by a need to master their environments; second, people can achieve independence and meet their basic needs if given adequate and appropriate supports (Cnaan, Blankertz, Messinger, & Gardner, 1988). These principles also are reflected in the community support system model, which recommends that services are designed so they are responsive to clients' needs as they define them, and that they are delivered in a manner that enhances clients' control over their own lives (Stroul, 1989, 1993). Indeed, assisting people to gain control over their own lives, an aim that can be compromised by the social reaction to serious mental illness, may be a cardinal value animating the field of psychiatric rehabilitation.

The field of psychiatric rehabilitation has implemented these principles through a commitment to self-determination visible in client participation in agency administration (Smith, Brown, Gibbs, Sanders, & Cremer, 1984), client involvement in the evaluation of rehabilitation services and community supports (Prager, 1980; Smith, 1984), and the empowerment of clients as their own advocates and as advocates of their peers (Chamberlin, Rogers, & Sneed, 1989).

The value placed upon client self-determination has several implications for the delivery of psychiatric rehabilitation services. One implication is that clients have the "... rights, ability, and knowledge to make decisions" (Cnaan et al., 1988, p. 65). Another implication is that psychiatric rehabilitation practitioners should avoid doing things in the "best interests" of the people they serve. Alternatively, people coping with psychiatric disabilities are to be encouraged to make their own decisions and to experience the consequences of these decisions as a means of moving toward independence (Cnaan et al., 1988). Despite the expanding ideology of client involvement and control over the rehabilitation process, many contemporary mental health systems, and even psychiatric rehabilitation programs, are searching for ways to become "consumer-driven."

In the realm of service system planning, a primary question is highlighted by Cohen and Anthony (1988): "What do clients want and how can they best be helped to get what they want?" (p. 69). In part, psychiatric rehabilitation and community support system models respond to this question by including advocacy and rights protection services as important programmatic components (Anthony & Blanch, 1989; Stroul, 1989). Yet there are several limitations of current rights protection and advocacy systems in assisting people coping with psychiatric disabilities to achieve the goal of self-determination (Freddolino, Moxley, & Fleishman, 1989).

Rights protection and advocacy services typically focus on substantive legal rights with a necessary emphasis placed on issues of abuse and neglect. Such an emphasis potentially ignores other client needs and wishes that are not being addressed by any segment of the mental health system. Another limitation is that federal and state mandates and the press of scarce resources have led rights protection and advocacy services to focus on state psychiatric hospitals and other congregate care facilities, thereby limiting the ability of these programs to address the community living needs of people who are not institutionalized. A third limitation is that rights protection and advocacy programs tend to solve client problems through legal processes rather than through other problem-solving approaches. This limits the allocation of resources to support individual-level self-help approaches. Finally, advocacy services typically are reactive, in that clients or people acting on their behalf must initiate contact to activate the advocacy process. Clients who do not have the motivation, skill, or accessibility to others to initiate complaints can be easily overlooked by rights protection and advocacy systems.

There is a need for an approach to advocacy that is proactive, and that encourages self-determination by promoting people's mastery, by assisting them to meet their needs in terms of how they themselves define them, and by respecting their wishes and preferences about the kind and intensity of help they desire (Cohen & Anthony, 1988). The purposes of this chapter are to outline a field-tested advocacy model that incorporates these aims and to identify the implications of this model for the field of psychiatric rehabilitation.

AN OVERVIEW OF THE CLIENT SUPPORT AND REPRESENTATION PROJECT

The Client Support and Representation (CSR) Project was designed as a randomized field experiment to implement and evaluate an innovative advocacy model. Funded by the National Institute of Mental Health, the CSR model was designed to assist participants in identifying their own needs for advocacy and then in addressing these needs. A guiding principle of the project was that these needs did not have to be related to the mental health status of the person or to the delivery of mental health services (Freddolino, Moxley, & Fleishman, 1989). Needs were seen as encompassing a broad range of resources and opportunities, the absence of which reduced the quality of life experienced by participants. By helping participants to identify the needs they perceived as important, and by supporting them to fulfill these needs, the project was seeking to increase the quality of life of participants.

The field test involved 473 men and women 18–65 years old who were about to be transferred or discharged from several different types of psychiatric facilities and residential programs in one urban northern California county. These participants were then randomly assigned to the advocacy intervention condition, to a placebo control condition, or to a "no new treatment" control condition in which they continued to receive services from the mental health agency with no services from the CSR project.

The participants in this study were generally representative of long-term clients served by the community services segment of the county mental health system. They included a variety of "chronic" diagnoses with 35.5% labeled as having schizophrenia, 26.4% labeled as having affective disorders, and 23.5%

labeled as having schizoaffective disorders. The sample was largely male (56.4%), predominantly white (77.0%), and generally young (66.8% were between 18 and 35 years of age). The participants were generally long-term consumers of mental health services, and all but 15% had experienced two or more psychiatric hospitalizations.

The intervention was implemented in the field by setting up a new division of an existing public interest law firm serving people coping with either psychiatric or developmental disabilities. Six staff members provided CSR services to the 222 participants who were randomly assigned to the CSR intervention. All advocates received training in mental health law, and in mediation and negotiation skills. CSR staff members were supervised by the attorney who directed the advocacy agency (Freddolino, Fleishman, & Moxley, 1987).

Because the organizational locus of CSR was outside of the formal mental health system, the advocates saw themselves as free to pursue client wishes without regard to the person's clinical treatment plan and without regard to the preferences of mental health professionals. Because CSR advocates were not employees of the mental health system, their potential clients were more likely to perceive them as being free from conflict of interest (Freddolino, Moxley, & Fleishman, 1989).

The actual characteristics of CSR advocacy made it a rather unique intervention and gave it a "consumer-driven" character. The goals of advocacy were based on clients' perceptions of what they wanted to achieve in key areas of daily living regardless of whether these needs were related to their mental health status (Freddolino, Moxley, & Fleishman, 1988). The advocate was a partisan of these consumer-defined needs but would not take action on an issue unless the client defined this action as desirable (Moxley & Freddolino, 1991; Freddolino & Moxley, 1992).

THEORETICAL RATIONALE OF THE CSR MODEL

The CSR model is based on a positive view of the person that precludes the use of deficit conceptions of social functioning introduced by psychiatric and diagnostic labeling. The client is perceived as a person who, like the advocate, has specific wants, desires, and aspirations. However, people coping with the effects of serious mental illness (especially social consequences) face very real environmental challenges, barriers, and resource problems in attaining these preferences largely because of the discrimination, stigmatization, and lack of support suffered by many people who are labeled as mentally ill.

The CSR process operates according to a strengths framework (Weick, Rapp, Sullivan, & Kisthardt, 1989) in which advocates work with their clients in a manner that promotes the latter's incipient capacities to help themselves, to activate or to develop the necessary attitudes and skills to achieve what they desire for themselves, and to use their own efforts, and support from others, to overcome the barriers preventing them from getting what they want for themselves. This framework is based on a humanistic view that individuals have strengths involving their abilities to acquire knowledge and pertinent information, assertiveness, and skills, and that these strengths can be set in motion or activated to assist them in successfully meeting personal and environmental challenges (Rapp & Wintersteen, 1989).

The theory guiding the CSR model builds on this strengths perspective. CSR theory views the advocate only as a catalyst who is available to assist clients in speaking for themselves, and to support them in assisting themselves. From the perspective of CSR, enabling clients to speak for themselves involves the capacity of clients to influence those events or factors that affect—either positively or negatively—their ability to address the fulfillment of their needs as they define them (Pinderhughes, 1983). Being able to speak for oneself and to build the supports that enable this to happen sucessfully (Ingram, 1988) contributes to empowerment, an important proximate outcome of CSR advocacy.

Within the context of the CSR model, empowerment occurs when people successfully confront the issues or barriers preventing them from achieving what they want for themselves (Ingram, 1988). Interactions between the client and the CSR advocate are a microcosm of the empowerment process. CSR advocacy provides the forum within which people can express their desires and can receive support that optimizes the chances of successfully achieving these desires.

THE PROCESS OF CSR ADVOCACY

CSR advocacy incorporates seven major processes. It makes use of rehabilitation practices with demonstrated effectiveness, including the use of tangible objectives, the task analysis of activities, contracting, homework, and the monitoring and evaluation of the provision of advocacy services. Each of the seven primary processes used within the CSR advocacy intervention is described below.

Engagement and Proactive Linkage

CSR advocacy requires a proactive linkage between advocates and users. This stands in contrast to the reactive character of traditional rights protection and advocacy services. The latter require the client or a significant other to report a rights violation or unfulfilled need in order to set the advocacy process in motion. Alternatively, CSR services were offered to a randomly selected group of clients immediately before their transition out of residential placement. Settings included a county-operated inpatient psychiatric facility (54.0%), two subacute residential treatment programs (17.3%), a respite program for people needing some time away but not hospitalization (10.6%), three locked skilled nursing facilities caring for more long-term and seriously disabled people (8.9%), and two transitional community residential programs serving people preparing for independent living (9.2%).

This proactive offer of advocacy services was implemented to assure that clients who might otherwise not have had the skills, resources, or information to obtain the assistance if they wanted it would not be deprived of the opportunity for CSR assistance. It also meant that some clients with no self-defined needs (13.0%) also received the offer of current and future advocacy support (Freddolino, Moxley, & Fleishman, 1988). The routine and unconditional offer of CSR services was an important first step toward the building of trust between two independent parties.

Broad-Based Needs Assessment

Advocacy needs were identified during the first contact through the use of an open-ended needs assessment instrument. The open-ended design of the interview instrument allowed clients maximum opportunity to identify their self-perceived needs without the formal structure of either the program or the advocate imposed upon them.

Nine daily living areas were covered by the needs assessment instrument: income and benefits; employment and training; health, mental health, and dental care; transportation; medication; legal problems; social, personal, and family problems; housing; and conservatorship. Participants were given opportunities to identify needs that did not fall within these categories. The needs actually identified by the 207 participants who completed needs assessment would be considered critical to successful community living (Farkas, Anthony, & Cohen, 1989). The most frequent need area was income and benefits (52.2%), followed by housing (36.7%), legal assistance (36.2%), employment (28.0%), and health care (26.6%) (Freddolino, Moxley, & Fleishman, 1988).

Although the CSR model was not designed to address the needs of any particular subgroup within the broad category of people with long-term psychiatric disability, this advocacy assessment process was successful in identifying the needs of individuals from the high risk group of people coping with both mental health problems and homelessness (Moxley & Freddolino, 1991). By far the most prevalent needs of the 40 participants who were identified as homeless and coping with psychiatric disabilities involved income and benefits (67.5%), while 47.5% wanted assistance in resolving housing problems and 42.5% wanted assistance with legal problems. Over 37.5% of this group wanted help with employment and 35.0% wanted assistance in resolving their health care needs. Unlike the broader sample, only 2.5% reported no needs (Chi Square=4.80, df=1, p<.05).

These data illustrate that when given a chance, people do identify practical and critical needs that are essential to their quality of life and standard of living. The successful and meaningful identification of these needs is a critical precursor to the formulation of consumer-driven advocacy objectives.

Setting Objectives and Identifying Tasks

Following the needs assessment, the clients and advocates worked together to formulate an advocacy plan. This plan consisted of prioritized objectives linked to issues identified in the needs assessment. It specified tasks for both the client and the advocate. For example, if a client was concerned about not receiving a General Assistance check, the objective might have been to contact the Department of Social Services (DSS). The client's task might have been to call DSS while the advocate's task was to encourage the client and follow up on this issue with the person in the next contact. Objectives reflected client wishes, which usually involved resolving unfulfilled needs or removing barriers preventing successful community living.

The specification of tasks formed the basis of the partnership between user and advocate. At the time of each contact, client and advocate jointly discussed the specific duties or activities to undertake prior to subsequent contacts or meetings. The emphasis throughout the intervention was placed on encouraging and supporting clients to take on as many specific tasks as they could handle in their own behalf. Except for emergency situations (which were quite rare), the general principle for advocates was not to do for clients what they could do for themselves, even if it took more time.

Maintaining Relationships across Time and Space

A fundamental practice of the CSR model involved efforts to make weekly contact with the client no matter where he or she was located within a 50-mile radius of the project office. If a client was committed to a psychiatric facility, or changed residential treatment programs, or moved to a board and care facility, it was a responsibility of the advocate to attempt contact. If a person wound up in jail, the advocate attempted to obtain permission to see the person if the latter desired to maintain contact. Although clients could choose to stop receiving CSR services, advocates were responsible for maintaining the offer of assistance no matter which other system—mental health, criminal justice, medical, etc.—the person entered.

In addition to maintaining relationships across space, staff were responsible for maintaining the offer of assistance across time. The intervention called for at least one contact each week for 22 weeks or for six calendar months, whichever came first. Explicit procedures were established to specify the pattern of attempts advocates were expected to follow to contact people who were not available for scheduled weekly contacts. The general pattern was for three weeks of contact by phone, then one in person. If additional meetings were needed this could be accomplished by phone or in person depending on the situation. One additional in-person contact occurred in the third week to facilitate establishing a relationship between client and advocate, providing a minimum of three in-person and two telephone contacts in the first five weeks.

Five weeks of contact was operationally defined as the minimum amount of service required to define a case. For those 169 randomly assigned CSR clients who reached the minimum level (81.6%), the average amount of exposure was 17.8 weeks with at least one contact. During these 17.8 weeks the typical client averaged 2.32 contacts each week.

Problem-Solving and Ongoing Needs Assessment

Implementation of an advocacy plan typically began with the advocate providing technical assistance and information on how to resolve each specific need or problem before any higher level of intervention was undertaken by either party. At the time of each weekly contact between client and advocate the two parties discussed progress made toward the fulfillment of objectives. If technical assistance did not appear to be sufficiently effective for a specific need, the advocate became more involved when the client requested it. For example, some clients requested the assistance of an advocate at administrative hearings, at face-to-face negotiations with landlords, or in meetings with employers.

Data collected on the advocates' use of various interventions illustrate that staff members emphasized teaching clients self-advocacy skills during the average of 17.8 weeks of contact with clients. Discussion (20.9 incidents per client); advice, instruction, and technical assistance (7.0 incidents per client); and providing specific information (5.4 incidents per client) were the most common intervention activities used by advocates. Activities directed toward third parties, including formal administrative representation (0.2 incidents per client) and mediation (1.8 incidents per client), were used by advocates on an infrequent basis and only when mutually agreed to by clients and advocates. No litigation was used by the CSR project in dealing with the problems identified by these clients.

A short needs assessment was completed during each weekly contact. The advocate inquired into how things were going in specific areas of potential need, determined whether the client wanted to address any other needs, and updated the advocacy plan accordingly. Frequent repetition of the informal needs assessment allowed the client and advocate to identify any needs that might have emerged after the first assessment.

The data reveal that income and benefits was the problem area most frequently identified by clients during the weeks after the initial needs assessment, with 162 problems identified in this area. Other frequently identified problem areas were housing (n = 114), legal issues (n = 84), health (n=59), and personal/social/family concerns (n = 54). Fewer than 50 total new problems were identified in each of the remaining areas: employment, conservators, medication, and transportation.

Monitoring of Problem Resolution

Maintaining frequent communication between the client and advocate was an important aspect of the advocacy process. Clients and advocates contracted for weekly telephone contact (once per month in person), with the purpose of discussing how things were going. Monitoring was not designed to assess whether the client was complying with the agreed upon plan under threat of some punishment or disapproval for failing to do so. Rather, its purpose was to determine whether milestone tasks were being reached and whether adjustments in strategies should be considered by the two parties.

Evaluation

The extent to which clients were satisfied with the resolution of their needs or problems was an important criterion used to evaluate the effectiveness of the advocacy effort. Although this may seem rather simplistic, the use of client satisfaction is consistent with the "consumer-driven" character of the model. This approach to evaluation prioritizes the perceptions of the participants. It respects their status as independent decision makers who have the capacity to determine when they have resolved a situation to their liking, and it reinforces the importance of participant reflection on the attainment of their own preferences.

Participants were generally successful in achieving the mutually agreed upon goals established for their problems. Their highest rate of success was in the area of income and benefits (94.2%), which is an area in which the formalized procedures of government programs lent themselves to the supported self-help efforts fostered by CSR. Alternatively, desires and needs in the employment area often required negotiation (e.g., with potential employers) in situations of limited options and resources, and with no clear rules for determining outcome. This situation was reflected in the lower success rate (67.0%) for this area of need. Overall, the mutually defined goal was achieved in 82.1% of all reported problems. Exactly half of all unresolved problems (n = 99) had been reported by clients who dropped out before final resolution of problems. It is not possible to determine whether there was a causal relationship between problems that went unresolved and discontinuation. It is known that geographical movement outside of the project's 50-mile range was the most frequently identified factor in program dropouts.

SUMMARY OF THE MODEL

In summary, the identification of consumer-defined needs and the implementation of advocacy activities that assist people in resolving these needs through their own efforts are distinguishing attributes of the CSR model. The model respects clients' preferences for how this resolution should occur, whereas issues pertaining to the mental health treatment plan and compliance with this plan are not meaningful aspects of the CSR process. Alternatively, advocates emphasize successful engagement and linkage with clients, the building of trust between two independent parties, and the implementation of action only when people specifically request this action. If clients identify no problems from their perspective, the weekly contact becomes a type of friendly support with continual opportunity to identify needs.

In this model, therefore, advocates do not work in the "best interests" of the client, but rather assist clients in realizing their own wishes. In this sense CSR is compatible with an emerging view within psychiatric rehabilitation that people must be assisted in identifying and achieving what they want for themselves (Cohen & Anthony, 1988; Anthony, Cohen, Farkas, & Cohen, 1988).

IMPLICATIONS FOR CASE MANAGEMENT IN PSYCHIATRIC REHABILITATION

Despite the contemporary ideology of the psychiatric rehabilitation field, case managers who work with people experiencing severe mental health problems often are involved in evaluating client wishes against the "best interests" of the client. These best interests evolve out of clinical and diagnostic judgments regarding the person's ability to act independently.

The dilemma of choosing between acting on client wishes or acting in the best interests of the client can result in role conflict for case managers and perhaps even conflict of interest (Dill, 1987). Although the psychiatric rehabilitation field has identified case management in a fashion that is very similar to CSR advocacy (Anthony et al., 1988), others insist that case mangement should serve important social control and surrogate parent roles (Kanter, 1985; 1988). The field-tested CSR advocacy intervention, on the other hand, clearly operationalizes a commitment to the empowerment of people independent of their mental health status.

Reflecting on these dilemmas raises some important considerations for the field of psychiatric rehabilitation. For example, in light of conflicting roles of case managers and other rehabilitation professionals, how do we define advocacy? Does advocacy mean getting people the services that are in their best interests? Alternatively, does advocacy mean protecting substantive legal rights, which may mean that the advocate may have to wait until a rights violation is reported? A third alternative is defining advocacy as acting on those goals, issues, and needs that clients wish to achieve for themselves. To practice case management in this manner may mean that quality of life becomes the advanced organizer of practice as opposed to service access or rights protection.

Clearly it is this third alternative that was embraced by the CSR project, and use of this definition led to a distinctive process of interpersonal helping and assistance. First, client perceptions of what they wanted for themselves were given primacy by project staff. Role definitions for CSR staff, therefore, were clear. The staff represented the clients and their wishes; they did not act in the client's best interests nor did they seek to control the person's behavior for the benefit of the greater community.

Second, CSR staff sought to develop consultative relationships with their clients that followed clients through time, regardless of geographic or programmatic changes in client situations. Sticking with the person was not a function of their involvement or enrollment in a specific service system. This meant that CSR advocates were available to follow the lead of clients who were expected to pursue their own goals, calling on the advocate when they desired support, technical assistance, information, or representation. When asked to take action, as good consultants, the CSR advocates would provide their clients with the knowledge and skills they required to try to resolve their own needs. However, CSR advocates were available to represent the person in forums in which the "status"of the person needed to be bolstered. Triggering this representation, however, was under the control of the consumer.

In addition to this general utility for clients coping with psychiatric problems, the CSR model offers other interesting possibilities as well. For example, a major issue facing the psychiatric rehabilitation field involves the acceptability of services to people who are homeless and who are coping with psychiatric problems, a group which frequently finds little value in how current mental health and rehabilitation services are delivered or offered to them. Successfully serving members of this population may mean that professionals must prioritize the perceived needs of consumers as well as building relationships that emphasize responsiveness to basic needs, trust, and engagement over treatment compliance (Freddolino & Moxley, 1992; Tessler & Dennis, 1989). CSR advocacy may be more acceptable to such a population of recipients than traditional community support and case management services.

The field of psychiatric rehabilitation is becoming increasingly characterized by "consumer-driven" perspectives as well as by service technologies that prioritize the involvement and participation of clients themselves. CSR advocacy can make a contribution to the evolution of the field as it attempts to identify and to act on client perceptions of needs and desires.

CHAPTER 10

ADVOCACY AND CASE MANAGEMENT PRACTICE

David P. Moxley and Shirley P. Thrasher

This chapter is an outcome of the authors' joint interest in the area of interpersonal advocacy and in the formulation of a relevant graduate social work course addressing the role of professional social workers as advocates. The model of interpersonal advocacy identified in this chapter emerged out of the design and teaching of a course, Advocacy in Social Work Practice with Vulnerable Populations, that represented a teaching collaboration of three years, halted by Dr. Thrasher's untimely death. Over this period of time the authors maintained a spirited dialogue as they sought to define what advocacy meant to social work practice, how they saw advocacy within the context of their practice, and how advocacy was related to case management. As Dr. Thrasher's research on homelessness grew, and Dr. Moxley's work in the area of psychiatric rehabilitation continued to expand,   a number of commonalities, both in thinking about advocacy and in its application to discrete fields of interest, were found that could contribute to the formulation of a model. This formulation also affirmed a connection between individual advocacy and systems advocacy despite their frequent conceptual separation in the social work literature. It was hoped that a linkage could be established between an individual advocacy response and a collective one, a linkage that is now a salient aspect of the model.

Advocacy has been included as a functional element of most traditional portrayals of case management practice. Indeed, advocacy, as an element of case management, is framed as an important if not critical aspect of practice although it has often been narrowly defined to encompass the identification of service needs, the achievement of access to services that are deemed necessary to the well-being of the recipient, and the troubleshooting of bureaucratic, organizational, and other factors actually or potentially frustrating the needs of consumers. The manner in which advocacy is defined by most case management programs highlights the strong service orientation these programs take to advocacy and its operationalization, often through brokering approaches to case management practice.

Yet advocacy is much richer than the service orientation adopted by many case management programs. Despite the relative consensus on the importance of infusing advocacy into case management practice (Anthony, Cohen, Farkas, & Cohen, 1988; Rapp & Hanson, 1988; Rose & Black, 1985; Moxley, 1989), there are several conflicting definitions of advocacy that reflect the lack of consensus on what advocacy in case management practice really is. As noted above, a traditional human service definition of advocacy involves assisting recipients in gaining access to need-meeting human resources, typically through brokering and linking activities (Moxley, 1989). Or advocacy may take on a more legal definition involving the protection of the rights of recipients (Raider, 1982). Advocacy can adopt a social control perspective by asserting the "best interests" of a recipient despite the possibility that the recipient disagrees or does not concur with the aims of the advocate (Gerhart, 1990; Belcher, 1988). Or advocacy may involve a partisan perspective in which the advocate case manager works with recipients to define their own aims and ends and the advocate takes action only in close collaboration with recipients (McGowan, 1987; Moxley & Freddolino, 1990; Rose, 1992).

There are few models of advocacy within case management practice that begin where consumers are at and that are designed to assist consumers in identifying their own preferences and then assisting consumers in bringing these preferences into reality. Models within the developmental disabilities field such as personal futures planning and "circles of friends" have demonstrated the importance of linking case management and community support alternatives to the visions and hopes of people we label as recipients. Also, in the field of psychiatric rehabilitation there is increasingly recognition that brokering approaches to case management are too limited and that the vision guiding advocacy often gets translated into linking people to "what is," not to "what is wanted."

The recovery movement within psychiatric rehabilitation argues for the need to pay close attention to the aspirations of consumers and to help them address the environmental barriers that frustrate the attainment of these aspirations (Anthony, 1994; Moxley, 1994b). In the social problem area of homelessness, advocacy that is oriented to a "partisan" perspective is seen as crucial since case management programs that embody such orientations are more likely to link with homeless people, to develop ongoing relationships with them, and to achieve outcomes that move people out of this most problematic status (Moxley & Freddolino, 1991; Freddolino & Moxley, 1992; Tessler & Dennis, 1989).

We embrace a partisan perspective in this essay and present its core elements through the formulation of an interpersonal model of advocacy. We begin with a working definition of advocacy derived from our own practice experience in case management and advocacy and informed by our collaboration as co-teachers of a course on interpersonal advocacy in the practice of social work that we designed and have taught now for several years. We then flesh out our model by identifying the principal elements and their integration into a working framework of interpersonal advocacy.

ENDORSEMENT OF PARTISAN ADVOCACY

We endorse a partisan approach to advocacy for several reasons. First, case managers frequently interact with people who experience oppression, which can manifest itself as a degraded sense of self, loss of self-esteem, and the internalization of a diminished status. A problematic aspect of this oppression, especially on a behavioral level, is that it can foster learned helplessness, and a reluctance or even an inability to articulate what one wants or desires to achieve (Freddolino, Moxley, & Fleishman, 1989). People may present themselves as incompetent, unmotivated, hostile and angry, or extremely obsequious. A partisan-oriented advocacy in case management practice will seek to offset this oppression by forming a new context supportive of a recipient's desires and aims and the action required by the recipient to achieve these ends.

A second reason we endorse a partisan orientation is in reaction to the tendency for case management to translate human needs into a service response. This is inherently conservative, because it requires the availability of an appropriate service and may give case management a people-processing character in which success is defined as linking a person to a service. When this is accomplished case management is completed for the time being. Such a service orientation also tends to focus the attention of case managers on their host systems, and it neglects to recognize that resources (rather than only services) exist within the broader community to meet the needs of recipients (Rapp, 1992).

Thus, the formal boundaries of the mental health system will define the availability of services for case managers working with people who are identified as seriously mentally ill. The formal boundaries of the child welfare system will define the availability of services for case managers working with adolescents. A partisan approach to advocacy, like the strengths model of case management (Rapp & Wintersteen, 1989), requires the case manager to understand what the consumer wants to achieve and then to take a broad orientation to the community in identifying ways to meet these desires. The attention span of the partisan advocate should not be bounded by the dimensions of a formal system of service.

Our third endorsement lies in the ambiguous nature of contemporary case management practice. As other chapters have emphasized, it is often confusing to identify who a case manager represents. Some forms of case management blur the lines between the recipient and a system of service, so that consumers may be legitimately concerned about who the case manager actually represents and to whom the case manager is ultimately loyal. In the partisan form of advocacy, and its implementation within case management practice, this question is clearly answered: the case manager is committed to the perspectives of the recipient and is willing to embrace the conflict that the exercise and attainment of these perspectives can create with service systems, bureaucratic authorities, and community gatekeepers.

A DEFINITION OF ADVOCACY

Partisan advocacy, therefore, emerges out of a context of oppression and diminished status experienced by people who bear the effects of serious social problems. It is not an accident that this form of advocacy is very much linked to the problem areas of serious mental illness, developmental disabilities, and homelessness. It is in these areas especially that people experience the full impact of the absence of life-sustaining and life-enhancing resources ostensibly available to everyone within our communities, and the limited resources available to promote quality of life offered through the American social welfare institution. It is in these areas that people can be encapsulated by total institutions whose impact on functioning can be restrictive, limiting, and destructive (Kozol, 1995). Partisan advocacy recognizes the enhanced relationship needed by our most vulnerable citizens in order to address ecological and environmental forces producing risk and subsequently negative personal effects for these individuals.

We identify within our definition the importance of the partnership or alliance between the advocate case manager and the recipient. Like several models of case management that are closely aligned with ours (Rose, 1992; Rapp, 1992; Moxley & Freddolino, 1990), the relationship is foundational to the model, and the values steering this relationship are fundamental to addressing the oppression felt by recipients.

Our definition also identifies the importance of the person's worldview, the stories that reflect this worldview, and the experiences that have helped to subvert the status of the person and to diminish this status. The dissatisfaction arising from this worldview is critical to the achievement of the direction of advocacy. We view this dissatisfaction as the energy that advocate and recipient can harness and use to identify what needs to be accomplished within the advocacy alliance. The level of satisfaction becomes a natural means for evaluating the success and achievement of this partnership (Moxley & Freddolino, 1990). The environmental and structural forces impinging on the person become critical objects of change rather than individual or personal characteristics.

Advocacy, from our perspective, is

> A partnership or alliance between two parties, one a recipient and one an advocate, in which the worldview of the recipient becomes the prism for defining a situation that is unacceptable to the recipient, and where the advocate assists the recipient in changing a situation to his or her level of satisfaction. The change is environmental or structural and not individual, although the recipient may want to change aspects of his or her behavior to address external barriers frustrating the achievement of a valued end state.

CORE VALUES GUIDING THE MODEL

The achievement of four core values strengthens the integrity of this concept of advocacy. These involve: consumer control over the aims of advocacy and the activities that constitute advocacy; concrete action designed to make an impact on a recipient's dissatisfaction; loyalty to the recipient on the part of the advocate case manager; and the achievement of an egalitarian relationship between recipient and advocate.

Consumer Control

We are assuming that the advocate case manager interacts with a recipient with high levels of social vulnerability. This means that recipients have experienced oppression manifest in labeling, stigma, and outright rejection if not actual harm. It is not unusual for recipients to have experienced institutionalization and regimentation, and as noted above, for these experiences to be translated into a loss of personal control.

Partisan advocacy must value consumer control as an initial means of establishing a new set of interactional rules. The partisan advocate is not in a position to apply expert assessment or diagnostic skills to the aim of defining the needs or problems of the recipient. Nor is the partisan advocate in the position to exercise control over recipients by telling them what to do and how to do it. Consumer control as a basic value of partisan advocacy means that the recipient, working with the assistance and support of the advocate, controls the process of problem definition or issue identification, the aims of the advocacy activity, the nature of action taken to make an impact on the situation, and the evaluation of the outcome of the advocacy activity (Moxley & Freddolino, 1990). Consumer control is recognized within the model as a means for offsetting problems emerging from the diminished status of the recipient and the assumption of control over the individual by people in positions of authority.

Action

This value recognizes that action in real social environments can make a substantial impact on people's worldview, motivation, and skill development, especially if this action produces successful outcomes. Indeed, most models that seek to assist people in developing capacities to overcome environmental barriers and to achieve self-defined ends value action in real social settings so that people can experience the consequences of their actions (Anthony, 1979; Brown & Hughson, 1987; Epstein, 1988; Maluccio, 1974).

Partisan advocacy underscores the importance of animation, defined by Lauffer (1984) as the activation of people to take responsibility for their own situations in order to achieve self-defined ends. Valuing action does not mean that recipients are left to their own devices for resolving the many environmental factors that they potentially face in addressing their dissatisfaction. This value unfolds within the alliance in which both advocate and recipient possess strengths and resources to address environmental factors and barriers that can frustrate the achievement of the recipient's desires. The valuing of action means that both advocate and recipient will undertake concrete and practical activities designed to make an impact on identified issues and to achieve proximate outcomes that make important contributions to the achievement of the ultimate ends defined by recipients.

Loyalty

This value addresses a vexing value problem created by case management. Kane (1988) emphasizes that some case management initiatives can create "mixed loyalties" in which the ultimate accountability of the case manager is ambiguous or ill-defined. A case manager who is employed by a mental health system may represent himself to the recipient as someone who is devoted to the concerns and issues raised by the recipient. But this same case manager may act later on in a manner that contradicts this loyal position by asserting that the recipient must do something that serves the need of the mental health system. For example, the recipient is told to live at an adult foster care facility that does not achieve the person's residential preferences or desires. Or the case manager may attempt to put limits on the sexual preferences of a recipient at the request of a family, a situation that can become very problematic if the family is paying the case manager to offer services to the recipient.

Our model of partisan advocacy attempts to reduce this ambiguity by clearly defining the loyalty of the case manager. The case manager is loyal to the recipient, which raises issues pertaining to the organizational auspices of practice, the position of the case manager in a human service system, the role definition of the case manager, and the ability of the case manager to resist authoritarian intrusion into the case management/advocacy relationship by a third party who attempts to exercise control over this relationship.

Egalitarian Relationship

By operationalizing the previous three values, we assert that the probability of an egalitarian relationship between recipient and case manager can be realized. Providing that the recipient truly exercises control over the purpose, aims, and activities constituting advocacy; that the recipient and case manager each take responsibility for action that is well coordinated; and that the case manager is indeed loyal to the recipient, then the chances that the case manager and recipient can create an egalitarian alliance are increased tremendously. An egalitarian relationship will be a product of ongoing work between case managers as advocates and recipients as they work together to identify the issues facing recipients, the factors creating these issues, what the recipient wants to achieve, the actions necessary to the achievement of a desired outcome from the perspective of the recipient, and an evaluation that captures the level of satisfaction realized by the recipient.

The notion of collaboration here is important, and it is incumbent on the case manager working as advocate to achieve this sense of collaboration. However, the success of collaboration, and its contribution to the achievement of an egalitarian relationship, is most likely contingent on the case manager capturing a valid subjective understanding of the worldview of the recipient and designing subsequent action using this worldview by encouraging an open dialogue about what the recipient wants to achieve through the advocacy relationship (Rose, 1992).

AN INTERPERSONAL MODEL OF ADVOCACY IN CASE MANAGEMENT

A model of advocacy is displayed in figure 10.1. The model captures the principal elements of our approach to case management. In addition to the core values discussed above, the model consists of six principal elements, involving (1) understanding, alliance, and direction; (2) activation and coordination; (3) recycling; (4) collective response; (5) the acquisition of "know-how"; and (6) release. Each of these principal elements is discussed in the following sections.

Principal Element 1: Understanding, Alliance, Direction

Most models of interpersonal helping place emphasis on assessment and diagnosis as the starting point of the helping process. We conceive of the starting point of interpersonal advocacy as involving the linkage between understanding and alliance. Understanding is a subjective process of gaining a deep sense of and appreciation for the recipient's worldview and especially gaining a sense for experiences pertaining to oppression, abuse, loss, and neglect. These first person accounts can come in the form of stories about anger and frustration, lost hopes and desires, and wounds that are most accessible to advocate case managers when they are attuned to these stories rather than looking for diagnostic signs and indicators. As Cole (1989) has observed, stories people offer us can shape our understanding and compassion for them and offer us a portal through which to gain a deep appreciation for what they have experienced and what they have had to overcome to arrive at our doorstep. Rose and his colleagues have observed that people who have experienced oppression often report hidden abuse involving mistreatment and sexual exploitation.

Cole reinforces the importance of approaching the act of understanding as a humanistic enterprise as opposed to an analytic or nosological one. Formalized systems of case management place great emphasis on collecting and collating data concerning needs and problems. But Cole suggests that we look for themes and issues people face and how they view their life circumstances in relationship to their hopes and aspirations. From our perspective, these life stories, and the events that shape people into who they are, serve as the building blocks of an alliance. From our perspective, a necessary aspect of understanding requires the advocate to gain an appreciation for a recipient's dissatisfaction with a subjectively defined situation and to gain an appreciation for how a recipient wants to change that situation, if he or she indeed wants it changed.

Understanding and the building of an alliance go hand in hand, because many people who feel the sting of oppression probably will be hesitant to enter a relationship with an advocate if they feel that they are not understood. Trust, confidence, and commitment can flow from achieving an understanding, and these qualities can in turn strengthen the alliance. Understanding then interacts with the establishment and fostering of an alliance, a dynamic and ongoing process operating throughout the duration of the advocacy work.

Recipients must control the alliance and decide when and under what circumstances they will pursue it. Recipients themselves must identify the frequency of contacts and the manner in which contacts will occur. Frequency of contact, therefore, is under the control of recipients, who will make use of the advocacy relationship in a manner that is consistent with their desires. However, it is incumbent upon the advocate to make contact with the recipient—not to check up on or to monitor the person, but to offer a friendly contact and to assure that the recipient is aware of the availability of the advocacy opportunity (Moxley & Freddolino, 1990). Recipient control of the alliance reinforces the consumer-driven character of this form of assistance and also assures that the advocate is reaching out so that people can trigger the advocacy relationship when they feel it is desired or necessary.

The concept of direction (Rose, 1992) is incorporated into the model to offer a broader framework within which to establish the purpose and ends of case management. Direction serves as a substitute for treatment or service plan because we want to place advocacy into a much broader framework and to offer a way to think about meeting people's needs as an alternative to the formalistic and narrow perspective of services and treatment. Direction is a rather simple and loose term. Yet it possesses a richness that is not communicated by goal or objective. Every enterprise needs a direction or else one can end up in an unintended place.

Establishing a direction will likely involve the recipient and advocate in identifying, from the perspective of the recipient, those issues that create dissatisfaction as well as the end that the recipient wants to achieve through the resolution of this dissatisfaction. Framed from a negative perspective, this dissatisfaction may mean that the recipient wants to leave what is seen as an undesirable situation. For example, a person may want to move out of an adult foster care facility that offers little choice and freedom. Or, from a positive perspective, the person may want to move into an independent living situation that is better suited to the person's values and preferences.

The value of the direction plan is found in the process of developing the actual direction. Successful formulation of a direction requires the recipient and advocate to work collaboratively in defining issues, dissatisfaction, preferences and values, and in satisfying end states. Formulation of a direction is a small yet important empowerment strategy that offers recipients opportunities to voice dissent about their circumstances as well as to identify values, preferences, and wishes. Direction focuses on a discrete issue that links dissent to resolution through the achievement of a recipient-defined outcome.

Principal Element 2: Activation and Coordination

The establishment of a direction offers the recipient and advocate an end point and serves as a framework for the organization of advocacy activity. A core value of the model demands action on the part of both recipient and advocate, who must undertake practical activity in order to achieve a recipient-defined end state. We refer to the initiation and continuation of this activity as activation. This concept means that activity must be initiated by both parties and that energy must be invested to engage in the work that will produce desired outcomes and subsequently a desired end state.

Each party to the advocacy enterprise brings distinctive roles and resources. Recipients are responsible for identifying issues and helping the advocate gain an understanding of their dissatisfaction. Advocates are responsible for

FIGURE 10.1

An Interpersonal Model of Advocacy

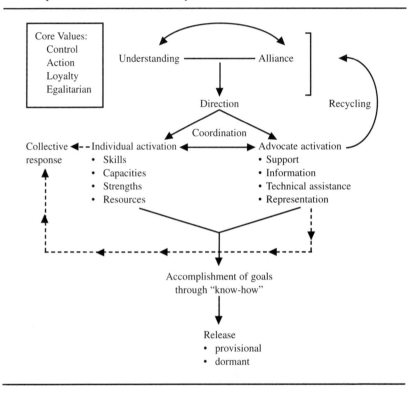

gaining an understanding of and deep appreciation for the life experiences of recipients. Both parties are responsible for maintaining and developing an alliance. And both parties are responsible for activation—that is, for undertaking relevant and concrete action.

The resources brought to the advocacy enterprise by the recipient are multiple, as indicated by figure 10.1. Recipient activation means that the person makes use of personal skills and strengths, capacities, and perhaps resources obtained through social network relationships to make a contribution to the positive resolution of the identified issue and the achievement of the desired end or outcome. The recipient can identify these strengths, skills, capacities, and resources in collaboration with the advocate, who is available to support the recipient's engagement in relevant activity.

The full involvement of the recipient serves four purposes. First, it can offer recipients a positive experience of issue resolution from which they can gain concrete knowledge about how to approach a problem (e.g., how to appeal a benefits claim). Second, such involvement can offset the negative personal effects of a social problem that can often dampen motivation and induce feelings of helplessness. Third, it ensures that the recipient is directly involved in the resolution of the issue and can experience the immediate positive consequences of overcoming a negative environmental situation, consequences that can reinforce positive self-regard and self-concept. Finally, it ensures that recipients are receiving feedback about the effectiveness of their efforts, and it offers them an opportunity to learn how to change a strategy and modify tactics based on the feedback they are receiving. Thus, activation serves as a learning opportunity for recipients, one that can offer opportunities for them to increase their problem-solving skills as well as their fund of know-how about how to resolve problems in the future.

Advocate activation recognizes that the case manager must be directly involved in undertaking relevant activities. The potential resources that the advocate can offer recipients are many. As mentioned above, the advocate can offer recipients ongoing support in the form of encouragement, troubleshooting, and stress management. The advocate can offer access to a body of information about resources, services, and people, all of which can be potentially invoked by the recipient and used as problem-solving tools. As a technical assistant, the advocate can offer recipients specific knowledge and skill about how to resolve a problem to their satisfaction. For example, an advocate may possess in-depth information on how a recipient can dispute a benefits decision, and the advocate can outline the specific steps the recipient must follow in filing an appeal of the decision.

Advocate activation can also take the form of representation. At the request of the recipient, the advocate may represent the recipient within bureaucratic, organizational, and community forums. As a representative the advocate works in presenting the case and circumstances of the recipient, and in making an appeal for a decision that favors the recipient and achieves the outcome desired by the recipient. For example, the advocate may represent the recipient in an appeal of a negative decision concerning unemployment benefits.

Activation can pose some serious threats to the integrity of the alliance between recipient and advocate. Advocates who are overwhelmed by work demands may use the individual activation of recipients to shift the burden of taking action from themselves to recipients and then rationalize the failure of recipients to follow through as a measure of their insincerity. Overzealous advocates may undertake too much action and overwhelm recipients by virtue of their pace or may communicate to recipients that they should be inactive and passive. Within this context, advocacy shifts from being an activity undertaken by two equal parties to an activity that is only the legitimate responsibility of the advocate case manager, who works in the interests of the recipient but who dominates the actual process of advocacy.

We incorporate the concept of coordination to communicate that activation is a joint undertaking of recipient and advocate, who must work in a parallel manner in order to assure that they are not working at cross-purposes, that the burden is not shifted to any one party in an inequitable manner, and that the recipient maintains control of the activity. This coordination can be achieved in several ways. It can be achieved when recipient and advocate jointly identify direction, establish the roles of each party in achieving this direction, and identify the actions that each party will undertake. It can be achieved during frequent meetings between recipient and advocate, the purpose of which is to assess the relevance and merit of the activities each party is taking and determine how recipient and advocate are working together. And it can be achieved by empowering the recipient to trigger the action of the advocate. In other words, the advocate will be unwilling to take direct action on behalf of the recipient unless the recipient has identified this action as desirable. So the advocate will not engage in representation unless the recipient desires this and decides that the advocate should serve as a representative (Moxley & Freddolino, 1990). Coordination as a concept integrates the alliance into the activation element of advocacy, and mitigates the possibility of unilateral action on part of a well-meaning advocate.

Principal Element 3: Recycling

Recycling emphasizes the ongoing review and evaluation of the advocacy alliance and the activation of recipients and advocates. The formulation of direction is based on the selection of a discrete issue from among a number of issues identified by recipients. Given the character of serious social problems, it is not unusual for recipients to identify a range of issues and to attach some urgency to each one. Reality dictates, however, that not all issues can receive immediate attention, since the attention and energy of both advocate and recipient are limited. This means that in the formulation of direction there is the necessity to give some priority to identified issues.

An aspect of recycling involves the ongoing look and assessment of issues faced by recipients and an opportunity to examine what issues should receive priority attention. Recipient-defined issues are fundamental to the realization of a consumer-driven model of case management and advocacy, and these issues must be preserved, updated, and evaluated on a frequent enough basis to ensure that they are addressed in a timely manner and according to the wishes of the consumer. Thus, recycling can lead to a mutual decision by recipient and advocate to abandon work on one issue and to initiate work on another, more pressing one, giving a dynamic quality to the formulation of direction. Recycling of issue identification becomes an important part of the meetings undertaken by recipient and advocate.

Recycling can make an impact on the advocate's understanding of the circumstances and world of the recipient. The recycling of issues identifies for the advocate the urgent situations faced by recipients and the environmental triggers of these situations. It can sensitize the advocate to how institutional structures may erect barriers that can frustrate the aims of recipients. Recycling therefore can feed back onto the strengthening of the alliance by increasing the sensitivity of the advocate to the environmental circumstances of recipients and by communicating to recipients an advocate's concern with the relevance of those recipient-identified issues that form the substantive agenda of the advocacy enterprise.

Principal Element 4: Collective Response

This element of the model demonstrates the possibility of linking individual and collective forms of advocacy practice, two forms of advocacy that are often treated as discrete and separate approaches to addressing advocacy in the human services. Recipient-defined issues and directions can form a systemic agenda for advocacy when these issues and directions are collated across people and groups. Recipients and advocates need to keep in mind that the issues they address are indicative of environmental factors and institutional structures that can frustrate people's needs, reduce their status, and limit their opportunities. Reflecting on opportunities for larger scale social action can link both recipients and advocates to groups and to movements that are addressing recipient-defined issues on a larger and more institutional scale.

Such linkage can offer recipients new reference groups and new communities with which to affiliate. As Lane (1992) points out in his book about the deaf community, such a community can offer its members protection from the greater society and foster the selfhood and identity of newcomers who have only experienced misunderstanding or rejection by the larger community.

Activation as part of a social movement can offer advocates and recipients additional tools, technical assistance, and resources to address recipient-defined issues. Recipient-defined issues can offer a social movement impact cases useful from a legal perspective to better define or expand rights, or useful from an issue-building perspective when case situations document the personal consequences of institutional and environmental forces. Systemic and policy-oriented advocacy can orchestrate the dissatisfaction of a great many people who can articulate corporately an agenda for social change (Freddolino & Moxley, 1994; Lane, 1992), an amplification that probably cannot be achieved through interpersonal advocacy alone.

Principal Element 5: The Acquisition of Know-How

Know-how involves pragmatic knowledge useful in achieving the often complex ends of advocacy. The acquisition of know-how by recipient and advocate will empower the achievement of recipient-defined ends and the resolution of recipient-defined issues, especially if this know-how is buttressed by rights codified in law (Freddolino, Moxley, & Fleishman, 1989). Many recipients simply do not have the power to confront alone many of the institutional forces within communities that control credit, housing, income, employment, education, training, and transportation. This relative lack of power means that recipients often lack the necessary knowledge to enable them to address effectively the rules and procedures governing eligibility, access to basic living resources, and appeal of decisions.

The availability of advocacy is designed to create more equitable circumstances for recipients, an observation that points out the importance of the advocacy program itself possessing the necessary technical and legal resources to strengthen the relative standing of the people it serves. Know-how is important because advocates and recipients will learn how to activate complaints, how to make appeals, how to take advantage of legal procedures, and how to capitalize on bureaucratic and institutional processes. This know-how will be available to other recipients and advocates as the advocacy enterprise builds its pragmatic knowledge base and as recipients offer support and assistance to other recipients while making use of the know-how of the program to increase the probability of successful outcomes.

Thus, our model reflects the importance of this know-how and its fundamental relationship to the accomplishment of recipient-defined ends. Each "case" cannot be viewed as a unique occurrence, although recipients should always be approached and understood as unique individuals. The know-how acquired from both negative and positive advocacy initiatives will contribute to the problem-solving capacities of the advocacy enterprise. Since most requests for advocacy will probably involve access and use of basic living necessities and the troubleshooting of institutional forces that prevent the attainment by recipients of these necessities (Freddolino, Moxley, & Fleishman, 1988), advocacy know-how will most likely cluster into the areas of housing, income, employment, education, training, health care, and transportation. The capacity of the actual program to translate know-how in this area into technical assistance capabilities will greatly enhance the expertise and effectiveness of interpersonal advocacy (Freddolino & Moxley, 1987).

Principal Element 6: Release

We do not envision the interpersonal advocacy enterprise to have a final ending point that is translated into a permanent termination of the effort. Indeed, the concept of termination is too final. Consistent with the ethos of this model, we envision a mutual release of recipients and advocates at a time when recipients feel they have completed their work. Hopefully, release will be driven by recipients' feeling that they achieved a satisfactory state and that they do not want to move into new areas of advocacy work. Release, however, is framed in provisional terms. Effective interpersonal advocacy should be easily triggered by recipients, and they can return to the service at any point when dissatisfaction reemerges and they want to address the issues creating this dissatisfaction. We invoke the term *dormant* to communicate that the recipients' relationships with advocates—and/or the host program—remain in place but inactive until recipients choose to trigger the help and assistance of an advocate. Outreach may be offered to recipients on a periodic basis, but it is done so in a casual manner as a friendly contact or as an opportunity to let former recipients know about the continued availability of the advocacy service rather than as an assertive strategy to track and monitor people.

IMPLICATIONS FOR CASE MANAGEMENT PRACTICE

Location of Advocacy Program

Given the consumer-driven character of the advocacy model we propose, the location of the actual program and its organizational auspices become important issues for the design of case management programs that incorporate advocacy as a form of practice. Most case management programs—especially those that embody a brokering form of practice—are embedded in human service systems such as those serving people with serious mental illness or developmental disabilities, or people who are aging. Such locations can produce some ambiguity by raising loyalty questions, especially when human service organizations define the purpose of case management as achieving the ends these organizations see as important or when case management is seen as responsible for controlling the behavior of consumers. It may be difficult for these programs actually to advocate for their recipients when they juggle both system-defined goals and consumer-defined desires.

Siting the case management program outside of formal human service systems may give advocate case managers a more autonomous role and offer them the latitude to represent consumer-defined goals and desires more authentically. Such an advocacy-oriented case management program does not have to be encumbered by the approach to human services defined by the sponsoring system. For example, case management programs within mental health systems may need to incorporate clinical and diagnostic procedures that highlight people's mental health status rather than issues and concerns identified and prioritized by consumers themselves. An advocacy-oriented case management program will most likely want to focus only on issues defined by consumers themselves and use these issues to frame the actual process of case management practice (Moxley & Freddolino, 1994).

Positioning the advocacy-oriented case management program outside of an actual human service system may enable it to resist coercion and pressure from this system. In some situations, the system may want the program to share information, coordinate services, and participate in individualized planning. An autonomous program can resist these demands and reaffirm its consumer-driven purpose, which suggests that the recipient would need to identify when it is important to share information or to coordinate services.

The potential organizational hosts of an advocacy-oriented case management program can be quite diverse. The host can be a legal advocacy program (Freddolino, Moxley, & Fleishman, 1989) or an actual organization run for and by consumers such as a consumer-run drop-in center or an independent living center. Community action organizations or disability groups committed to social change may also serve as auspices or hosts of such a case management alternative.

The ideological and philosophical orientation of the host is important. A consumer-driven program most likely will incorporate empowerment perspectives based on a world view that the need for case management and advocacy emerges out of oppression and the negative social reaction experienced by people who bear serious effects of complex social problems. This form of case management practice may be actually linked to broader social movements like disability rights, empowerment of people with serious mental illness, and the expansion of benefits for people coping with serious physical or medical conditions. Thus, a commitment to social justice and the capacity to understand and act on the broader social conditions faced by the identified recipient population may be important capacities for a host to offer. These capacities demonstrate the ability to link interpersonal advocacy and a broad orientation to helping people organize essential daily living resources to a more systemic strategy for changing the social status of the people who are identified as recipients.

Anticipated Outcomes

One of the most important outcomes that an advocacy-oriented case management initiative offers consumers lies in the legitimization of disputes and dissent (Moxley & Freddolino, 1990). People who experience oppression and social neglect may view themselves as unworthy of attention by people in authority. Alternatively, they may be angry, but these feelings may be diffuse and unrelated to a specific issue or object in the person's environment. One outcome of interpersonal advocacy is a recognition by the recipients that they have legitimate disputes and that they have many feelings tied to these disputes. The advocate and recipient can work closely in identifying the nature of these disputes and the issues that are tied to them. Opportunities for dissent offer people an outlet for expressing their feelings as well as a means of exercising choices and the values and preferences underlying these choices. Choice-making—especially when it is not nominalistic—itself may be an important outcome of advocacy.

We also want to identify quality of life as an important outcome. The subjectivity of quality of life must be respected, for each individual must define what they mean by this as an outcome. A broad orientation to consumer-defined issues, needs, and desires sets the stage for helping consumers make choices about quality of life. It is likely given the consumer-driven character of the advocacy model we propose that quality of life issues will become central features of advocacy practice, and that as recipients make critical choices about housing, work and employment, income, involvement in the community, and education, these choices will have direct consequences for their quality of life. Thus, we assert that advocacy-oriented case management must ultimately be measured through the subjective perceptions of recipients concerning their quality of life.

CONCLUSION

Our model of interpersonal advocacy certainly holds many implications for the structuring of case management programs and systems. The adoption of such an approach to practice can redefine what we mean by case management and its purpose and role in contemporary human services. Indeed, case management practice based on advocacy is very different from case management based on the ethos and logic of brokering, gatekeeping, or clinical practice. Case management practice based on advocacy focuses more on the societal reaction to the social problems experienced by recipients, and it focuses on the relationship between the recipient as citizen and the organizational and bureaucratic structures monopolizing contemporary human services. The forces emanating out of these structures and the diminished status often experienced by recipients vis-a-vis these forces become the focal point of this form of case management and offer case management a stronger and more salient social purpose than other forms of this practice.

Advocacy itself must embody an empowerment process. Thus, the core value of consumer control becomes a critical feature of the model and is central to framing the efforts of the advocate and recipient in their efforts to overcome social forces that can frustrate recipients and that can undermine their status as citizens who are striving for dignity and respect. It appears to us that operationalizing this value is fundamental to making each step in the advocacy process an effective one. We do recognize that some individuals may not want to exercise this control (Kane, 1988). This itself is a choice that can be made in close collaboration with the individual who serves as advocate, and arrangements for respecting this choice can be made. Nonetheless, it is incumbent upon the advocate to ensure that basic consumer control over the advocacy process is at the forefront of the model and is offered to each recipient.

CHAPTER 11

FIVE PRINCIPLES FRAMING CASE MANAGEMENT PRACTICE WITH HOMELESS FAMILIES

Shirley P. Thrasher and David P. Moxley

In this chapter, previously published in the proceedings of the conference *WHAT WORKS?: Synthesizing Effective Biomedical and
Psychosocial Strategies for Healthy Families in the 21st Century*,
sponsored by The Indiana University School of Social Work, Dr.
Thrasher's concern for homeless families and Dr. Moxley's concern
for responsive human services combine to craft a statement of how
human services and case management systems can respond more
proactively to the emerging problem of homelessness among families. The five principles identified in this chapter can be adopted by
professionals practicing in an array of settings serving people and
families who are homeless. These principles are consistent with the
framework of advocacy proposed in a previous essay. Putting them
into practice successfully requires all of us concerned with families
who are homeless to commit to the adoption of a consumer-driven
framework, one that offers families a comprehensive support system
designed to prevent the recurrence of homelessness.

The changing landscape of homelessness from one of older unattached adults to
homeless families poses a significant challenge to helping professionals. The
emergence of homelessness among families points to the significant stress that
many families are experiencing in the United States as changes accelerate in our
social structure and as many social stressors accumulate to push some families
into a status that once only involved our most marginalized citizens. In the past
decade the increase in homeless families has accelerated to such an extent that in
a survey of twenty-seven cities conducted by the U.S. Conference of Mayors in
1989, approximately one-third of the overall homeless were families (Bassuk &
Cohen, 1991), and in some cities the proportion of the homeless who were fam-

ilies exceeded 50 percent (e.g., New York City, New York; Portland, Oregon; Norfolk, Virginia; and Trenton, New Jersey) (Bassuk et al., 1990). Women with children are the largest subgroup of homeless families (Axelson & Dail, 1988; Bassuk, 1989; Bassuk & Rosenberg, 1990; Bassuk & Cohen, 1991; Hagen, 1987; Kozol, 1988; Solarz, 1988), indicating the very serious nature of this social problem.

Poverty and the severe shortage of affordable housing are leading causes of this new phenomenon of family homelessness, and some believe it is an outcome of significant and substantial change in our social structure that has made accessible health care, good housing, employment, training, and child care almost impossible to obtain for a large segment of our citizenry. In addition to these leading causes, research on homeless families has established other problem areas: substance use, social disaffiliation, family violence, social service cutbacks, emotional difficulties, residential instability, and educational and vocational problems (Bassuk & Rosenberg, 1988; Dail, 1990; Mills & Ota, 1989; Thrasher & Mowbray, in press). The recurrence of family homelessness is also a major problem. According to the Citizens Committee for Children of New York (1992), families who leave shelters often return to them, move from place to place, and are in need of ongoing support services designed to enable them to stabilize their housing situations, address critical problems facing them, and reduce those stressors that if left unaddressed can result in families rejoining the ranks of the homeless.

In response to this increasing problem of family homelessness, helping professionals and concerned citizens must adopt a comprehensive strategy that moves human services beyond addressing merely the crisis and emergency needs of homeless families. This strategy must be designed to prevent the recurrence of homelessness while also connecting families to community support systems that will nurture them, help them to troubleshoot and successfully resolve the problems and stressors they experience in daily living, and achieve a quality of life that is satisfying and productive. In other words, helping in this critical area must not stop at the resolution of crisis and emergency but must establish an ongoing capacity to address the needs of families, using a longitudinal time frame. Such a comprehensive strategy can be achieved by providing to homeless families service-enriched permanent housing that links families to networks of community services, social supports, and other families who can offer nurturing and caring attention.

In this chapter, we propose an approach to case management that is designed to organize the services and supports necessary to help homeless families to stabilize their lives in permanent housing situations. We propose five program design principles on which to base a case management effort, and within these principles we organize state-of-the-art case management ideas relevant to working with homeless families. Our goal is to offer a framework of practice that promises a relevant response to this serious social problem and to the families who bear the effects of it.

A CONCEPTION OF CASE MANAGEMENT

There is considerable variability in case management systems, reflecting the plethora of definitions attributed to this form of human service practice (Moxley, 1994a). Some forms of case management seek to make human services more efficient and cost-effective, with primary emphasis placed on controlling the behavior of consumers as one means of reducing the consumption of expensive services and supports. Often this approach to case management incorporates gatekeeping roles designed to enforce control over consumption and utilization. Alternatively, case management has gained another character by virtue of the efforts of consumer activists and advocates who have sought to make human services more responsive to people who experience serious social problems and who often have unfulfilled basic needs created by a serious illness, disability, or condition as well as by the social stigma and discrimination that often accompany many social problems (Anthony, Cohen, Farkas, & Cohen, 1988).

Homelessness among families represents a situation in which case management must be responsive and consumer-driven. The situation in which homeless families find themselves is complex and is characterized by many interacting social forces that create the social status of homelessness. Like those with many other complex human service problems, such as serious mental or physical illness, people who are homeless are seen as needing a representative who will work with them in an almost tireless manner to address and fulfill a range of needs created by the status of homelessness that likely will result in neglect and further decline of the family if left unaddressed (Moxley & Freddolino, 1991). Rather than conceiving of the role of the case manager in work with homeless families as that of a gatekeeper seeking to forge a more efficient human service system, we envision this role as taking the form of an advocate who works with families both in the short and long term to resolve housing emergencies, develop a plan for stabilizing their housing, and implement an ongoing proactive strategy for improving outcomes vital to creating a viable home life (Moxley & Freddolino, 1991).

We view case management as a collaborative effort undertaken by a person or team designated as a case manager and a family, who work jointly to resolve issues, barriers, and needs identified from the perspective of the family in order to achieve successful housing outcomes. Basic values must be identified since they are the primary building blocks of our framework, and they should serve as the advanced organizers of our principles and the practices that flow from these principles. We envision six values underlying the approach to case management we propose. These are:

1. *Responsiveness.* We must struggle to create a service and support system that is truly responsive to the family and to the qualities, desires, and aspirations of the family and its members.
2. *Environmentalism.* We must address proactively those environmental forces that create family homelessness and amplify for those people who control resources in our communities the role of these forces in perpetuating this social problem.
3. *Strengths.* We must create a framework of case management service delivery that makes use of the strengths of homeless families and that assists these families to make use of these strengths in their efforts to stabilize their housing situations.
4. *Advocacy.* We must adopt an advocacy orientation designed to collaborate with families in identifying and resolving family-defined needs and in responding to bureaucratic and community impediments that can frustrate their fulfillment.
5. *Distal Temporal Orientation.* We must adopt a long-term time frame guiding action, one that is sensitive to the prevention of housing crises and to those forces that can disrupt a family's housing, and one that builds toward the achievement of stabilized housing consistent with the family's vision of itself.
6. *Consumerism.* We must undertake the evaluation of helping efforts and their effectiveness from the perspectives of consumers and focus on the competence of the case management system to achieve successful housing outcomes.

THE BASIC PRINCIPLES OF THE MODEL

Principle 1: Case Management Must Focus on Environmental Circumstances of Homeless Families

Much of the research in the area of homeless families highlights the deficits of these families, especially those of principal caregivers who are too often women. These studies may highlight observations concerning substance abuse, psychopathology, and diminished parenting skills. Yet from our perspective, these issues and problems are not causes of homelessness but rather are likely responses to the high levels of stress created by the experience of homelessness and the related social structural problems that can interact to create this problem. From a social problem perspective, these individual problems are best seen as covariants of homelessness among families. Perhaps one hypothesis that we can propose is that such problems will be reduced in significance and salience as daily living stressors are reduced and as the housing situations of homeless families are stabilized over time through the use of enriched services and supports.

Homelessness among families may represent the failure of our collective efforts to support families and, therefore, the capacities of communities to support all families must be brought into question. Families without resources and supports, and those whose income is in jeopardy, are under considerable stress, and it is the role of any intervention strategy to understand both the immediate situational environment of these families as well as the greater environmental context in which families must function. It is an overstatement that the economies of our local communities can produce sufficient housing for every family. This is especially true if we heighten our expectations and criteria of success: many communities—themselves confronting massive levels of socioeconomic change and stress—are more than challenged to offer housing that is embedded in safe and crime-free environments and that is linked to accessible and decent educational, health, and employment resources.

If we point to homeless families and say they are inherently unhealthy, and that it is these unhealthy behaviors that push them into homelessness, then we neglect to identify those critical dimensions of communal life that fail to meet the needs of these families. In other words, we cannot assume that housing can be offered independent of supports designed to help families obtain and hold on to the vital resource of housing. It is difficult to conceive of homelessness among families independent of the communal functions needed to foster good family life. Housing and community support must go hand in hand.

A case management effort the purpose of which is to reach out to homeless families and to help them change their status (i.e., from homeless to housed) must assume an environmental perspective. Those helpers serving in case management roles must gain an understanding of the stressors impinging on a family and the resource inadequacies that can exacerbate stressors leading to homelessness. Gil (1976) offers simple yet meaningful concepts for thinking about these resources by differentiating between life-sustaining and life-enhancing resources. An environmentally responsive case management model must address, at a minimum, those needs required for survival. Among these are safety, housing, nutrition, clothing, income, and transportation (Moxley, 1989).

A case management model that is responsive to quality of life concerns cannot stop at merely addressing survival. It must identify life-enhancing resources that may be found in the quality of neighborhood life, the availability of training and work, opportunities to gain long-term employment and to participate in career development, and activities relevant to leisure and family development.

According to ethnographic research conducted by Thrasher and Mowbray (in press), finding a home is a difficult enterprise for homeless families. Barriers like the absence of a security deposit, unavailability of the first month's rent, a poor credit history, and shelter rules that fail to offer childcare alternatives so parents are free to search for housing, can frustrate the attempts of homeless families to get settled. A relevant case management effort will prioritize enabling measures designed to facilitate a family's successful search for housing they see as valuable.

A pathology of too many case management programs is their preoccupation with crisis and emergency. Often people can only activate some case management efforts through a crisis. Helpers filling case management roles focus on these crises and measure the success of their efforts by their resolution. The work with the family is then terminated. Yet if we are truly to help families who are homeless to change their status and to hold on to their housing, then we must pursue four aims. We must (1) be prepared to offer assistance in obtaining both life-sustaining and life-enhancing resources; (2) be fully cognizant of the role of environment and of those factors external to the family that can lead to the disruption of housing; (3) adopt a broad orientation to what constitutes support, and help families to find communities that can offer them nurturance, protection, and ultimately membership; and (4) adopt a time frame whose horizon is well beyond the effort it takes to help people move into housing and that truly offers rich follow along to address stabilization of the family. In other words, we must adopt helping strategies that respect the difficulty and challenge presented by the social problem itself. For many, homelessness is not a situational or time limited problem. It can be enduring and it can recur.

Perhaps a public health model is one of the most relevant organizing frameworks we can apply to the development of a case management effort suitable to addressing a problem as serious as family homelessness. We can view the families themselves as hosts of the problem. This helps us to understand the multiple personal and interpersonal problems that often serve as the principal foci of human service intervention as the symptoms or effects of a much larger environmental problem. Homelessness is embedded in an environment that fosters neglect of families and tolerates the absence of strong societal and community policies that would legitimize the provision of essential resources to families, buffering them from stress and preventing their disruption.

These environmental conditions interact with other serious environmental circumstances such as poverty, racism, and sexism, thereby creating a very complex social matrix of cause and covariation. Agent factors—those factors responsible for transmitting or triggering the problem—are numerous, including a diminished supply of housing, violence, limited job opportunities, poor child care, and retrenchment of essential social services. Homelessness among families living in marginal circumstances can be triggered by marginal changes in our communities. Case management must become effective in recognizing the environmental influences of this problem and in responding to these environmental challenges.

Principle 2: Case Management Must Adopt a Strengths Perspective

To simply focus on the host and the problems that the host exhibits heightens the probability that a case management effort will adopt a deficit perspective. Indeed, contemporary human services can be characterized by such a perspective, as helpers focus on the interpersonal and intrapersonal qualities of individuals in need rather than focusing on either the role of environment in the creation and sustenance of stress or the interactions among people and their environments. The assumption underlying such an intervention approach often involves the conception of people as creating their own problems. State-of-the-art practice in case management is calling for a mastery or strengths perspective in which people are seen as striving to cope with circumstances that are challenging at best, or life-threatening at worst (Rapp, 1992). A strengths perspective in human services demands that helpers work with people in efforts to identify personal, situational, and community strengths and assets and to incorporate these assets into the process of helping people to fulfill self-defined needs.

The strengths perspective applied to the problem of homelessness among families recognizes the functional adaptations that homeless families have developed in response to adverse conditions. These conditions call for the use of survival skills and daily problem-solving efforts that can tax the mental health, coping, and interpersonal skills of even the most heroic among us. Thrasher and Mowbray (in press) conducted an ethnographic study of homeless families in Detroit. Rather than focusing on their deficits, these researchers examined the coping efforts of homeless mothers from a strengths perspective. Their findings illuminate the strengths of these mothers in seeking shelter residency, caring for children, finding new housing, and obtaining and remaining connected to essential support systems. In addition to their own personal fortitude, motivation, and persistence in resolving their housing dilemmas, these women demonstrate how to make use of basic resources that can be found in social networks and that may be ignored by helpers who only focus on linking families to formal entitlements. Rather than experiencing disaffiliation and lack of social networks, Thrasher and Mowbray (in press) found their informants maintained contact with a wide variety of individuals, from immediate family members such as mothers, fathers, and siblings, to former boyfriends. Relatives in particular served as principal supporters who offered child care, respite care, and small amounts of money.

The adoption of a strengths framework can reframe the actual design and implementation of a case management effort (Rapp, 1992; Rapp & Wintersteen,

1989). It enables case managers to build an alliance on a foundation of positive forces rather than negative ones. Needs assessment and service planning instruments framed from a strengths perspective will communicate to family members a respect for their struggle and for their attempts to cope successfully. Such an approach will honor the efforts of families to master the difficult situations in which they find themselves. In addition, it offers the helper the opportunity to reinforce how difficult the situation of homelessness actually is and how overwhelming it can be. Certainly, a case management effort does not want to demoralize the family, but such a negative and unintentional outcome can be avoided by identifying barriers, the resources available to support the family, and the strategies that families can undertake to use their strengths in overcoming barriers.

Case management incorporating such a strengths perspective has been used successfully with people who are coping with serious mental illness. Strengths-oriented practice also demonstrates that a strengths perspective can be integrated into a model of rehabilitation that focuses on barriers in the environment and a joint formulation by client and case manager of mutually agreed upon strategies to attack and overcome these barriers. Such an approach recognizes the importance of the availability of meaningful resources designed to facilitate successful achievement and mastery of barriers (Rothman, 1992). A case management model designed, for example, to assist families to overcome homelessness would have control of the following resources:

1. Rich information about housing options to meet a range of family preferences and situations, and practical technical assistance on accessing these options successfully.

2. Monetary assistance adequate to help families make deposits on housing; to pay the first month of rent or even several months rent, if needed; and to obtain services from utilities.

3. Flexible transportation assistance designed to help families conduct a proactive housing search and make timely contact with agents who control housing.

4. A person to accompany the family, if desired, who can serve as a supporter of the family during the housing search process, can serve as a "surrogate consumer" in helping the family to make decisions about housing, or can troubleshoot problems that may arise between the housing agent and the family.

5. The availability of start-up funds designed to assist families to obtain the necessary material resources to operate a household. Certainly clothing, cooking utensils, groceries, and basic furnishings must be obtained, and families need flexible funds to address these needs.

Principle 3: Case Management Must Adopt an Advocacy Orientation

Fulfillment of the two principles stated previously does set the stage for the achievement of an advocacy orientation by the case management effort. If we assume that environmental forces really do create and perpetuate family homelessness, and that agent factors can trigger the manifestation of this social problem among families who are most likely already dealing with marginalized situations within their communities, then advocacy must become a salient attribute of any proactive model of case management. The adoption of a strengths perspective moves us further toward the embodiment of an advocacy orientation, since we will be building on the strengths of families as they define them and as they exhibit them through their coping with a very difficult and challenging if not life-threatening family situation.

To paraphrase Wolfensberger and Zauha (1973), our conception of advocacy requires case managers to "represent the interests of families as if they were their own." This does not mean that advocates define these interests (Moxley & Freddolino, 1990). We envision the need to respect the autonomy of the family. Our approach to case management requires helpers to work very closely with families in defining their needs and desires, identifying their preferences, and crafting strategies that incorporate the efforts of two parties (family and case manager) who come to this problem-solving enterprise as equals (Freddolino, Moxley, & Fleishman, 1989; Moxley & Freddolino, 1990).

Advocacy on the part of the case manager is undertaken in concert with the family and is driven by the preferences of the family as defined by this intimate collective or by its principal spokespeople. Thus, underlying the case management effort is an orientation to advocacy that requires case managers to (1) obtain a clear understanding of the family's experience of homelessness and how members want to address this situation; (2) form an alliance with the family that is characterized by the values of consumer control on the part of family members and loyalty of the case manager to the preferences of the family; and (3) take, along with the family, tangible action designed to change the status of the family from homeless to housed (Moxley & Freddolino, 1994).

A direction plan is formulated based on this alliance that (1) leads to activation of the family through the support of its strengths, the development of housing-relevant skills and capacities, and the incorporation of social network resources; and (2) involves the activation of case managers through their provision of tangible support information and technical assistance to the family, and of representation by case managers in forums to assure that those individuals or organizations who control resources needed by families do not frustrate their needs or violate their rights.

A case management effort that is truly designed to work with homeless families from an advocacy perspective must control or link to specific advocacy resources. First, it must have available legal resources to address the legal status of families as homeowners or tenants. The case management effort must have available the technical expertise or know-how to address conflicts that are generated between the family and community agents who control access to housing, income, health care, or other necessary resources (Moxley & Freddolino, 1991). This means that the case management effort has lawyers or paralegals with relevant expertise available either through advisory boards or through a legal staff. Pro bono arrangements or linkage to appropriate public interest or legal rights organizations are other ways of assuring availability of legal resources.

Second, operationalizing an advocacy perspective requires the case management program to have rich knowledge of housing resources and of supportive social services desired by the family, and to possess the expertise and perhaps the authority to activate these resources in a manner that is consistent with a support system driven by the preferences of families. Third, the case management program must have a capacity to link families quickly to housing alternatives that are satisfying to the families served by the program and consistent with their preferences (Tessler & Dennis, 1989). Fourth, the case management program defines long-term outcomes and has the capacity to work with families consistently over time once they are settled in to their housing, in order to troubleshoot problems that can become major threats to housing and family stability. Case managers are readily accessible to families, and it is easy for families to trigger a response from the case management program when they perceive a need for help. And fifth, the case management program has the availability of staff members who, in addition to sharing the demographic or social characteristics of homeless families served by the program, can easily demonstrate empathy and compassion, and achieve sensitivity to the perspectives of families, skills they have perhaps gained through personal experiences with homelessness themselves.

An individual advocacy orientation embraced by the case management program can grow into a collective one. By working with individual families the case management effort continually collects data on the issues, problems, and barriers these families face in choosing suitable housing, getting it, and holding on to it. These issues offer an aggregate portrayal of the problems and circumstances faced by homeless families, and they can be used by the case management program and its allies to make community decision makers aware of resource deficits, access issues, and systemic problems that face families coping with homelessness. Adopting this collective advocacy orientation may offer the program a means of orchestrating a larger scale alliance for social change among families, human service professionals, community activists, and sympathetic citizens. Collective advocacy is a salient means of addressing the environmental and agent factors that can trigger and sustain homelessness among families.

Principle 4: Case Management Must Operationalize a Strategy of Long-Term, Responsive Work with Homeless Families

The research on homelessness reveals that this problem is often best understood as a career. This means that people may move into and out of a state of homelessness, and they may experience various degrees of homelessness over time. Weaknesses in the so-called social safety net of programs and services may exacerbate this career and turn the attention of helpers to viewing family homelessness as a crisis state—one that must be addressed from a tertiary level of intervention. Certainly homelessness is a crisis and a serious emergency for families. We do not want to discount this. However, our concern is with the extent to which homelessness is placed into a long-term horizon of intervention and the extent to which it is viewed as demanding preventive work.

Case management must not be sporadic and rationed as a short-term intervention. How does a case management program create a form of practice that values the outcome of housing success? Working effectively with homeless families requires a generous time frame—one that respects the seriousness of the problem and the possibility that homelessness can become a career among families if the basic environmental influences and agent factors triggering and sustaining it are not addressed over time. There are several qualities of service that must be incorporated by a case management effort to address the possibility that homelessness can become a career. The case management program has outreach capacities so that helpers can link to families who seek refuge in shelters and also can link to families who reside in cars, in parks, on the streets, and with relatives.

The capability to establish meaningful and long-term relationships with families is important, and within this context case management staff follow procedures that require continual identification of needs and preferences, and that offer families continual opportunities to evaluate their satisfaction with their current circumstances and the outcomes produced by the case management program (Moxley & Freddolino, 1990). The continual identification of needs and desires should also incorporate an analysis of barriers so that the family and case manager can revisit their plans frequently and assure that these forces are addressed on a timely basis and do not disrupt the housing status of the family.

Simply to assure that families are housed is a necessary but not sufficient measure of case management success. The nature of case management intervention in this context does indeed call for helpers to establish a long-term vision guiding work with the family that infuses the hopes, desires, and preferences of the family as a unit into the helping process. For example, the current housing status of the family may involve residence in an inner city apartment, while the long-term vision of the family may be to reside in a single family home located in a middle class suburb. A responsibility of the case manager is to help the family craft a vision. It is the responsibility of the family, supporters of the family, the case manager, and the case management program and its sponsor to translate this vision into reality. We see the very real possibility of prevention and long-term housing success linked to the formulation of these visions and to their subsequent achievement.

The individual and collective advocacy efforts of the case management program may result in its programmatic elaboration achieved by the addition of emergency and long-term housing resources that can be easily triggered by case managers. The case management program may need to control a certain number of emergency housing placements as well as an array of supportive housing alternatives that are under corporate sponsorship of the case management program or an affiliated organization (Tessler & Dennis, 1989). The effectiveness of homeless service programs is often an outcome of whether these programs offer quick access to housing for the people with whom case managers work.

Choice of an appropriate organizational auspice can be a critical decision in crafting a case management program capable of creating long-term housing success. A homeless shelter may seem an obvious choice as this auspice. Yet the culture of such an agency may work against achieving a programmatic focus on long-term housing success, since homeless shelters may design their services around the objectives of crisis intervention, the offer of transient and time limited shelter, and the framing of the intervention problem as confined to the expeditious resolution of the immediate emergency. Other organizations like mental health or counseling services may tend to focus on framing the problems faced by homeless families from a diagnostic, personal, or interpersonal perspective, and they may fail to address the broader environmental forces setting the stage for homelessness among families. In addition, mental health organizations have not demonstrated the capabilities to muster housing resources to address the needs of their service constituents.

Perhaps the best organizational auspice of the case management program we envision is a human service agency that has specialized in the development and delivery of housing services and supports that are integrated with social services and community supports. Such an organization does not necessarily have to operate these housing alternatives, but it must be able to offer the technical expertise to create housing alternatives, to create partnerships with landlords and housing management firms to offer good housing, and to support families in housing they find through their own efforts. These auspices will recognize the importance of developing and providing housing within the context of social services and will recognize the importance of forging linkages with those community services that offer education, child care, transportation, nutrition, family development, training, and employment services. In addition, such an organization will support outreach to agencies involved in case identification, emergency shelter, and income maintenance.

Thus, we envision a case management program embedded in an organization committed to serving people in poverty—one that is also comfortable with taking community action in collaboration with the people it serves. The overarching vision of these organizational auspices is not confined to the provision of emergency shelter alone but incorporates measures that operationalize the importance of working with families over time to prevent emergencies, to improve their housing status, and to foster family development.

Principle 5: Evaluation of Case Management Must Be Driven by Consumer Perspectives

Too often in human services, the evaluation of intervention efforts incorporates those values important to system-level decision makers and fails to incorporate those directly relevant or meaningful to consumers themselves. Evaluation can be used as an empowerment strategy so that consumers can reflect on the effectiveness of services and supports from their perspective, and can use this activity as a means of informing service providers and decision makers about their preferences and the merits of the program that is designed to serve them. As noted above, case management too often is designed to achieve system-defined objectives and aims, while an emphasis on understanding whether a given service produces benefits valued by the actual users is overlooked (Moxley, 1994a; Freddolino & Moxley, 1993).

In order to assure that the case management program is consumer-driven it is critical to evaluate it from the perspectives of consumers themselves on an ongoing basis (Freddolino & Moxley, 1992). Indeed, the literature on providing sensitive consumer-driven case management services highlights the importance of incorporating a brief evaluation of the direction case management is taking within each contact between helper and consumer. We envision that evaluation would be conducted in four ways. First, at each contact homeless families would be asked to evaluate the actual helping effort by reviewing (1) how the case manager and family are working together; (2) the actual outcomes that are being realized; and (3) whether prioritized needs or desires are effectively addressed within the interactions between family and helper. Second, the case management program samples families several times annually and conducts focus groups that will offer input into the program concerning specific ways that it can improve the delivery of services and supports, achieve better outcomes, and respond to emerging needs. Third, the program conducts an annual survey of its participants to examine the degree to which it is offering services and supports to families in a satisfying manner and whether it is truly addressing the quality of life of families. Fourth, the program collects and uses outcome data indicating the extent to which the program is helping participants to achieve their housing preferences and whether the effort is helping families to stabilize and maintain their housing.

By virtue of this approach to evaluation, a case management effort designed to serve families who are homeless defines its accountability directly to the consumer. It also offers families who are too often unempowered a voice concerning how case management should be undertaken and the outcomes such a program should produce. A well designed and maintained database will enable the program to engage in continual consumer-based planning in order to refine its program and to elaborate its responsiveness to specific subgroups of families formed by important factors like race, ethnicity, and family structure.

CONCLUSION

Achievement of the five principles represents the necessary psychosocial means supporting the implementation of a proactive case management service that forms a family-driven strategy. Our own discipline and profession of social work is struggling with these concepts in its efforts to define family work through policies guiding professional practice, the socialization of graduate students into the profession, and the creation of social programs that are effective and meaningful to their recipients. But too often our own colleagues engage in practices that merely focus on patching families together—ones that may actually constitute a form of "blaming the victim."

How do we foster the health and well-being of homeless families as we move rapidly to the beginning of a new millennium? One salient conclusion is that we cannot ignore the necessity of strengthening supports. We must recognize, however, the systemic features of such support: We must struggle with offering these supports in the context of a healthy community. Hancock (1991) identifies the importance of building healthy communities simply because healthy communities form the contexts in which family well-being is achieved. The World Health Organization has proposed a concept of community health: such communities offer their citizens justice, sustainable ecology, peace, housing, food, education, and income (Hancock, 1991). We imagine that any normative definition of community health will incorporate the ability of communities to generate housing and to create homes for people. Housing, homes, and family development go hand in hand—all three cannot be easily overlooked as fundamental qualities of communities that function well.

In addressing homelessness among families, we cannot separate the family from the community, and the community must be the framework within which case management is implemented. Effective case management programs developed in this social problem area cannot confine their attention solely to the linkage of families to housing; they must conceive of a broader agenda of community and neighborhood development. Why? Because ultimately family well-being will be tied to community health. Perhaps case management programs will not be the principal leader in fostering better communities, but they should be meaningful participants in amplifying the nexus between homelessness among families and community capacities so as to offer long-range supports to families—especially the most vulnerable ones.

Housing families, and preventing homelessness, must ultimately become a collaborative effort of committed human services, enlightened community leaders, an activated citizentry, and the people who experience the problem directly. According to Kretzman and McKnight (1993), we must focus on working with communities from the "inside out" and through this work realize that human service professionals are only one group that must reckon with a problem as serious as homelessness among families (Hancock, 1991).

Those case management programs designed to address homelessness among families and adopt a systemic mission will seek to become meaningful and visible participants in community dialogues concerning the needs of all families. Certainly programs that exemplify the five principles will have families as allies; possess data that will enable them to document and portray family desires, and the barriers that obstruct the fulfillment of these desires, in an ecologically valid and rich manner; and possess in-depth information concerning the unfulfilled needs among families. Following the five principles can help to amplify the voice of homeless families.

Those of us concerned about homeless families must remain cognizant that to work with this social population means that we are working primarily with children and women. These demographic realities do indeed influence how we undertake our work and the nature of the support systems we seek to create to respond to homelessness among families. For example, case management programs must practice within a social problem context created by children living in poverty and women dealing with sexism.

Working with families is a challenging enterprise. Working with homeless families is profoundly challenging. The salience and seriousness of this problem, however, cannot be ignored by a society committed to democractic culture. As we move rapidly toward a new century, we risk the normalization of homelessness as an expected and accepted part of our social structure. Professionals and citizens committed to promoting health among all families cannot tolerate these circumstances. To paraphrase Ralph Nader, such a situation must arouse our indignation.

CHAPTER 12

SERIOUS MENTAL ILLNESS AND THE CONCEPT OF RECOVERY: IMPLICATIONS FOR CASE MANAGEMENT IN SOCIAL WORK PRACTICE

This chapter is based on observations I made at the National Forum on Recovery for Persons with Serious Mental Illness sponsored by the Ohio Department of Mental Health and the Center for Mental Health Services. Held in Columbus, Ohio, during April 1994, those invited to the forum included consumers, family members, researchers, and state and national mental health administrators. As the forum facilitator, I had the opportunity to observe directly the two days of presentations and dialogue that occurred in a roundtable format. The content of this chapter is based on the papers delivered at the conference, my notes concerning the dialogue, and my observations of the content of the forum. This chapter does not represent the policies or positions of the Ohio Department of Mental Health or the Center for Mental Health Services. A version of this chapter was published as a monograph in 1994 by the Boston University Center for Psychiatric Rehabilitation.

The National Forum on Recovery for Persons with Severe Mental Illness could not have come at a more fortuitous time. Those of us involved with serious mental illness, whether as consumers, providers, family members, researchers, or policy makers, need a new vision orchestrating our work and commitments in the vital field of mental health. Whether the idea of recovery meets the need for this vision waits to be seen. The forum really did not answer this. But the National Forum did achieve one of its ends: *it stimulated a sustained dialogue among consumers, family members, providers, and others involved in the area of serious mental illness about what is needed to improve the lives and well-being of people who are labeled as seriously mentally ill.*

I have chosen the phrase "labeled as" to capture one of the important themes of this forum. That is, serious mental illness is as much a social and cultural construct as it is a biomedical one. Recovery, therefore, must incorporate personal and social factors either as curative and healing forces or as barriers to the recovery process. In grappling with the idea of recovery, forum participants moved from multiple planes trying to unravel something as complex as recovery. Biomedical, social, cultural, interpersonal, and transpersonal aspects of recovery were considered. A number of participants saw recovery as a movement back to "normality" from a diseased state. Synonyms for recovery here included rebuilding, restoration, and reconstruction. Others saw recovery as a process of transformation: a transformative movement—or a journey—a person makes through a state we refer to as mental illness to a new state of being, and to a new understanding of the self. A synonym for recovery here involved metamorphosis.

Disagreement among major stakeholder groups seemed to prevail. Perhaps the only common ground was the recognition that the idea of chronicity may have lost its relevance to understanding serious mental illness; that the movement out of the status of serious mental illness is possible for many people; that this movement is not so much an end state as it is a process that varies across people, can be very individualistic, and requires well articulated support but not necessarily in the form of mental health services; and that mental health systems, society's reaction to serious mental illness, and the actions taken by uninformed or uncaring professionals who view people as having little potential for development can compound people's problems, and can very likely degrade their daily lives and prevent the realization of recovery.

Many perspectives about recovery were shared at this conference, but I have chosen to highlight the perspectives shared by consumer participants primarily because it is my feeling that these views rarely get a hearing within professional social work forums. Also, I was very impressed with the direct implications of these perspectives for the development of our profession, which are especially important considering the large numbers of social workers who offer services and supports to people with serious mental illness. It is critical for social workers to listen carefully to these first person perspectives about recovery. By doing so we may be able to think about our practice in mental health with more creativity and relevance.

EMBRACING A NEW VISION

The Concept of Recovery

Anthony (1994) offers recovery as a vision that we can embrace as a new platform on which to base mental health service delivery and practice. He offers us a caveat, however: recovery should not be seen as the disappearance of suffering or the restoration of functioning to a "premorbid" state. Alternatively, recovery must be seen as a process. According to Anthony (1994), recovery is best viewed as a "deeply personal, unique process of changing one's attitudes, values, feelings, goals, skills, and/or roles" (p. 559). Recovery is grounded in the direct experiences and perspectives of consumers, and involves the adoption of new ways of living as well as the personal creation of meaning and purpose in one's life.

The subjectivity of recovery is an important characteristic of this process. As a mental health outcome, recovery involves the change of self expressed in qualities like empowerment, life satisfaction, self-determination, self-care, and self-efficacy. Achieving recovery, according to Anthony, requires helpers to assist people to achieve "more," such as more meaning and purpose, as well as to achieve "less," like decreased symptoms and coping problems.

A full appreciation of recovery as a concept also requires us to recognize that stigma, iatrogenic treatment systems, and societal discrimination are as much a cause—or maybe more of a cause—of disability as biomedical factors (Anthony, 1994). People with serious mental illness face serious barriers to recovery found in discrimination by employers, menial work opportunities, poor housing, impoverished social supports, low expectations by treatment personnel, and fear on the part of community members produced by a misunderstanding of serious mental illness. We cannot understand recovery if we neglect to address the social consequences of serious mental illness.

The very nature of serious mental illness characterized by its multiple influences and implications requires us to understand this problem as involving impairment, disability, and discrimination. It is often hard to draw discrete lines between biomedical symptoms, role functioning problems, and problems arising from social stress and discrimination. It is not surprising, therefore, that the concept of recovery is an ecological one, and that the vision of recovery emerges at a time when we have more understanding of the need to integrate biomedical services, social supports, developmental opportunities, and rights protection into "systems of recovery." The community support system model, psychosocial rehabilitation, and peer self-help and support all share a common theme: the relevance of tailoring a variety of supports to assist people with serious mental illness to craft their own recovery.

Driving Forces Supporting the Relevance of Recovery

Several driving forces have made recovery a contemporary possibility and a necessary vision. First, our conception of disability is changing dramatically. In several fields of practice, including psychiatric rehabilitation, mental retardation and developmental disabilities, and neurological and physical disabilities, the old assumption that disability precluded growth and development and prevented people from full citizenship and community participation is quickly fading. Contemporary conceptions of disability question whether the impact of disability must be serious or limiting for individuals, especially when social supports and personal coping resources are increased and readily accessible. Recently the American Association on Mental Retardation (AAMR) reformulated its definition of mental retardation to include a third factor to supplement its traditional two-dimensional definition involving intelligence and adaptive behavior. The AAMR definition recognizes that social and personal supports offered within the context of self-determination and cultural sensitivity can reduce the extent of people's disabilities and increase their functioning in critical realms of everyday life.

Similarly, in the area of psychiatric rehabilitation, the buffering role of social and personal support has long been recognized as an essential factor in preventing or reducing the impact of disability resulting from mental illness. Effective role functioning must be seen as emanating from a matrix of supports and services that are driven by people's preferences, values, and life aims. By establishing and articulating this personalized matrix for each individual, the field of psychiatric rehabilitation frames disability in a situational manner, as something that does not have to be an ongoing, lifelong reality. Thus, the very term chronicity equated with disability may be an anachronism. Perhaps, as Anthony (1994) suggests, by replacing chronicity with recovery as an overarching concept we will have a new, positive vision guiding rehabilitative work in the 1990s.

The emergence of consumerism in the field of serious mental illness is a second driving force. Both the antipsychiatry movement, whose members condemn the mental health system, and the consumer movement, whose members seek more egalitarian and collaborative roles with mental health professionals, have produced more assertive individuals who are critical of the performance of mental health professionals and mental health systems. Often this criticism involves issues of input and the involvement of consumers in the process of mental health service delivery. Many times this criticism involves issues of service relevance and responsiveness. However, perhaps the greatest contribution of consumers has been to model for mental health professionals meaningful and relevant services as evidenced in the increasing adoption by mental health systems of self-help, peer support, and self-advocacy approaches. Increasingly, local mental health service systems are involving consumers in the actual governance of these systems, a testimony to the importance of first person perspectives about serious mental illness.

A third driving force is the reengineering of many of our state and local mental health systems. This reengineering is another recognition of how mental illness cuts across biological, cultural, social, and personal planes and requires a complex and integrated approach to intervention. The reengineering of community mental health systems started with the demise of the Mental Health Systems Act at the beginning of the Reagan administration, and the subsequent prioritization of services and supports to people with serious mental illness by a number of state governments (Moxley & Taranto, 1994). The coalescence of a movement composed of consumers and survivors, family members, and informed professionals initiated local dialogues among these key stakeholder groups concerning the improvement of the standard of living and quality of life of people with serious mental illness.

The use of rehabilitation and community support ideas directed the attention of these stakeholder groups to consider the introduction of vocational and employment services, housing, socialization and developmental opportunities, and advocacy activities into established mental health systems. The reengineering of local mental health systems may now be seen as a project involving the integration of multiple approaches designed to address the consequences of serious mental illness involving consumerism, social services, rehabilitation, and medical and health care. Professionals cannot undertake this reengineering alone, not only because of the growing assertiveness of consumers and family members (Freddolino & Moxley, 1994) but also because consumers themselves must define the recovery process given the personalized and individualized character of this process (Anthony, 1994). The concept of recovery may make possible the successful integration of these four different and somewhat incompatible, but necessary, approaches to supporting people with serious mental illness.

RECOVERY AS AN ECOLOGICAL CONCEPT

Perspectives of Consumer Participants

Consumer participants in the forum articulated many different perspectives on what constitutes recovery. I have attempted to capture major themes and identify these below.

Multiple Pathways to Recovery

In classical systems theory the principle of equifinality posits the existence of multiple pathways to an outcome. Consumer participants emphasized that there are multiple ways to move through the process of recovery and to achieve a positive life outcome. Some consumers articulated a *heroic* approach by placing considerable emphasis on the use of personal strengths and the mastery of very difficult situations by invoking and using these strengths. The importance of spiritual beliefs and practices was highlighted, as were faith and hope in oneself.

Finding personal meaning in what can be a very isolating and frightening situation was reported by several consumer participants to be an indispensable resource.

The several consumers who articulated this approach to recovery discussed the importance of reframing the experience for themselves, and perhaps fighting the meanings given to them about this experience by professionals. Their aim was to give the experience of mental illness personal meaning and to find purpose. According to several participants, viewing the situation of serious mental illness as a personal transformation involving an awakening, a discovery of what lifestyle to pursue, or decision making about personal commitments and relationships, gave a distinctive purpose to the experience.

An alternative approach can be characterized as a *supportive* one in which people experiencing serious mental illness are fortunate to have productive encounters with others who accept, support, and nurture them. Unfortunately several consumers reported that such encounters were not necessarily the rule with mental health professionals who, according to some consumers, could often treat people in ways that objectified and depersonalized them. Consumers endorsing the supportive approach noted the importance of acceptance by others and the helpfulness of profound listening and empathy offered by other people. It was not unusual for these encounters to occur with other consumers and/or survivors, whose personal experience with serious mental illness helped to make these encounters even more sensitive and productive. Productive contacts with other consumers were reported within the forum as a basis for connection and safety that appeared to be absent in some interactions with trained mental health professionals.

A third approach is based on the availability of *opportunities*. Consumers articulating this perspective highlighted the importance of a safe refuge and the opportunity to manage the stressors in their lives in a personally constructive manner. Opportunities may mean access to essential and basic living resources (such as housing and food) or it may mean the opportunity to find a safe and quiet haven in order to spend time alone and to contemplate. The term sanctuary was suggested by several consumer participants to capture, I believe, the need for opportunities that offered peace and solitude, qualities that may be absent in inpatient and outpatient mental health programs.

I do not offer these three different approaches as a typology. I want to illustrate the diversity of approaches to recovery as articulated by consumers themselves and to highlight the necessity to personalize what we mean by the process of recovery. Recovery as a process, as noted by Anthony (1994), may mean different things to different people. For some individuals it may mean the use of their own personal resources and strengths; for others it may mean getting the support they want; while for others it may mean having opportunities to reach a sanctuary and address those needs they see as vital at the moment.

Recovery and the Degradation of Everyday Life

Consumer participants implied that mental health professionals are too preoccupied with the impairment dimension of mental illness and not its social and personal consequences. In one presentation, a consumer assertively framed what people with serious mental illness are recovering from: unemployment, stigma, absence of sanctuary, and "crushed dreams." It is one thing to recover from an illness. It is another to try to recover from the loss of status and outright discrimination. A number of consumers identified the role issues involved in serious mental illness and they noted that one's role as worker, homeowner, and student can all be jeopardized with serious negative, long-run developmental consequences.

Many consumers noted the close correspondance between employment and recovery. Certainly they discussed the implications of employment for gaining self-respect, identity, and social contacts. But a major concern was the link between employment and standard of living. Without good employment that pays a competitive wage, is available to people with serious mental illness, and offers supports that do not increase stigmatization, recovery may be an elusive aim for a number of people with serious mental illness. One presenter noted that he finds substantial meaning in his current work since it enables him to maintain a decent standard of living, something he is unable to do on disability income. In addition, he can exert considerable control over his job and choose his own hours, pace of work, and extent of social contact during the day.

Consumers who were concerned about the quality and standard of everyday living know firsthand the limitations of talking about recovery when people have inadequate food, housing, and work opportunities. Assisting people labeled seriously mentally ill to increase their standard of living with supports that help them to achieve a decent lifestyle may be one of the most significant challenges facing the recovery movement. Meeting this challenge successfully was identified by several consumers at the forum as a vital aspect of the process of recovery.

Recovery and an Expanded Role Set

Several consumer participants underscored the importance of moving beyond a narrow view of a consumer's role as a recipient of services to an expanded conception of—and appreciation for—the many contributions consumers can make to their own recovery and to the recovery of their peers. Consumerism within mental health systems means that an expanded role set can be available to all consumers. Included in this set are roles like researcher, provider, peer supporter, nontraditional recipient, and activist.

As *researchers,* consumers can work with their peers and providers in identifying relevant research questions and implementing research and evaluation projects within mental health systems. Already several systems are employing consumers in peer research, consumer-driven marketing studies, action research, and evaluation studies, with the aims of sensitizing professional staff to first person accounts of service quality and the needs of consumers. From a recovery perspective, "consumer as researcher" enables the recipient to take a more active, critical, and empowered role within mental health systems.

Consumers as providers received considerable endorsement at the forum. Consumer participants noted the importance of creating meaningful roles that paid competitively and that recognized the important contribution consumers can make to recovery through peer support, crisis intervention, case management, and the support of employment and vocational development. Affirmative employment is not only a means of increasing the sensitivity of mental health systems to recipients; it also serves as a strategy for linking consumers to peers and thereby enhancing the relevance and variety of support available to recipients (Mowbray, Moxley, Thrasher, & Associates, in press).

Closely related to affirmative employment is the role of *peer supporter*. Consumer participants emphasized the need to expand programmatic alternatives within mental health systems so that a variety of support options exist, especially relating to self-help, vocational development, and socialization. These options need to be run for and by consumers and have as their aims the creation and provision of flexible supports that are available during evening, holiday, and weekend hours. The peer support role is fundamental to the realization of recovery because, from the perspective of consumer participants, it makes available to consumers people who have firsthand experience with serious mental illness and the problems that mental health systems can create for recipients.

The role of *nontraditional recipient* recognizes that recovery is not compatible with passive consumers who accept what professionals want for them. Consumer participants identified the need to introduce rehabilitative and clinical approaches that support people in articulating their desires, making choices about treatment, and evaluating the quality and relevance of the services they receive. The role of nontraditional recipient, according to consumer participants, is relevant to recovery because it encourages people to become critical of the care that is offered, and to become more decisive about the nature and quality of the supports they want for themselves.

Finally, the *activist* role recognizes the importance of direct consumer involvement in the governance process of mental health service organizations and systems. The availability of the activist role suggests that consumers have perspectives that must be factored into governance, whereas the absence of these perspectives will lead to systems that fail to offer meaningful, desired, and relevant services and supports. Consumer participants identifying the importance of the activist role argued that if mental health systems are designed for consumers, why shouldn't consumers have significant roles in the governance of these systems?

All of these roles are consistent with a metatheme of the conference: *the achievement of an active voice on the part of consumers is perhaps the most vital ingredient of the recovery process.* The achievement of voice is linked to self-determination, empowerment, and self-efficacy. An active voice combats impairment, disability, and discrimination. If these are the outcomes of recovery then we have to recognize the close correspondance between the achievement of an active voice and the diversity of the role set, the viability of the roles composing this set, and the support consumers receive for effective role performance.

Recovery and the Achievement of Systemic Purpose

Consumer participants were very articulate about questioning the ultimate purpose of mental health systems. Some consumers at the forum boldly questioned whether mental health systems are indeed relevant to people labeled seriously mentally ill. They recognized that their well-being was not dependent on their involvement in mental health service, and underscored the necessity of distancing themselves from the status of mental health recipient in order to achieve recovery. For other consumers, maintaining a relationship with mental health systems was seen as important, and yet they were very concerned about the purpose these systems were pursuing in the name of community support—whether these systems were actually designed to be responsive to consumers or merely to control them.

Certainly the concept of recovery serves as a lens through which to view the purpose of contemporary mental health systems. And as we move further into the 1990s, we must ask some fundamental questions about what mental health systems should assist people labeled as seriously mentally ill to achieve. A new recovery-oriented mission of mental health systems may speak to the role these systems serve in helping people to define their own form of recovery and to support their own personal process of recovery.

The Ecology of Recovery

I was puzzled that more dialogue did not emerge about the role of mental health systems in national health reform and managed care, and whether the concept of recovery should be aligned with changes in our national health policy. At this writing, the situation of people with serious mental illness is not really getting the attention it requires in the national health care debate, and innovative approaches to the recovery process are not getting an enlightened hearing at the national level.

Yet I conjecture that the absence of this type of dialogue within the first National Forum on Recovery signals the broad ecological conceptualization of this idea. Recovery includes much more than health and medical care. To treat serious mental illness solely as a biomedical condition will limit our creative thinking about the range of resources, structures, opportunities, and roles needed to make recovery the ecological conception suggested by the diverse array of forum participants. Several potential ecological hypotheses concerning recovery were suggested by forum participants, and they are consistent with the role that social work and case management can assume in this vital area:

1. Recovery will be most successful when the nature of the supports that are made available to people is consistent with the personal meanings they have given to the experience of serious mental illness and to their recovery.
2. Those recipients who have opportunities to expand the supports available to them according to their own preferences and values will experience a corresponding increase in their recovery.
3. Recovery will be enhanced when mental health systems address and resolve many of the social, interpersonal, and cultural factors that serve to degrade the daily lives of recipients.
4. Those recipients who experience an increase in their standard of living and quality of life will experience a corresponding increase in their recovery.

AN AGENDA FOR CASE MANAGEMENT IN SOCIAL WORK PRACTICE

How can social work make use of the variety of these observations in case management? Certainly the observations themselves call for a critical look at how social workers are practicing with people who have been labeled as seriously mentally ill. Three major areas, articulated at the forum, are salient to the profession and deserve close examination. First, the role of peers in the recovery process stands out as a salient issue, and raises the possibility of recruiting to the profession people who are considered to be seriously mentally ill. Second, there are salient issues pertaining to practice education. And third, there are implications for the infusion of consumerism into case management in social work practice.

Recruitment to the Profession

From the perspective of consumer participants in the forum, peer assistance and understanding appear to be critical aspects of the recovery paradigm. Mental health systems have become increasingly enlightened about the possibility of extending mental health services, increasing their sensitivity, and offering new opportunity structures to consumers through the augmentation of consumer service roles, programs, and supports (Mowbray, Moxley, Thrasher, & Associates, 1996; Mowbray & Tan, 1992). However, these policy and programmatic efforts on the part of mental health systems have highlighted the limitations of affirmative employment. Consumers are often relegated to roles as helpers, assistants, and paraprofessionals, and often fail to receive the supports necessary to move into professional roles and responsibilities (Mowbray, et al., in press).

Social work can benefit from recruiting into its professional ranks individuals labeled seriously mentally ill, given their firsthand experience with serious mental illness and with the service system. Several consumers attending the forum were themselves mental health professionals holding doctoral degrees, master's degrees, and other professional credentials. Mental illness does not necessarily create cognitive and intellectual limitations that can prohibit successful completion of professional social work education. As a social work educator, I have witnessed firsthand the tenacity, courage, and commitment of at least six graduate social work students who creatively managed manic depressive illness or schizophrenia in order to complete professional education.

Progress in psychiatric rehabilitation has demonstrated the promise of supported education programs designed to offer critical supports helpful to people with serious mental illness in managing stress that can interfere with the completion of academic requirements and successful role performance as a student (Moxley, Mowbray, & Brown, 1993). Specific supports can be offered to higher education students so they can make career choices and commitments. The Michigan Supported Education Project, a research demonstration supported by the National Institute of Mental Health, has found that a number of students who have been labeled as seriously mentally ill want to pursue professional education in social work, substance abuse counseling, and other mental health disciplines. If the profession sensitizes individuals labeled seriously mentally ill to ways they can use their backgrounds as consumers as a practice asset, we may be able to increase the overall sensitivity and commitment of the profession to addressing the daily living and quality of life problems created by serious mental illness. Professional commitment to address practical daily living needs like employment and housing issues, and experiences of discrimination felt by people labeled seriously mentally ill, comprise a vital dimension of the recovery paradigm (Anthony, 1994).

Practice Education

Many graduate social education programs incorporate clinical paradigms into their mental health curricula. This clinical emphasis may not be relevant to a recovery paradigm given the many environmental problems faced by people with serious mental illness that, when left unaddressed, often create stress, unwanted symptoms, poverty, abuse, and discrimination. Given consumer perspectives on recovery articulated at the forum, what is the most relevant approach to practice education that social work can adopt in order to make recovery a vision of social work practice in the mental health field?

Answering this question is certainly complex. Yet we have some basic ideas articulated by forum participants. First, we must create practice education opportunities in which students develop competencies in assisting consumers to articulate their own personal meanings of recovery. Understanding consumers' personal constructions of their mental illness, their stories about their daily lives, and their hopes and visions for productive futures (Coles, 1989) all may be necessary competencies on the road to becoming competent and effective consumer-driven practitioners. These competencies may have little to do with understanding psychopathology, formal diagnostic systems, and symptom management strategies. They may have more to do with the humanization of social work practice and the reduction of social distance between practitioner and consumer.

Second, the material from the forum suggests that social work should concentrate its efforts on collaborating with consumers to address social and interpersonal factors that can block or otherwise frustrate recovery. Discrimination, rights violations, inadequate entitlements, and closed opportunity structures (like meaningful employment and homeownership) may be very appropriate targets for a social work of recovery. Practice education in mental health may need to (1) strengthen students' knowledge of housing systems, entitlements, vocational development, training, employment, transportation systems, and self-help opportunities; (2) equip students with the systems change skills to create and/or enhance these types of supports; and (3) assure that students can address injustice when these systems are unresponsive to the needs of people labeled seriously mentally ill.

Practice education driven by a recovery paradigm can make social work more distinctive than other disciplines in the mental health field. By decreasing clinical aims of practice, and by increasing social support and social development aims, social workers can bring their professional mission closer to that of psychiatric rehabilitation. A recovery purpose offers social work the opportunity to pursue the mission of assisting people with serious mental illness to achieve success in roles and environments of their own choosing (Farkas, Anthony, & Cohen, 1989). The realization of such a professional purpose and mission may be achieved through the integration of advanced generalist ideas into a social problem framework of serious mental illness.

Consumer-Driven Social Work Practice

Social work practice that values consumerism will emphasize sensitivity and responsiveness to consumer desires and wishes. Whether consumer, family member, or professional, many participants at the forum emphasized that coerced mental health care can seriously hinder recovery. Many participants appeared to endorse the idea that mental health systems needed to be driven by the desires and wishes of consumers and not by what professionals say consumers need (Cohen & Anthony, 1988).

Assessment of these desires and wishes reveals their centrality to the achievement of a decent standard of living and quality of life (Freddolino, Moxley, & Fleishman, 1989). Not surprisingly, these desires and wishes cluster into the basic areas of employment, vocational training, income, and housing (Freddolino, Moxley, & Fleishman, 1988). They reflect the necessity of linking the "choosing, getting, and keeping" of basic opportunities and resources, the availability of which can be taken for granted by many citizens, to the purpose of advanced social work practice in the mental health field.

Social work practice that values consumerism will recognize the importance of using self-help alternatives, consumer-run initiatives, and consumer employment opportunities as core programmatic qualities and not as mere adjuncts to service. This means that social workers involved in program development and administration will find ways to foster and sustain these alternatives. And they will find ways to make visible to the community the contributions of these alternatives so that consumerism becomes a venerated and honored dimension of mental health service delivery (Moxley & Taranto, 1994).

Finally, social work practice that values consumerism will endorse consumer control and evaluation of service provision. Strategies that enable consumers to control directly the individualized purchase of mental health services and supports through creative and flexible case management alternatives are vital aspects of consumerism. This also means that mental health care or support is not defined by its locus—in other words, it does not have to be offered by mental health professionals—but rather by its functional outcome. This means that consumers can forge personalized recovery plans that make use of innovative and creative inputs offered by mental health, rehabilitation, education, employment, and other service sectors of our communities. Accountability of provider performance and the benefits of the plan will be judged by consumers against an array of criteria, including the acceptability of professional effort and the meaningfulness of functional outcome. In other words, from the perspective of consumers, did these efforts contribute to their movement along a personalized pathway of recovery?

CONCLUSION

The National Forum on Recovery for Persons with Serious Mental Illness offered multi-stakeholder perspectives on the idea of recovery as an organizing concept for the mental health field. Several participants warned against turning this idea into a "sacred cow," the richness of which may be lost when researchers attempt to operationalize recovery, or when administrators or policy makers attempt to author guidelines and procedures to define it. What can be a provocative concept with a potential of encouraging considerable dialogue among consumers, family members, and providers can devolve into yet another short-lived mental health fad.

Social work, however, should examine the relevance of this concept and consider whether it can offer guidance to the profession in creating a form of practice that is more relevant to addressing the many issues created by the social problem of serious mental illness than an emphasis placed on clinical practice. As implied by Anthony (1994), recovery is not a biomedical idea. Rather, it is an ecological one. By focusing on the ecological dimensions of recovery, perhaps social work practice can reinvent environmental intervention in a manner that is consistent with a framework of consumerism and consumer-driven practice.

PART IV

EDUCATING CASE MANAGEMENT PERSONNEL

INTRODUCTION TO PART IV

The two chapters composing this part of the volume are devoted to the education and training of case management personnel. Chapter 13 presents a course that I designed for graduate social work students. The chapter examines the core content of the course and then relates this content to the professional development of graduate social workers. Two essential tasks for social workers are identified in this chapter. First, they must gain an understanding of the transdisciplinary character of case management, and second, they must integrate case management into the core of their practice. The first task evolves out of my assumption that case management is not the sole domain of any one discipline in the human services. The second task evolves out of the reality that many graduate social workers will serve as case managers, lead case management teams, and/or supervise programs with a case management component.

Chapter 14 changes the focus to the core practice competencies of case management personnel who work at the confluence of two social problems: serious mental illness and homelessness. The content of this chapter is derived from the research literature and from a demonstration project implemented in Michigan.

I hope these two chapters encourage readers to reflect on the professional development needs of case management personnel. They are not designed to exhaust all the educational possibilities that can be offered and that can contribute to the preparation of effective personnel. However, these two chapters do speak to an essential aspect of case management: effective programs will not be realized without considerable energy invested in the preparation of good personnel at all levels of professional development.

CHAPTER 13

PREPARATION OF GRADUATE SOCIAL WORK STUDENTS IN CASE MANAGEMENT

This chapter examines a course on case management developed and taught at the Mandel School of Applied Social Sciences at Case Western Reserve University. A version of it appeared in *The Journal of Teaching in Social Work*. Although the course was designed for the preparation of graduate social workers, many of the students came from diverse practice settings and represented diverse domains of practice. Some students worked in clinical settings in mental health while others worked on the streets in outreach roles. Other students were involved in various roles either in rehabilitation, educational, developmental disabilities, aging, or health care settings. However, most of the students had the same questions: What is case management? What is case management within the service context in which I practice? What variables or factors influence or otherwise shape my practice as a case manager within human services? And does case management really constitute professional practice? This chapter struggles with some of these questions to identify the relationship between case management and the core of social work education.

The growing complexity of case management in health and human services reflects a vastly changing service environment characterized by policy concerns involving cost containment, service effectiveness, and responsiveness to people who experience serious social and health problems (Donovan & Matson, 1994). Preparing graduate students in health and human service disciplines to assume case management roles has never been more challenging as increasingly case management is seen as a core element of preservice preparation in social work (Rose, 1992), nursing (Del Togno-Armanasco, Hopkin, & Horter, 1993), rehabilitation (Roessler & Rubin, 1982), and medical education (Hurley, 1986).

Social workers, in particular, must gain an understanding of case management since it represents a growing arena of contemporary professional practice. The proliferation of case management approaches and models, as well as the diverse applications of case management, calls for focused preservice education in this area so that students gain a critical perspective on this emerging form of human service practice. Case management approaches have emerged in a diversity of fields like primary health care (Like, 1988), long-term care (Applebaum & Austin, 1990), aging (Steinberg & Carter, 1983), child welfare, serious mental illness (Dill, 1987), serious physical illness, developmental disabilities (Wray & Wieck, 1985), and head injury rehabilitation (Dixon, Goll, & Stanton, 1988). These are certainly areas representative of the vulnerable populations the profession of social work is committed to serving (Gitterman, 1991).

This list can be extended since case management is seen currently as a preferred approach for addressing service delivery problems created by the diffusion of accountability, the decentralization of human services, the privatization of care, and the scarcity of resources (Moxley, 1989). Most of these attributes seem to characterize every contemporary field of human service. They suggest to policy makers the need for client-level system strategies designed to coordinate, integrate, or manage the provision of an array of health and human services in order to address effectively the situations of people who experience the multiple and interacting effects of complex social problems (Barker, 1987; Raiff & Shore, 1993).

Social work probably cannot and should not claim exclusive domain over case management. Some may argue that certain disciplines, like nursing, may more appropriately fulfill case management functions created by serious physical illness than other disciplines, while, for example, social work may be more appropriate in other situations, like those created by community support of people with psychiatric disabilities (Johnson & Rubin, 1983). But even in these two examples, one can persuasively argue that such problems are not the exclusive domain of these disciplines, and that case management can be undertaken by a variety of disciplines—or stakeholders (like family members or recipients themselves)—a reality that has given an interdisciplinary and transdisciplinary character to this form of practice.

Social workers, however, are heavily involved in case management roles both at the BSW and MSW levels of professional preparation, and they can benefit from preservice education in case management that helps them to understand this form of human service practice. Given the complexity of most health and human service problems that call for well coordinated responses by multiple professionals, case management is probably best recognized as a transdiscipline. That is, the body of case management knowledge is not unique to any one discipline (Levine & Fleming, n.d.). Multiple disciplines can contribute to the advancement of case management practice, and the emerging body of knowledge can be used to address social and human problems (Weil & Karls, 1985) by a variety of professionals who work with colleagues of similar disciplinary affiliations, within interdisciplinary arrangements, or in situations that do not emphasize discipline identity at all. In a transdiscipline, there is a core set of skills that can be used by a variety of disciplines.

The complexity of case management poses a significant teaching challenge. Graduate social work students must not only learn about case management within the context of their own discipline; they also must learn about case management as a transdisciplinary element of health and human service delivery so they are better able to integrate case management into their professional roles as they move into autonomous practice. Without such a broad understanding of case management, professionals with strong disciplinary orientations may subsequently drop out of these roles (Applebaum & Wilson, 1988).

This chapter identifies five elements of a specialized course on case management practice that offers graduate social work students an introduction to case management as part of their core curriculum. From the perspective of the author, these five elements serve to define the transdisciplinary character of case management and offer graduate social work students, as well as other graduate health and human service students, a meaningful preservice introduction and orientation to the growing complexities of case management practice. Following an overview of the domain of the course, I discuss the five core elements, and then I examine the implications of these elements for making case management a salient dimension of the professional development of graduate social work students.

THE COURSE DOMAIN

Course Background

The specialized course on case management was developed in the early 1990s as a core curriculum offering to graduate social work students enrolled in the intensive semester option at The Mandel School of Applied Social Sciences at Case Western Reserve University. Students enrolled in the intensive semester option complete their course work through intensive weekend courses. They are individuals who are working in professional positions typically within local mental health, developmental disabilities, aging, and long-term care service systems, and who are coming to graduate school to obtain advanced training and education while they continue to practice.

The course was developed with the support and involvement of the Cuyahoga County Mental Health Board, which wanted its personnel educated in state-of-the-art case management concepts, ideas, and practices. The author worked collaboratively with representatives of the mental health board and the Mandel School to identify the essential content of the course and to create the initial course plan.

Scope and Aims of the Course

The purpose of the course is not merely to equip students with case management skills. Students are to develop a critical perspective on case management and a broad understanding of its role in the *improvement* of human service delivery systems (Applebaum & Wilson, 1988; Steinberg & Carter, 1983). The course examines the emergence of case management within complex community service arrangements and the contributions case management can make to the effective functioning of these systems (Anthony, Cohen, Farkas, & Cohen, 1988).

Normative and *prescriptive* elements of case management are examined in the course. Social systems theory is used to identify the information processing and integrating role of case management in complex delivery systems and to develop a rationale for the need for case management in the creation of service systems that are functional for users. The prescriptive element of case management is highlighted by emphasizing its role in the improvement of service systems on behalf of individuals, or groups of individuals, who frequently are dependent on benefits they may not control or even understand. The scope of the course involves both the "systems" role of case management in its efforts to assure that service systems perform in an appropriate manner, as well as the "client level" role of case management in its efforts to organize an effective service response to the individual needs, characteristics, and preferences of people served.

A third aspect of the scope of the course resides in *critical reflection* on the possible contradictions inherent in case management practice. The systemic and client level functions of case management are examined through the lens of street level bureaucracy, which posits that case managers fill critical roles in operationalizing social policy and in allocating social benefits through their face-to-face transactions with citizens in need (Lipsky, 1980). The street level bureaucracy framework is used to examine such contradictions as the strain between rationing and access; the conflict created by advocating for people who are not seen by providers as desirable or perhaps worthy candidates for service; and the ethical dilemma of mixed loyalties—that is, whether the case manager represents a system seeking to contain costs, or clients who want responsive services (Freddolino & Moxley, 1993).

Thus, the scope of the course offers students a broad point of view on case management. Normative, prescriptive, and critical postures are intermingled throughout the course to encourage students to look at the assumptions of this human service form and to analyze critically their roles as case managers. Assignments complement this journey by offering students opportunities to examine case studies of case management, to identify and track consequences of poor case management practice, to explore how good case management outcomes are realized, to formulate a theory of case management, and to demonstrate how this theory should work in practice.

Three principal aims are addressed by the course. The first aim is to offer students a critical understanding of the emergence of case management and how case management as a human service reform is indicative of major structural, legal, and programmatic shifts in the human services (Linz, McAnally, & Wieck, 1989). Students demonstrate their achievement of this aim by identifying and explaining the social forces that account for the emergence of case management. The second aim of the course is to assist students to increase their knowledge of the multiple, and sometimes conflicting, purposes and goals of case management, and of how these are embodied by different models of case management (Moxley, 1994a). Achievement of this aim is demonstrated by students through their identification of at least two alternative ways of thinking about the purpose of case management and about how specific goals of case management and related case management models cluster within these purposes. The third aim of the course is to help students to increase their understanding of the practice of case management and of how issues of context, role definition, intra and interorganizational networking, and ethical issues create serious challenges to the effective delivery of case management. Students demonstrate the achievement of this aim by identifying specific choices they can make in the design of case management programs and systems, and the challenges that they will have to address as a result of making these choices.

Content of the Course

The content of the course is divided into five major elements, all of which reflect necessary requirements of case management program development. Students first consider the policy environment of case management and the social forces that have influenced, and continue to influence, case management as a human service form. Within this topical area students consider problem formulation and the nature of how problem definition influences the substance and configuration of case management service delivery and practice.

A second element of course content focuses the attention of students on case management purpose and models (Freddolino & Moxley, 1993). Students explore the principal purposes of case management and the policy and program aims that are related to these purposes. They also examine multiple models of case management and compare and contrast these in terms of relevance, adequacy, and effectiveness in relationship to service problems that they choose as professionally meaningful to them.

The context of case management is the third element of the course. Students explore how different contexts can influence the success of case management. In particular, students examine the relative influence of community context, system context, and organizational context on the alternative configurations of case management, and the implementation and effectiveness problems created for case management by these different contexts (Moxley, 1994a).

Role definition and staffing implications constitute the fourth element. Here students consider the relative merits of professionalization and deprofessionalization of the case management role (Levine & Fleming, n.d.), ways of extending case management through role innovation (Mowbray, Moxley, Thrasher, & Associates, in press), and issues concerning how role definitions influence the power and authority of case managers (Dill, 1987). The fifth element of the course addresses ethical aspects of case management practice (Kane, 1988). Students examine how case management configuration, program design, and practice can create ethical challenges that can compromise or otherwise threaten the effectiveness and propriety of case management practice.

AN EXAMINATION OF FIVE CORE ELEMENTS

These five elements comprise the core content of this specialized course. The elements take students from a broad consideration of the policy and problem framework of case management, through program considerations, and then on to practice. The ultimate aim of the course is to produce practitioners who have a fundamental and balanced understanding of case management, who have insight into the distinctive contributions this human service form can make to the fulfillment of people's needs, and who recognize how to integrate case management into their professional discipline and the professional roles they will eventually assume in their practice.

Core Element 1: Policy Environment and Problem Formulation

Students are exposed to a broad perspective on case management by first examining the policy environment influencing this form of human service practice and also by examining problem conceptualization and the role that case management plays in addressing specific human service problems. Four aspects of the policy environment of case management offer students a framework for understanding its emergence in contemporary human services.

Historical Influences

First, case management is placed in historical context so students understand that the forces influencing the emergence of case management have been operating in human services for some time now (Weil & Karls, 1985). Nineteenth and early twentieth century efforts to rationalize human services and to promote their efficiency through coordination activities are reviewed to illustrate that local efforts to manage case services, and the allocation of social benefits, have been a classical theme in human service practice. Innovations in social policy and programs and their implications for the emergence of case management are examined, including the child guidance movement with its emphasis placed on interinstitutional coordination of services and the incorporation of multidisciplinary services; the involvement of family service agencies to promote the social integration of returning World War II veterans; the colocation of multiple human service providers as part of the Model Cities program of the 1960s; the service integration efforts of the 1970s; and the service coordination efforts that emerged during the 1970s and 1980s to address deinstitutionalization. These innovations are analyzed by students to identify their policy implications for case management and to understand the mixed—and potentially contradictory—goal set subsequently linked to case management, including policy goals that focus on the control of consumption and utilization, the promotion of access, and the enhancement of social participation and integration.

Three Problem-Program Areas

A second aspect of the policy environment of case management focuses on the emergence of case management within specific problem-program areas, especially those of aging, developmental disabilities, and serious mental illness. The aging movement in the United States is examined, and the role of case management in promoting access to and use of social services and supports as social utilities by older Americans is considered (Steinberg & Carter, 1983). Innovation in community living alternatives and the functions of case management in the integration of services for people living in community settings is juxtaposed against case management as a strategy for controlling utilization and costs in long-term care.

Consumerism in the developmental disabilities movement also is introduced as a theme so students gain an appreciation for the influence of efforts by family members, people with developmental disabilities, and sympathetic professionals to expand community living arrangements and to promote the access of people with developmental disabilities to normalized social benefits and opportunities (McKnight, 1989; Wray & Wieck, 1985). The developmental disabilities movement illustrates for students the conceptualization and implementation of case management as a way to increase the social integration of people with these disabilities, thereby giving case management within this field a strong advocacy and consumer orientation (Skarnulis, 1989).

Case management in the area of serious mental illness is examined to illustrate how this human service form emerged as a means to respond to deinstitutionalization and community support of people with psychiatric disabilities (Granet & Talbot, 1978; Intagliata, 1982). Students learn about the role of case management within the community support model as a means to integrate, within a local community, an array of personalized supports for people with serious mental illness, including access to entitlements, mental health and health care, housing, socialization opportunities, and vocational development and work opportunities (Stroul, 1989, 1993; Turner & TenHoor, 1978).

A review of case management in each of these three problem-program areas reveals for students that the policy environment of this human service form is dynamic and has influenced the emergence of different types of case management designed to serve different purposes. However, rather than interpreting case management solely as an innovation linked to discrete problems, students delve into the linkage between case management and a contemporary change in our understanding of what constitutes disability, the third aspect of the policy environment of case management.

A New Paradigm of Disability

The aging, developmental disabilities, and psychiatric rehabilitation movements have influenced and benefited from changing notions of disability. Disability, which was once thought of as residing within individuals and as resulting only from medical impairment, is now seen as heavily influenced by physical, social, and interpersonal environments (Institute of Medicine, 1991). Disability is now seen as a dynamic concept emanating from medical impairment but dramatically modulated by the environmental context of the person (Farkas & Anthony, 1989). Disability can be heightened when these environments are not supportive of people's functioning, especially when they engender iatrogenic treatment, discrimination, stigma, and prejudice (Anthony, 1994). People's disabilities can actually be obviated when supports are increased or otherwise enhanced, as can be witnessed when architectural barriers are eliminated, health care is made accessible, assistive technology is provided, and in-home supports are arranged to aid successful execution of daily living tasks (Moxley, 1989, 1994b).

The role of support is now so intimately linked to the reduction (or perhaps elimination) of disability that we have seen the recent change of diagnostic systems to address the positive effects these supports serve in the lives of people who are labeled as disabled, and the need to consider the influence of supports in assessing the extent of a person's disability (Flexer & Solomon, 1993; American Association on Mental Retardation, n.d.). In addition, we have seen critical changes in contemporary sociolegal thinking that call for the necessity to make supports accessible to and usable by people with disabilities as a matter of right (West, 1991; Wehman, 1993). Case management can be conceptualized as a basic technology for the assessment, organization, and implementation of supports designed to obviate disability. Case management therefore is very much a part of a disability rights movement that calls for the enhancement of the social status of people with disabilities and the provision of resources to make integrated community living a real possibility.

The Influence of Managed Care

A fourth aspect of the policy environment of case management involves the growing acceptance of managed care as a health care cost containment strategy (Feldman & Fitzpatrick, 1992). Case management within managed care has as a major objective preventing, reducing, or averting costs and, therefore, represents a major effort to introduce the social control of health and human expenditures as an important thrust of contemporary social welfare policy. Health care, substance abuse treatment, long-term care, and mental health care are all increasingly coming under the purview of a form of case management that may represent more a policy to rationalize and control services than a policy to advocate for more responsiveness to the desires of consumers (Borenstein, 1990). However, unlike the use of case management to respond to equity issues created by reduced access to, and availability of, services and supports, a form of case management that actually may increase some costs, case management occurring within a framework of managed care will seek to reduce risks to the system of uncontrolled costs created by poorly managed utilization, behaviors on the part of clients that can result in the need for more costly services, or social control problems that can result in high costs for a community (Feldman & Fitzpatrick, 1992; Jacobs & Moxley, 1993).

A Complex Goal Set

The complexity of the policy environment, and the multiple roles case management has assumed within health and human service systems over the past thirty years, may create somewhat of an enigma for students. "What is case management?" is a likely question. But the teaching aim here is to sensitize students to case management as a metaphor for an approach to practice that attempts to make service systems either more rational, efficient, responsive, or effective. Nonetheless, students must confront the reality that contemporary case management may itself lack an exclusive, clearly defined focus, and that many different types have emerged to address different aims. The goal set of contemporary case management is pluralistic, and while some goals are complementary or compatible, some goals may create such a strain that they conflict in practice and their achievement may be elusive (Moxley, 1994b).

This goal set demonstrates to students the sheer diversity of contemporary case management systems. Which goals are actually legitimized and prioritized may depend on the conceptualization, purpose, and role assigned to case management within a specific service system. This illustrates the strong possibility of goal conflict and displacement emerging within case management systems when there is an attempt to optimize incompatible goals, or when the purpose and mission of case management are not clearly identified and operationalized.

Core Element 2: Conceptualizing the Purpose and Models of Case Management

Since there are multiple models of case management, and a diversity of applications, it is important to sort out the purpose of case management so that students can begin to understand more clearly this form of human service practice and its implications for their practice. One way of accomplishing this is to examine the multiple aims of case management through the lens of who is the principal beneficiary of case management activities. A basic question that must be raised here is whether case management is "system-driven" or "consumer-driven." System-driven forms of case management are framed for students as those that seek to achieve outcomes for a health and human service system as their principal aim, while outcomes for recipients are valued but are a somewhat secondary consideration. Consumer-driven forms of case management are framed as those that seek to identify and achieve the preferences of recipients despite costs to the system.

Although this dichotomy is somewhat black and white, it does offer students a heuristic for sorting out different models of case management and analyzing either the system-driven or consumer-driven characteristics of a particular case management application. Considerable attention in the course is invested in the identification of the properties of both system-driven and consumer-driven case management and the use of these properties to gain a more thorough understanding of case management applications.

System-Driven Case Management

System-driven approaches seek efficient solutions to client needs and, by virtue of the adoption of efficiency as a primary value, this form of case management emphasizes administration of cases, gatekeeping, and the management of consumption—especially the control of costly alternatives—with the aim of reducing costs for the funders of services. Certainly system-driven approaches to case management are consistent with managed care, but they may also be found in sectors of human services where behavioral management is a primary policy goal, as in child welfare, corrections, or community support of people with mental illness. Here case managers attempt to exert control over behavioral constellations that can create significant social control problems and related costs if left unmanaged (Surber, 1994). In system-driven case management the "client" is most likely the funder of the service or benefit, or is an organization that is administratively responsible for the care of a specific group of individuals.

Consumer-Driven Case Management

Consumer-driven approaches to case management seek the development of a more responsive system of services and support. Often the case managers act as representatives of people who may have substantial functional limitations and who, consequently, may be unable to represent themselves. Also, these case managers may serve as collaborators seeking to increase the power and status of individuals who may often experience neglect, discrimination, and stigmatization by bureaucratic systems. Case managers adopting consumer-driven approaches invest considerable energy in assisting recipients to identify their desires and expectations of service situations and what they want to achieve for themselves.

Whereas efficiency is an important value for system-driven approaches to case management, acceptability of the service response to the person is considered to be an essential defining value guiding the work of consumer-driven case managers (Freddolino & Moxley, 1993). Consumer-driven approaches will emphasize the necessity of developing strong face-to-face working alliances with recipients rather than merely relating to them administratively (Rapp, 1992). Thus, this form of case management takes on a very personalized advocacy orientation, with advocacy defined as helping people to achieve what they see as important for themselves (Freddolino, Moxley, & Fleishman, 1989). The purpose of this form of case management, therefore, is not to create an efficient, rational system of care. Rather, it serves as a check and balance on human service systems that may engage in self-serving behavior and administrative manipulation of recipients and, as a consequence, fail to respond to what consumers say they want (Anthony, Cohen, Farkas, & Cohen, 1988). This approach to case management seeks to offset bureaucratic power and to empower the perspectives and "voice" of recipients. It is a strategy for humanizing human service systems.

Five Models of Case Management

Using these two approaches students examine various models of case management and analyze their system-driven and consumer-driven properties. Five models are examined from the perspective of their purpose and mission, role in service systems, and principal practices. Utilization-focused and clinical case management are reviewed as exemplars of system-driven approaches given their emphasis, in the former case, on controlling costs of service utilization, and in the latter, on controlling costly behavior of people who may present significant challenges to clinical management. Case management that is primarily characterized by brokering is examined for its role as a people-processing strategy in systems that define success in effort terms—usually as merely linking people to services. Rehabilitation case management is examined as an exemplar of the consumer-driven approach since it places an emphasis on learning about what people want and forming working strategies that help people use their strengths to overcome barriers frustrating the achievement of their desires (Farkas & Anthony, 1989). Advocacy-oriented case management also is examined as a person-driven exemplar characterized by a broad orientation to the identification and resolution of quality of life issues prioritized by recipients as important to their well-being (Moxley & Freddolino, 1994).

All of these exemplars are operating in contemporary human service systems, and most students are able to identify specific applications within their own local service systems. An assignment devoted to reviewing critically the system-driven and/or consumer-driven attributes of these applications serves to reinforce for students these basic concepts and related properties, and enables them to expand their critical understanding of case management practice as well as the ultimate aims this practice serves within human service systems.

Core Element 3: Context of Case Management

Students' critical understanding of case management as a form of human service practice can be further developed through a consideration of the multiple contexts in which case management systems and programs often are embedded. Students consider three principal types of context involving the community in which the case management program is operating, the health and human service system within which it is implemented, and the specific organization that serves as the host to the program. The aim here is to educate students about the forces that shape or otherwise influence the case management program and the resources that are available to the program and its clients through these different contexts.

Community Context

Students are sensitized to the necessity of examining closely the community context of a case management initative and the salient or hidden strengths, as well as limitations, of each community. The rural or urban character of a community serves as a relevant heuristic since there are a number of students who are practicing in each kind of community, and class exploration of "community type" typically reveals dramatic differences among urban and rural communities. Students examine the relative strengths of their communities through needs analyses and resource inventories that are undertaken as environmental scans. They focus on understanding the extent to which socioeconomic and sociodemographic change is taking place within their communities and the implications of this change for resource availability, for influencing problem formation, and for creating risk and vulnerability for the groups that are traditional users of case management services. Examination of the community context links case management to community practice for these students and reminds them that case management is not necessarily clinical in character or interpersonal in focus.

System Context

Another aspect of context considered by students is how the case management program is organized within a human service system. Students consider the implications of an internal case management system that functions as a "manager of service" with the authority to monitor service delivery and to make decisions about service process and outcomes. Students explore the role of internal case management systems from a normative and rational organizational perspective of systems theory that calls for an internal correction to the system by feeding back information concerning various factors, including performance; the adequacy, appropriateness, and efficiency of service effort; and the effectiveness of the service response. Quality management is introduced as part of this context, and the role of case management in quality improvement is examined by students.

Case management within interdisciplinary service settings is considered here, and the internal service coordination role of case management is looked at from the perspective of integrating a complex system on behalf of a client whose needs require attention from a diversity of professionals. The "politics" of systems work are examined, and typically discussion focuses on the power of discipline, professional authority, and interdisciplinary conflict and collaboration.

Students also consider the systemic conditions under which case management assumes an external orientation. Those systems that cannot meet the needs of recipients comprehensively may establish case management programs to link recipients to entitlements, benefits, social supports, and services that the system does not provide. Students explore the implications of this system context for the creation of a case management effort that offers follow-along and monitoring services and assures that clients are linked to needed services and obtain necessary supports.

However, the "encapsulating" effects of human service systems are examined so that students have an opportunity to explore how systems can define what constitutes adequate and legitimate responses to need, and the likely possibility that case management personnel will confine their work to those responses that are considered legitimate and minimal by the system. Failure to explore and use other community resources and limiting their efforts to help people transition out of the system without having community supports in place are two other system problems that students consider. Various case situations from mental health care, homelessness, and AIDS are used to examine how social workers practicing as case managers can help extend systems of care and support into communities to support people's functioning and quality of life.

Organizational Context

Students consider the organization that serves as the host of the case management program as a significant element of context influencing case management practice. The placement of the case management program within the organization is considered as an important variable supporting the salience, authority, and power of case managers. Whether the organization's culture values certain disciplines over others, and whether it adopts a strict disciplinary focus, are considered by students as important factors in understanding who is empowered to undertake case management roles and activities and the degree of authority these individuals exercise over case situations. For example, in medical settings, strong and broad internal case management roles may be assigned to physicians, while social workers assume specific but limited external responsibilities for service coordination with other organizations. However, in mental health settings, social workers may have broad case management role sets that give them case authority for internal and external case management activities.

Students consider the factors that can influence competent practice within case management and the empowerment of its role, especially within interdisciplinary settings. These include substantive knowledge of the problem, substantive knowledge of particular cases, a track record of creative solutions, motivation to get involved and stay involved with particular case situations, and skills in formulating effective teams. Thus, students invest some time in considering the organizational dynamics of case management practice and exploring how these dynamics can be used to work effectively—as a strategic actor rather than a passive one.

When considering context, students look at a number of different exemplars and the influence of community, system, and organizational context in shaping the character of a particular expression of case management. Students look at the policy dimensions, purpose and models, and multiple contexts of case management in gaining an understanding of these exemplars. They are sensitized to the reality that case management is not a unitary construct but may be quite elaborate in terms of its form, functions, and auspices. The potential sophistication of case management program design, therefore, becomes quite apparent to students as they struggle to unravel the enigma of what constitutes case management practice.

Core Element 4: Functional Elements, Role Definition, and Staffing

Assessment, planning, intervention, monitoring, and evaluation are widely considered the core functions of case management (Rubin, 1987) and are often incorporated into professional standards guiding the implementation of case management (Rose, 1992). How these functions are ultimately implemented in practice may depend on the mission of the case management program; for example, in system-driven case management, assessment and planning are most likely undertaken exclusively by a gatekeeper acting independently of the consumer, whereas in consumer-driven forms of case management there is often considerable collaboration between case manager and consumer in the execution of assessment and planning functions (Moxley & Freddolino, 1990).

Students gain an appreciation for the reification of case management by comparing conceptual models of case management to the emerging research base of this field (Rothman, 1992). Most functional portrayals of case management are conceptual, and actual programmatic experiences with these functions likely diverge from idealized designs. Evaluative data, for example, suggest that case managers often engage in crisis intervention work—both directly with recipients and indirectly with family and community members and with other providers (First, Greenlee, & Schmitz, 1990)—yet crisis intervention often is omitted as a functional element from many conceptual models of case management. Students learn that the selection and prioritization of certain case management functions will be influenced by the needs of the intended beneficiaries as well as the purpose/mission of the case management program and its defined role in a service system. For some functions, such as linkage to income maintenance or housing, case management roles and assignments may have a very specific focus and embody considerable specialization. Students learn that this type of case management role definition contrasts sharply with a generalist approach in which all case managers undertake comprehensive functions and activities with little specialization.

The specific staffing of a case management program returns the focus of the course to the issue of discipline. Here students explore the implications of taking either a disciplinary, interdisciplinary, or transdisciplinary orientation to case management practice. The limitations of a strict disciplinary orientation are reviewed; these include the likely introduction of role conflict (Mizrahi & Abramson, 1985), failure to build a broad base of knowledge concerning the multiple determinants of recipient problems, and a failure to expand the skill base of a case management program. Case management as interdisciplinary practice is examined by students as a strategy for blending multiple professionals, fostering collaboration, and gaining opportunities to cross-train. Transdisciplinary practice is introduced to students as a strategy for recruiting professionals to case management who have the most appropriate skills, personal attributes, and experiences rather than basing recruitment on formal credentials or on a narrow conception of role.

Role innovation, including its implications for staffing, is introduced to students as a strategy for expanding the sensitivity of case management services and for increasing the range of services and supports available to consumers through the case management program. Researchers have explored the expansion of the roles of consumers, family members, and laypersons in case management activities (Mowbray, Moxley, Thrasher, and Associates, in press; Seltzer, Ivry, & Litchfield, 1987). These efforts change the focus of professionalism: from one driven by discipline and degree to one driven by personal qualities, functional skills, and outcome. "Consumers as providers" can enhance the sensitivity of case management to clients' needs and problems and may increase the personalization and responsiveness of the service to recipients. Consumers as case managers may be more flexible than professionals in executing certain case management activities—especially those pertaining to community support. Students can benefit from understanding the conditions under which different conceptions of professionalism can be incorporated into case management design.

Offering students opportunities to view case management role definition and staffing from multiple perspectives can expand their vision of the potential diversity of case management program design and of how case management can be configured so that it is truly responsive to the needs of its recipients and/or constituencies. Content that focuses on interdisciplinary and transdisciplinary practice helps students to view the delivery of case management from a broad, functional, and flexible perspective. In addition, the introduction of content on consumerism demonstrates to students the necessity to address the potential flexibility of the case management role and the possibility of limiting this role by placing an inordinate emphasis on professionalization and credentialing.

Core Element 5: Ethical Challenges to Case Management Practice

Content on ethics reduces the tendency for students to view case management solely as a technical enterprise without serious ethical implications for practice. Ethical issues are raised within the course at every juncture to assure that students consider the implications of their decisions about the purpose, aims, configuration, and practice of case management. System-driven case management raises rationing and cost containment as ethical challenges, and the need to inform consumers fully of these aims of the case management program must be considered by students (Kane, 1988). Students discuss how to offer informed consent and examine the implications of fully defining case management for consumers and apprising them of the risks and benefits potentially created by their involvement, including the prevention of access to a desired service, diversion from some forms of care, the rationing of a service, and the eclipse of privacy.

Students consider the ethical challenges created by consumer-driven forms of case management. Students look at the implications of advocating for a service system to meet fully the preferences of a particular person when such action reduces access to resources for other consumers (Kane, 1988). Intensive individual advocacy may introduce what Senge (1990) refers to as "tragedy of the commons." By allowing individuals to overutilize common resources, the availability of these resources for others may be substantially reduced. Students also grapple with empowerment, self-determination, and autonomy, which are highly valued within the consumer-driven form of case management but may not be valued by some who want to be dependent on providers, or who want case managers to undertake major responsibilities for making and implementing decisions as a strategy for buffering or reducing stress created by the demands of daily life.

Finally, students consider the consequences of incorporating social supports, informal resources, and multiple providers into a case management effort (Moxley, 1989). The involvement of family members or significant others as surrogate service providers may shift the burden of responsibility to these individuals and can create stress and costs that they may not have considered when they volunteered to be involved in social support roles (Senge, 1990). Here students must again address informed consent—but this time with respect to significant others in addition to primary consumers. Also, consumers and significant others may need to be apprised of the potential infringement of privacy and confidentiality when case managers seek to disseminate clinical, medical, and lifestyle data to other providers as a means to promote coordination and integration of services.

IMPLICATIONS FOR PROFESSIONAL DEVELOPMENT OF STUDENTS

Presentation of case management as a transdiscipline should not prevent students from understanding the strong relationship between this form of human service practice and professional social work. Indeed, the course offers students ample opportunity to place case management into the context of the profession, and for students to explore the many linkages between case management and social work. Students should achieve two outcomes when they complete the course. First, they should understand case management broadly and critically and understand the relationship of case management to the professional core of social work. Second, they should craft a statement of their own personal practice framework that operationalizes case management using values, perspectives, and practice knowledge consistent with the profession of social work.

Linking Case Management to the Professional Core

As part of their professional development within the course, students examine social work's perspective on case management throughout the course. They make use of the NASW statement on social work case management standards to gain an understanding of how the profession frames case management and the standards that professional social workers must follow in the delivery of acceptable case management services. Students also make use of the profession's code of ethics in appraising propriety in the delivery of case management services. In addition to their use of the social work literature on case management (Rose, 1992; Vourlekis & Greene, 1992), students make use of NASW statements on case management and ethics to frame the distinctive roles, functions, and activities of case management within interdisciplinary and transdisciplinary contexts. Some students may undertake comparative work by contrasting professional social work statements on case management with those of other disciplines such as nursing, medicine, and rehabilitation.

Linking case management to the professional core of social work also is facilitated through the examination of the practice framework of the profession. The mission of social work, with its focus on improving people's situations and functioning, as well as the strengthening of resource systems that support human development, is examined in relationship to the purpose of case management and its various aims in human service systems. Ecological systems theory and the use of a person-in-situation approach as a means to formulate and implement assessment, intervention planning, intervention delivery, and evaluation of intervention effectiveness are offered as overarching frameworks in thinking about the contribution of social work to case management practice and in framing case management practice from a broad perspective of professional practice.

A segment of each class session is devoted to examining the implications of case management material for thinking about professional social work practice and the implications of social work practice for thinking about case management. Students are able to articulate an appreciation for the distinctive contributions social work can make to case management, and to identify the leadership role that the profession can potentially serve in this area (Johnson & Rubin, 1983), especially regarding what professional social workers can offer other disciplines within the interdisciplinary or transdisciplinary matrix of case management.

Personal Practice Framework

Many of the students taking this course come from different practice backgrounds, are involved in different human service systems, and are employed by different organizations. They come together in the course, however, because they are all preparing for advanced practice in social welfare, and case management is recognized as a form of practice that they should at least understand if not begin to master in preparation for leadership practice within the context of a case management system or program.

To accommodate the diversity of backgrounds, perspectives, and professional aspirations represented by the students enrolled in the course, and to offer students an assignment to support their exploration of case management and its linkage to their professional development, each student prepares a personal state-ment of case management practice as a final course product. This course product consists of a framework because it should identify, critically examine, and orga-nize essential concepts and data useful in helping students integrate their under-standing of social work as a profession with case management as a human ser-vice function.

This assignment offers students an opportunity to make a personal state-ment about case management that captures the professional aims, values, and perspectives of students themselves. Given the broad perspective presented on case management within the course, and the documentation of the many differ-ent forms of case management, students craft their own statement about this form of human service practice within a context they choose as significant to their pro-fessional development. Using key concepts and ideas from professional social work practice, students identify the policy forces creating a perceived need for case management, the purpose and mission of case management within a specif-ic human service system and/or problem area, the goals that case management should achieve, the configuration of the case management program, the staffing of the program, the know-how and competencies that will have to be offered by the program, the organizational auspices of the case management entity, the prac-tical implementation of case management, the ethical challenges that are antici-pated, and the performance criteria that will be used to assess the merit of case management. Within this paper students are encouraged to discuss the distinctive contributions that social work can make to either the interdisciplinary or trans-disciplinary practice of case management.

This assignment assists students to achieve the three principal aims of the course. First, it offers them an opportunity to demonstrate a critical understand-ing of case management in a specific area of human service practice. Second, the assignment offers students an opportunity to examine relevant models of case management, to assess their relative strengths and limitations, and to incorporate this knowledge into their papers. Third, the assignment offers students an oppor-tunity to examine case management practice issues and ethical challenges within a specific field of practice of their own choosing. Thus, the formulation of a per-sonal practice framework assists students to integrate the five major elements of the course: policy environment and problem formulation; purpose and models; context; functional elements, role definition, and staffing; and ethical challenges.

CONCLUSIONS

This course offers graduate social work students one opportunity to prepare for case management practice roles in human service systems that have increasingly become interdisciplinary or transdisciplinary in their staffing patterns and use of personnel. Perhaps a strength of case management lies in the hope for collaboration and cooperation it offers health and human service systems whose diversity has grown over the past twenty years resulting in systems characterized by multiple—oftentimes competing—disciplines. Students learn through the course that social work has much to offer case management programs and systems but that social work will not be the sole discipline filling these roles.

There are a number of relevant conclusions here. First, graduate social work students need an understanding of the transdisciplinary content of case management and an appreciation of the contributions social work as a profession has made historically to this knowledge and practice base, especially in the areas of environmental intervention, service coordination, and the development of community resources on behalf of vulnerable populations.

Second, many graduate social work students will move into roles that are framed by the logic of case management, including roles as team leaders and supervisors, continuing treatment team members, and clinicians who work on the basis of community outreach. Thus, course work that equips students for these relatively new and perhaps novel service roles will have to be increasingly offered by graduate social work programs. Case management, in particular, reflects the necessity of integrating interpersonal and social development elements of the curriculum and highlights the relevance of an advanced generalist orientation to social work practice.

Third, courses on case management do indeed focus the attention of graduate social work students on the profession's commitment to working with populations of recipients who experience the primary effects of complex social problems and the stigma, discrimination, and oppression that create or otherwise intensify these effects. Some graduate social work students express a dislike for case management because they experience stigma themselves evolving from their close affiliation to members of populations who are devalued by society. A course on case management offers a portal both to the attitudes and stereotypes students may hold about certain populations, and to the manner in which our society devalues members of vulnerable populations.

Fourth, the course documents the complexity of case management and reinforces for students the need to view case management as a product of the vast changes that are occurring in contemporary social welfare policy and programs. Students who participate in the course cannot merely dismiss case management as deprofessionalized human service technology that is limited in scope and does not really represent sophisticated social work practice. Many students do realize that case management represents an emergent form of practice containing new practice elements taken from social administration and organizational and community practice, but they also recognize that case management represents, in some ways, "old wine in a new bottle," and that it can incorporate some of the best practice traditions of the profession.

Finally, students gain an appreciation for the many contradictions operating in case management practice, and learn that a balanced understanding of the assets and limitations of case management is needed so social workers can put it to effective use. The ethical content infused into the course sensitizes students to the hidden problems that can arise, for example, from efforts to achieve goals that may displace one another in practice; advocacy that may reduce the availability of resources; and the innovative use of resources, like social supports, that can potentially shift the burden of care from those who have a professional mandate to offer support to laypersons who already may be coping with high levels of personal stress.

These considerations make a course on case management a timely offering by any graduate social work program. In some ways case management reintroduces into interpersonal work the environmental dimension of practice and, therefore, may be essential content in graduate social work curricula that focus on preparing social workers for practice with vulnerable populations. Although case management is certainly no panacea for the serious structural problems in human service delivery and the inadequate resources that create considerable stress in many people's lives, it can offer social workers one approach to practice that assists the profession to operationalize its mission of improving the life circumstances of people in need.

CHAPTER 14

IMPLICATIONS OF RESEARCH ON HOMELESSNESS AND SERIOUS MENTAL ILLNESS FOR THE CORE PRACTICE COMPETENCIES OF CASE MANAGEMENT PERSONNEL

Carol T. Mowbray and David P. Moxley

This chapter is a product of the authors' shared interest in drawing implications for the improvement of human service practice from social, behavioral, and evaluative research. The focus here is on the research on homelessness and serious mental illness. The authors use the research to dispel myths about this serious and complex social problem, and they examine the research to identify "basic truths" about this problem area that are useful in framing case management and human service practice in this area. What is most salient in this chapter is that "typical human service practice" is not relevant to combating this problem if we take the evolving research base concerning homelessness and serious mental illness into consideration. The research suggests a form of practice infused by the values of consumerism, collaboration, and the development of community resources. This form of practice indeed may be antithetical to the ways we are preparing human service professionals in many of our preservice education programs.

Since the emergence of the "homelessness problem" some fifteen years ago, media images and long-standing stereotypes have deluged public consciousness so that an understanding of the true nature of homelessness in postmodern America may be rare among most of the populace. This situation of inaccuracy is compounded for the subgroup of homeless people with serious mental or emotional problems (Mowbray, 1985). Without specific training or practice experiences, case management personnel may assimilate the same mythology as the general population, misunderstanding the "old versus the new homeless" (Rossi, 1990) and selecting practice and intervention strategies targeting the wrong problem.

A considerable body of research knowledge has now accrued on the characteristics and needs of people who are homeless and mentally ill, as well as practice experiences from demonstrations of innovative service delivery approaches. The preparation of case management personnel working with this often misunderstood population must include an awareness and understanding of this information as well as its implications for the provision of case management services and supports. In this chapter, we offer such a summary and discussion. Following this, we suggest core practice competencies required to best respond to the characteristics of this population and to the service needs and barriers often encountered. We then conclude with a discussion of the implications for the preparation of case management personnel, and the necessary programmatic and system level changes needed to develop and sustain these core practice competencies.

BACKGROUND

The knowledge and experiential conclusions we present concerning people who are homeless and mentally ill are gleaned from the expanding research and clinical literature about this population, as well as from our experiences in carrying out an NIMH-funded research demonstration project. This project, Mental Health Linkage, was sited in two mixed, urban/suburban communities and operated as a demonstration for about three years, providing outreach, case management, housing, and other services necessary to engage, stabilize, and provide eligible individuals with needed mental health and other services on an ongoing basis (Mowbray et al., 1992). Specifically, services delivered included assessment of clinical needs and housing preferences, provision of temporary and permanent housing, case management, training in activities of daily living, and linkage to community services and resources.

The program identified the target population from three recruitment sources: shelters, public psychiatric hospital discharges, and imminently homeless community mental health clients. A quasiexperimental research design along with a comprehensive implementation and process evaluation were utilized to assess the project's operational success and effectiveness. Mental Health Linkage was intended for persons with a severe mental illness, with high levels of residential instability and/or imminent or actual homelessness. The characteristics of our eligible population (270 people) indicated that this intent was actualized: during the baseline year (prior to service receipt), 47% had moved three or more times, nearly half had experienced a psychiatric hospitalization, and 38% had experienced at least one shelter stay. Demographically, the eligible participants were characteristic of the catchment areas and/or other research samples of persons who are homeless and mentally ill, for example, 56% male, 63% white, with a median age of 34 years.

Information from the research literature on mental illness and homelessness and from our project results will be presented: first, by addressing the most frequently encountered false assumptions concerning those who are homeless and mentally ill; second, by the presentation of the truth about service delivery for this population; and third, by outlining value and attitude issues encountered in attempts to deliver appropriate services.

FALSE ASSUMPTIONS AND RESEARCH REALITIES ABOUT HOMELESSNESS AND MENTAL ILLNESS

Homelessness has become a highly politicized issue. Its nature and complexity now is also dramatically different from the depiction of hobos, derelicts, and vagabonds by sociologists some forty years ago. Given these two facts alone, one might expect that misperceptions about homelessness would be frequently encountered. We delineate the most frequent assumptions about people who are homeless and mentally ill that have permeated mental health service delivery and about which we now have more factual data for refutation.

A common assumption concerns the homogeneity of "the homeless mentally ill," an assertion that is refuted by our data. Our research and many other studies indicate that this population is quite heterogeneous (Bachrach, 1992; Dennis, Buckner, Lipton, & Levine, 1991; Newman, 1992; Streuning & Padgett, 1990). Through our research in Michigan we found a wide range of scores on symptomatology and community functioning variables, such as work capacity, deviancy, psychoticism, hostility, etc. Data analyses identified significant differences between subgroups based on recruitment source, gender, age, and substance abuse. As a heuristic approach to capture this homogeneity, we employed cluster analysis to identify empirically and group together individual participants with similar patterns on a core set of these variables (Mowbray, Bybee, & Cohen, 1993).

The cluster analysis produced a solution reliably assigning participants studied to four meaningful types:

Cluster 1. Individuals who were characterized as hostile psychotic constituted 35.2% of the sample studied and had the highest mean scores on aggression, psychoticism, problems in community living, and deviancy. Participants had the lowest mean scores on work capacity, financial management, and a global assessment of functioning (GAS, Endicott, 1976). Individuals in this cluster overrepresented shelter referrals and underrepresented those on current CMH caseloads. They were more often over age 40 and diagnosed as schizophrenic.

Cluster 2. Individuals who were characterized as depressed constituted 18.5% of the sample. They had the highest mean score on depression, and average functioning on community living variables. They also had the lowest level of substance abuse, were predominantly diagnosed with mood disorders and borderline personality disorders, overrepresented CMH caseloads, and tended to be disproportionately female.

Cluster 3. Individuals who were characterized as "best functioning," at 27.8% of the sample, had relatively fewer than average problems on community living and symptomatology scales. They had less baseline psychiatric hospitalization, were least likely to have been recruited as hospital discharges, and came mainly from shelters.

Cluster 4. Individuals who were characterized as "substance abusing" and constituted 18.5% of the sample. This group was characterized by the highest mean score on substance abuse, and the second highest on depression. Surprisingly they had the highest functioning scores on work capacity and medication management, and average scores on other variables. They were more often age 30 or younger, and tended to be disproportionately male, recruited from CMH caseloads, and diagnosed as schizophrenic.

The diversity of participants from the Michigan project challenges another common assumption: that the population of homeless/mentally ill people is uniformly difficult to serve. In fact, this stereotype applies primarily to Cluster 1 (those individuals characterized as hostile and psychotic). Outcome results did indicate that at four months, persons with this classification were least likely to have achieved the project expectation of living in a permanent type versus temporary setting (shelter, street, jail) (Bybee, Mowbray, & Cohen, in press). Service data from the project also suggested difficulties with substance abusing clients, in that those with substance abuse problems received more total service hours. However, those in the "best functioning" and "depressed" clusters constituted nearly half of the sample. Overall, of the eligible referrals, 73% were successfully engaged and accepted some project services—also refuting the difficult-to-serve assumption.

Of course, many of these participants presented challenges. According to focus group sessions held with project staff, the following client-associated barriers each made up 10% or more of the following: disturbing but nondangerous behaviors; rejecting help; affects like fears, suspicion, or anger; substance use; and delusions and hallucinations. Staff were also able to identify strategies for addressing these barriers. But it is important to underscore that nonclient barriers—those operating within the service system—were mentioned with nearly as much frequency as the client barriers (Mowbray, Thrasher, Cohen & Bybee,

1994), suggesting that there were very real environmental factors that created problems in addressing client needs.

A third, frequent assumption is that persons who are homeless and mentally ill need to be institutionalized, or at least placed into supervised residential living. While the latter may be an appropriate consideration for Cluster 1 clients, it ignores the fact that the community functioning of the majority of clients was adequate, as well as findings reported in the literature about the importance of consumer preference and choice in maintaining stable housing (Barrow et al., 1989). Our project utilized outreach staff to systematically collect data on participants' opinions about desired housing and needs for support and assistance to remain housed. Responses to questions about types of living situations indicated normative preferences. The vast majority preferred living in an apartment or house (77.2%), in the city or town (78.6%), alone or with a romantic partner (81.2%), and not with other consumers (68.6%) (Yeich, Bybee, Mowbray, & Cohen, in press). There were variations in self-reports of their desire to help in finding housing, and in managing daily life, the size of their crisis resource network, and satisfaction with their living situation. At the baseline data collection, the latter variable significantly related to living in a supervised care setting: that is, those in such settings expressed less satisfaction (Yeich, Mowbray, Bybee & Cohen, in press). We also found that most dimensions of consumer housing and support preferences had stability over four- and twelve-month time periods.

Many assessment and placement approaches for programs addressing homelessness and mental illness exclusively focus on personal characteristics, usually deficits, and ignore the contexts in which people are embedded. In contrast, in many of our research results, variables at the community level were more likely to be predictors of outcomes than were client-level variables. For example, in predicting who was successfully engaged with the project (e.g., who accepted assessment and/or some initial form of project assistance), neither gender, race, age, substance abuse at screening, nor any data on baseline residential history showed a significant relationship. What was predictive of engagement was recruitment source, differentially for one county and not the other. Thus, at the Factorytown site, fewer than expected numbers of eligibles were recruited from shelters. And, while a good proportion of eligibles were recruited from hospital discharges, less than a quarter of them were fully engaged (Mowbray, Cohen & Bybee, 1991). Service utilization data analyses, like engagement, showed few significant relationships with client-level variables (only with substance abuse at screening and having a baseline experience in a temporary setting). In the service analyses, as in the engagement analysis, the community-level variable of recruitment source also showed a significant relationship: those recruited as hospital discharges had more overall project contact hours; those recruited from shelters had proportionately more time spent on case management and on linkage services. Finally, the analyses of residential outcomes at twelve months also found recruitment source to significantly predict the likelihood of participants living in permanent type versus temporary settings; among client-level variables, only age group was a significant predictor.

Research studies have produced some substantive data on homelessness and mental illness that is relevant to service provision. This population is quite heterogeneous, including some members with severe functioning problems and some members with supervisory needs, but many with adequate community living skills. Although many clients present service challenges, staff are able to successfully employ strategies to address these, so that the population is not uniformly difficult to serve. Housing preferences of individuals who are homeless and mentally ill can be adequately assessed; they present diversity on some dimensions, but on others reflect normative expectations to live independently, alone or with significant others. And finally, the problems and characteristics of this population cannot be treated without an awareness of the geographic and service system context in which they are located, and that context may be more important than individual-level variables in some regards.

REALITIES ABOUT SERVICE DELIVERY: FINDINGS FROM THE MENTAL HEALTH LINKAGE PROJECT

Experiences from our project and others like it are now beginning to amass some shared wisdom about appropriate service delivery approaches for individuals who are homeless and mentally ill. While outcome research has not yet established the effectiveness of these approaches, common experiences and process evaluations lend credibility. These conclusions are presented with citations to other studies and with examples from the Michigan project.

It is generally well agreed that services to persons who are homeless and mentally ill need to be provided through an outreach modality, in that these individuals' priorities, transportation needs, and lifestyle choices usually preclude their coming into a mental health setting (Barrow et al., 1991; McQuistion, D'Ercole & Kopelson, 1991). Our project's experiences were that outreach and identification strategies needed to differ by recruitment source (shelters, hospitals, or community mental health agencies) and to be tailored to the varying expectations, capacities, and operations of each setting. Thus, in Factorytown, we were able to improve the number and percent engaged from shelters and hospitals (respectively) by tailoring the recruitment process to each setting; for example, having a more consistent presence at the shelters and consistently interviewing those guests approaching their maximum length of stay, and having a more formal presence and role in the discharge process at the hospitals (Mowbray et al., 1991).

Attention to the *engagement* process is also an agreed-upon element of successful service provision to this target population (Cohen, 1989; Drake, Osher & Wallach, 1991; Susser, Goldfinger & White, 1990). Yet others have noted that the process may be slow (McQuistion et al., 1991) and that the percentage successfully engaged versus the number contacted may be small (Barrow et al., 1991). Our project's experiences were that engagement was possible for a majority of clients referred and found eligible (73%), but not necessarily easy. Our success may reflect strategies utilized to coordinate with and provide supports to referral agencies such as spending time and/or socializing with agency staff; having a formal, scheduled presence in agency operations; and providing consultation and training to shelter staff (Mowbray, Thrasher, Cohen, & Bybee, 1994; Mowbray, Cohen, & Bybee, 1991). It may also reflect an approach to clients that was individually tailored, accommodating client preferences and meeting client-defined, basic needs; offering a range of housing options with an emphasis on living independently; minimizing entry requirements and demands; and often, presenting with repeated exposures (Mowbray et al., 1992). These strategies are necesarily staff-intensive and require small caseloads. Even though the overall engagement rate was quite high in comparison to other studies, there was a subgroup of those engaged (about 21%) who received very minimal service amounts. Nearly half of the engaged participants returned to the project with repeat episodes within the twelve-month follow-up time frame, suggesting the need for persistence and the inappropriateness of a set time frame for service provision.

These results are congruent with conclusions from other homeless projects, that effective services must incorporate *flexibility* in service intensity and in duration (Cohen & Tsemberis, 1991; Sheridan, Gowen, & Halpin, 1993). Specific data on service use in the Michigan project indicated that total hours of contact ranged from less than one hour to 141 hours, with a median value of 14.5 hours. The duration of contact ranged from less than one month up to twelve months, with two to three months being the modal period. Most individuals had one contact episode, but over 30 percent had two episodes and about 14 percent had three or four.

As should be expected, the greatest amount of client service time in our project was spent on *housing;* this was the systems-level barrier most often mentioned by staff in focus groups. Also consuming a substantial amount of time was *case management,* followed by assessment, and case planning and conferencing. Two categories of service that are oftentimes assumed to be critical to this population, mental health treatment and skill building, were farther down on the list. *Obtaining services outside of community mental health,* including entitlements and representative payees, required about four and a half hours, on average, per client—nearly as much time as assessment. The amount of time spent on obtaining these services, on case management, and on case planning is not surprising, given the heterogeneous nature of the population and the diverse array of needs they present (Newman, 1992). The time and effort that staff must invest in order to successfully negotiate such linkages was reflected in the high number of barriers from external agencies that they mentioned in the focus group sessions.

Finally, the literature also seems to agree that most clients with mental illness who have been homeless will need *continued mental health treatment or easy access to services in the future.* Because these clients often have problems establishing trust, continuity through the homeless service project should be assured (Lamb, 1984). In the Michigan Project, Linkage staff would frequently accompany clients to several visits with their new case managers, to make sure that the service referral would "stick." It was not uncommon for clients to come back to Linkage service, or for clients to go into crisis when a case transfer was about to be completed. At one site, the community mental health agency often resisted serving referrals from the homeless project, until the project's placement in the agency was changed to provide it and the ongoing case management program with a common supervisor. Thus, integrating a homeless project administratively with other core mental health services like case management may be a critical aspect of service success.

VALUES AND ATTITUDES NECESSARY FOR APPROPRIATE RESPONSES

While the knowledge base about client characteristics and needs, relevant contextual effects, and service delivery strategies may be well enough developed to warrant agreement on the conclusions previously offered, implementing improved services still presents multiple barriers. Some of these can be addressed through training and support for specific core practice competencies. Other systemic issues require administrative changes in mental health and collaborating agencies. Still others may require systems-change advocacy that seeks to increase housing benefits and options. However, it should also be recognized that fundamental barriers can be presented by values and attitudes discrepant with those required to optimize service delivery effectiveness for this target population. These discrepancies involve valuing consumer choice and empowerment, adopting holistic and constructive attitudes toward clients, and legitimizing a practice focus on environmental as well as individual change.

As described in a number of practice articles (Cohen, 1989; Drake, Osher & Wallach, 1991; Susser, Goldfinger & White, 1990), engagement is a necessary first step in providing services to individuals who are homeless and mentally ill. To engage people successfully requires the use of techniques antithetical to the hierarchical, medically driven, and deficit-oriented approaches that often typify traditional mental health service provision. Rather, workers must be prepared to establish rapport with clients through assurances that their own expressions are accorded significant meaning in determining service needs and in planning service provision. This means that serious time and effort must be spent on assessing consumer preferences for housing and support needs. However, since many of the individuals of the target population have had limited experiences in decision making, it also may mean providing guidance and feedback about choices that are realistic and appropriate.

In the Michigan project, the Linkage workers were required to collect structured interview data on a Consumer Preference measure (see Yeich et al., in press). This information was to help inform the housing search, through a negotiated process that also took into account the client's clinical and service needs and housing availability. The supervisory efforts expended to ensure that project staff collected and utilized the data appropriately were unexpected, to say the least. At one site, great resistance to even asking about housing preferences was encountered; staff felt that it would give carte blanche to clients and undermine staff leverage to make clients accept what was offered. They also believed client preferences were often time-limited and lacked long-term utility. At the other site, a nearly opposite response was encountered; staff took client responses to literally dictate the housing search—no matter how clinically inappropriate or logistically infeasible. Abandoning their own judgments and assessments, they often gave out exactly what was preferred without negotiation. Many arrangements quickly failed, particularly with those clients identified as "personality disordered," for whom limitless accommodation triggered symptoms of crisis proportion. Substantial training and consultation were required to assist staff in understanding how to ask about housing preferences so that unrealistic expectations were not reinforced, and how to use and help people develop more appropriate preferential expressions that could become realistic goals.

A second important value issue that was identified in the Michigan project involved staff consistently employing a constructive attitude toward clients and a holistic approach to their working with them. Problems in doing this are suggested by the implementation and outcome data vis-à-vis differential success with those clients referred from shelters. As previously described, these differences appear to reflect staff practices in being able to work as successfully with shelters as they did within their own community mental health agencies. It may also reflect staff attitudes differentially valuing clients who are literally homeless and having such a history. These people may be seen primarily in terms of their apparent inabilities to take care of themselves and live on their own, rather than through an open attitude exploring the functioning possibilities—and the functioning barriers—these people have experienced in the past or can experience in the future. Certainly these deficit-oriented attitudes were confronted by the homeless project attempting to get referrals from hospital discharges. By and large, hospital staff often felt that individuals who had no place to live post discharge and/or a history of residential instability should be confined to supervised, dependent care. These conclusions were unswayed by client preferences to the contrary, and often ignored clients' demonstrated abilities to live in the community on their own. Thus, there was a constant push from the project to get hospital referrals.

The practices of the homeless project staff also showed some problems in attitudes toward clients. At one site, staff strategies detailed through focus group data collection were more likely to include control mechanisms (e.g., giving medication, controlling funds, commitment), disconnecting strategies (asking clients to leave, sending them to the Mission), and rule orientations (e.g., drawing boundaries). At the other site, the use of personal relationships (e.g., showing friendship, establishing trust) and instructional techniques (skill building, joint problem solving) were more common. These differences were attributed to less experience with mental illness and less clinical training in the former site. Workers there seemed less able to maintain firmness, tolerate clients' disturbing behaviors, and work on clients' behalf without a punitive or control veneer. They were thus less able to utilize a holistic perspective that maintained clients' strengths in their frame of reference.

Finally, our experiences in operating Mental Health Linkage also identified problems in valuing a practice model that supported environmental as well as individual change. Initial recruitment efforts focused solely on meeting with potential clients, assessing them for eligibility, and proceeding to engage them in the project's services. Yet, particularly at one site, this approach quickly was seen to be unworkable with shelter and hospital staff; addressing the context and changing the social environment between the project and these settings proved to be necessary. There were similar experiences in service provision phases with clients, especially in locating and maintaining housing. Staff quickly identified the benefits of community networking so as to identify landlords who were willing to rent to project clients at affordable prices. They also found that maintaining good relationships with these landlords (even in providing assistance regarding tenants that were "not theirs") could help assure the continued availability of rental units. The importance of this community and resource orientation was not fully appreciated by the project developers at its inception, in that the majority of positions were identified as outreach workers; only one staff was assigned to housing and community development. In reality, the tasks of service coordination, outreach to settings and community contacts, and interorganizational networking were significant aspects of the work done by all project staff members.

IMPLICATIONS OF THE RESEARCH FOR CORE PRACTICE COMPETENCIES

Implications of the research and practice knowledge gained from the Michigan homeless project and other reports in the literature can be summarized in terms of the core practice competencies that are needed by staff to work successfully in programs for persons who are homeless and mentally ill. These competencies reflect skills in working with individual clients and on their behalf, in interfacing with other programs and systems, and in self-management. These competencies are all very relevant to the preparation and training of case management personnel working with people who are homeless and mentally ill.

Competencies for Individual-Level Work

As in much of human service practice, relationship building competencies are significant and important in working with persons who are homeless and mentally ill. Engagement involves establishing rapport and a climate of mutual trust and respect, so as to decrease fear, anxiety, and suspicion—with a clientele who have good reasons to feel all three. The target group probably presents more challenges to relationship building than most clients in terms of past disaffiliation with services and the diversity of their characteristics.

With such diversity, there is no easy formula for the development and sustenance of good working alliances. Threats to the creation of such alliances are many and include environments that are not free of distractions, people who may have problems attending and listening because of unfulfilled basic needs, and, at times, hostility directed toward workers as representatives of systems that have often failed to take people seriously or to respond proactively to the needs they present. Workers have to call on different strategies to build good alliances, including concrete offers of needed goods and services; showing friendship rather than offering counseling; and listening to the hardships and problems people have experienced and are experiencing in their daily lives. Valuing the homeless person's expressions about their current situation, and working with competencies and strengths, are foundational strategies that can assist workers to put in place a good working relationship.

Outreach and Case Finding

These competencies are founded on core relationship building skills and require the ability to communicate effectively with referral sources and potentially eligible clients. They require workers to understand the mission and purpose of the project, and to be able to talk concretely with people about what the project can offer people who are homeless and mentally ill. Effective outreach and case finding require clinical skills in screening basic indicators of homelessness and the severity of serious mental illness. Differential screening competencies can also be important aspects of outreach and case finding when workers must differentiate disorders which reflect alcohol or drug use only, or the effects of extreme physical deprivation.

These competencies must also include knowledge of the community. Workers must have in-depth knowledge about where homeless persons with mental illness are likely to be located, the community networks within which homeless people may be involved for other supports and life-sustaining resources, and other providers of mental health and community services undertaking outreach with this population.

Outreach and case finding offer workers opportunities to capture information about people who are homeless, and about potential community support networks. A strengths approach to outreach becomes crucial since early contact can offer concrete information about how individuals have coped with deprivation and the potential hostilities of the streets. Community strengths—such as indigenous helping resources, church networks, and activities undertaken by law enforcement personnel—may not be obvious, but may be subsequently identified when people discuss how they have survived and how they cope with the demands of homelessness. Outreach and case finding are complex activities, and the competencies they require for effective work with homeless people must not be discounted.

Assessment and Service Coordination

The findings from the Mental Health Linkage project indicate the importance of these competencies to effective practice in the area of homelessness and serious mental illness. Given the large percentage of time staff spent on these and related activities of case management and case planning, the importance of assessment as a broadly defined and complex competence demanding a holistic perspective, the incorporation of clients' perspectives, a focus on strengths, and the need to address the heterogeneity of the people served all become apparent. Assessment and service coordination must be integrated with outreach and case finding, since workers must take actions to help people once they link with them. It requires considerable patience and understanding in working with people who are homeless and mentally ill to support them in articulating their preferences in housing, and in identifying the supports they want.

Service coordination requires the cognitive ability to integrate this information into an action plan, and into service activities that can address identified needs and preferences—ones that are most likely complex and difficult to fulfill. Communication and negotiation skills are also required for the development of a workable service plan that is truly collaborative in content and process.

Support, Empowerment, and Advocacy

These competencies are necessary to actualize what is in the service plan. The literature as well as our personal experiences within the project suggest the importance of developing a sense of personal control and improving problem-solving capacities for persons who are homeless and mentally ill (Cohen, 1989; Witheridge, 1991). Workers need to move individuals toward self-reliance. At the same time, they need to be sensitive to the deficiencies some individuals have in terms of opportunities to exercise choices, and to provide support and practice as these skills are developed. They also must be aware of the fragmented nature of many service systems. These problems can present access challenges for even the most experienced and assertive professionals.

The notion of advocacy in this area is consistent with the use of advocacy in other chapters within this volume. Advocacy has a tripartite character. First, it highlights the importance of understanding how people conceive of their own problems, what they want to do about the issues created by these problems, and the manner in which they want to resolve them. Understanding the perspectives of consumers is vital to the realization of consumer-driven case management practice, and given the very real challenges social forces can create for engagement and relationship building with people who are homeless and mentally ill, the achievement of this sensitive understanding is vital to support, empowerment, and advocacy.

Second, advocacy requires close collaboration between workers and people who are homeless. This close collaboration evolves out of understanding, effective outreach, and good assessment, with the latter focusing on the true understanding of personal and community strengths, and leads to the integration of these strengths into a plan offering consumers something that is truly valued and meaningful. Collaboration that takes its direction from such a plan can set in motion true empowerment.

Third, advocacy requires an attitudinal openness to perceiving the many structural and social forces acting on people. The "biographies" of people served are understood within the context of community systems, social factors, and postmodern realities that have established very real limitations on the availability of life-sustaining resources. Enlightened workers cast a suspicious eye on simplistic explanations that pinpoint the reason for homelessness in the deficits of the person experiencing this treacherous problem. Workers embracing an advocacy orientation understand how social forces have deep personal consequences, and that the symptoms and "limitations" of the person are likely effects created by serious social causes.

Thus, workers who are advocates are always willing to seek remedies, opportunities, and benefits that establish a good support system within which a person can address and resolve issues of personal importance. Understanding, collaboration, and the recognition of the potent role of social forces in shaping and sustaining homelessness offer workers and clients opportunities to craft a respectful, dignified, and empowering approach to advocacy. This approach can strike a balance between encouraging people to advocate for themselves, and actuating interventions by outside authorities who can negotiate and advocate on behalf of people who are homeless. It is this balance between supporting self-help undertaken by homeless people, and taking action within the social environment, that gives practice a very strong generalist character.

Competencies in Program and System Interface

Advocacy that is informed by the social and organizational factors that influence service access is not easy to realize. Core competencies in the area of programmatic and system performance are important if not crucial to the success of homeless outreach and service. Knowledge of the importance of context in the lives of the target population, along with a valuing of community resource orientations and activity, leads to recognition of the importance of staff attaining competencies in working collaboratively with entities inside and outside of the mental health system. Results of staff focus group sessions in the linkage project suggest that system-level and external agency barriers present substantial challenges, and increase the severity of client-level barriers. Yet staff were much less able to identify strategies to overcome them. Effective practice with persons who are homeless and mentally ill requires a unique combination of interpersonal skills and community and organizational skills—usually addressed by separate tracks in professional training programs. Given the diverse characteristics and multiplicity of needs of the target population, a wide array of service sectors needs to be effectively involved with a homeless outreach program. These include programs for the homeless (shelters, soup kitchens, crisis centers) and a wide array of church-sponsored, voluntary, and governmentally operated programs. Also critical to homeless outreach for persons with mental illness are law enforcement, substance abuse, and vocational and employment services, an array that demonstrates the vigilance required in the organization and development of appropriate support systems.

Housing, of course, usually presents the biggest challenge (Hagen & Hutchinson, 1988). Required activities can represent anything from individual-level collaborations with landlords, to business ventures with community groups in refurbishing or developing housing, to attempts to access large public housing programs at local, state, or federal regional levels. As we discovered in the Michigan program, gaining access and entry to settings even less diverse than these (e.g., privately operated shelters versus hospitals) can require substantially different strategies and methods. Furthermore, the homeless outreach worker is often confronted with having to overcome historically based animosities between mental health and other sectors: shelters, for example, that allege that community mental health is "dumping" deinstitutionalized clients at their doorstep; or vocational rehabilitation, which has been accused of "creaming" and refusing to serve persons with psychiatric disabilities because of their unpredictable prognoses; or substance abuse services, which have been seen to reject dually diagnosed individuals because of an inappropriate antimedication policy. Substantial skills in organizational relations, in understanding diverse organizational and service cultures, and in addressing organizational barriers at the client level are definitely required to negotiate these interorganizational issues, as are abilities in resource development methods.

Working collaboratively with other units in a community mental health agency can also present substantial demands on systemic practice. On the one hand, a close working relationship can afford easy access to needed services like clinical case management or outpatient care on an ongoing basis. Such a close working relationship, however, can produce cooptation and a tendency to most readily serve community mental health-referred clients rather than those individuals who present the most serious challenges and who may not be readily known to the system until successful outreach has been undertaken. This situation prevailed at one of our sites (Mowbray, Cohen, & Bybee, 1991). On the other hand, a more detached relationship with community mental health units can mean greater difficulty in assuring that clients usually seen as difficult and resistant by more traditional mental health staff become fully linked with the ongoing services they need (e.g., medication, payees, case management). Thus, negotiating optimum performance in homeless outreach programs that are integrated versus freestanding vis-à-vis mental health agencies can also require extensive competencies in organizational relations, and in interagency or interdepartmental collaboration.

Self-Management

The qualities and skills required by staff providing outreach services to individuals who are homeless and mentally ill have included patience, persistence, realistic expectations, and a nonjudgmental attitude (Buckner, Bassuk, & Zima, 1993; Sheridan, Gowen, & Halpin, 1993). The roles and functions that these individuals must provide are multidimensional, and specialized knowledge concerning homelessness, clinical work, and community work are essential, a testimony to the complexity and seriousness of this social problem. Yet survey data on the characteristics of personnel who serve homeless people indicate that they are relatively inexperienced. This was true for one of our two sites.

These facts suggest there is a high probability for stress and burnout

•

among homeless outreach workers. Information obtained from staff focus groups held at the Michigan project sites provided elaboration on this potential problem. Although not specifically solicited through focus group questions, staff cited feelings relating to boundary issues (personal responsibility for clients; feeling like you let them down; not knowing where to draw the line). Other feelings involved personal competency (worries about whether a response to a client was right or wrong; not knowing what to do on the job) and fears (safety, humiliation, frustration).

Unfortunately, staff mentioned few personal strategies to deal with these feelings, e.g., humor, time management, letting go, prioritizing, or turning to the team. Self-management competencies are a neglected area for human resource development. Particularly in the work with a vulnerable, and disenfranchised group like the homeless, which can be politically charged and emotionally laden, this need is especially salient. Adding to this the expectation for high levels of skill and expertise, relatively low wages, and the diverse competencies expected, suggests that self-management and personnel development need to assume a high profile in selection, training, supervision, support, and ongoing education of staff.

CONCLUSION

The core competencies needed by case management personnel are as complicated as is the very nature of homelessness as a social problem. It is difficult to call case management in this field any one thing because, given the findings from the research, the actual provision of effective case management appears to be an amalgam of different forms of practice involving community development, interorganizational collaboration, and interpersonal intervention. In the language of social work education, preparation in this field may require advanced generalist credentials with a specialized focus in poverty and social marginalization.

The character of case management practice emerging from this research base is consistent with the reality that what we call case management in contemporary human services has much to do with working in the so-called safety net. Are case managers dealing exclusively with mental illness? The answer to this is no, of course. Case management is responding to the interaction of serious mental illness with poverty. Homelessness is a postmodern or postindustrial expression of the absence of basic life-sustaining resources felt by many people coping with serious mental illness.

The complexity and sophistication of case management practice at this interface reveals the need for our very best practitioners to move into this domain of practice. Practitioners with the requisite community, organizational, and interpersonal skills are needed for this most arduous duty. In addition, these qualities of case management demand a vigilance on the part of administrators and organizational leaders to encourage promising and effective case managers through staff development programs that help these personnel to develop, refine, and retain the competencies needed for effective practice. Can we rise to these personnel preparation and human development challenges? What will happen if we don't?

PART V

―――

CONCLUSION

CHAPTER 15

THE ORGANIZATION OF HUMAN SERVICES AND THE FUTURE OF CASE MANAGEMENT

In this chapter I return to the theme that case management means different things, and that we all need to be vigilant in identifying what is meant by case management as an approach to human service practice. It is not a unitary conception. Its sheer diversity signals a changing context in the design, provision, and intended outcomes of human service delivery. Many issues have been reviewed in this volume as we moved from a consideration of the role of case management in the human services through a consideration of both the development and improvement of case management service delivery, then on to an examination of the consumer perspective in case management, and the preparation of case management personnel.

In this concluding chapter I consider the various scenarios that can influence case management in the next five years. I base these scenarios on a basic assumption, one that we may overlook in our efforts to "patch up" the delivery of human services. This basic assumption is that the form case management takes is contingent on the organization of human services or on the emergent organization of human services. Or, to be more precise, perhaps the form that case management takes is contingent on our vision of what human services should achieve, now and in the future.

In this chapter I offer five different scenarios of the organization of human services and the role case management plays within these scenarios. Most of these scenarios are operating today in one form or another. These scenarios are not meant to be revolutionary but perhaps enlightening, because these various scenarios can motivate us to reflect on what we want human services to be and to do, and can motivate us to examine the values and assumptions that underpin the practice of case management within the human services.

There are a number of possible alternative futures of case management within the human services, and the seeds of these futures have been apparent for some time now. These alternative futures reflect the many definitions of case management as well as the various conceptions of human services that serve as the underpinnings of this form of practice. Predicting the actual form of case management in the near future is difficult if not impossible. Nonetheless, it is useful to ponder the form case management can take, since anticipating change will perhaps motivate policy makers and the implementers of policy to become more deliberate and intentional in designing the role of case management within human service systems.

I craft five different scenarios to represent these various futures, and within each scenario I consider (1) societal forces shaping human services; (2) the character of human services serving as the host of case management; (3) the linkage between the human service model underpinning the scenario and case management; (4) the role of case management within the human service context; and (5) negative and/or positive consequences potentially created by the human service and case management scenario. These scenarios are intended to be crude pictures or snapshots of the near future and are designed to capture some of the critical forces both within society and within the human services that set the stage for the particular form of case management identified within the scenario. Each scenario contains three important aspects:

1. Case management is presented within the context of a human service system that is very much influenced by the sociocultural context of our communities and ultimately by the sociocultural context of our society. Thus, the label attached to the scenario is designed to communicate the substantive character of case management within a particular scenario of human services.

2. Case management reflects a particular model of human services that can be abstracted from the substantive character of case management within the particular scenario. I implore the reader to embrace the idea that to endorse a specific form of case management means also to endorse a particular model of what human services "should be" within our communities and how these services should perform.

3. Endorsement is an act of valuing, and we must be clear on what values are embodied by various, and often divergent, approaches to case management. Our preoccupation with making case management perform well—

and for a specific purpose—may create blindspots. Thus we may overlook basic questions about ultimate purpose, and the values that give meaning (either negative or positive) to the enterprise of case management practice.

Well, enough said. Let's plunge into the five scenarios.

FIVE SCENARIOS OF CASE MANAGEMENT

Scenario 1: Community Support and the Organization of Support Systems for People with Disabilities

Human service systems enjoy some legitimacy within their communities, and they are recognized as a frontline resource in addressing the needs of people with disabilities. Citizens and political decision makers recognize the importance of these systems in adding to the quality of life of individual recipients as well as to the overall quality of life of the community. There is widespread understanding of what these systems do, and how they should perform. Thus, the development of these systems is seen as something desirable and needed.

Case management is intimately connected within the positioning of human service systems to address complex human problems and to address a range of human needs, supports, and opportunities created by both the actual consequences of the problem as well as the social reaction to the problem. Human service systems grow more sophisticated in their capacities to address long-term, serious social problems as well as more complexity in the range of services and supports, and their arrangements. Service systems in the fields of mental health, child welfare, developmental disabilities, and aging continue to develop around the theme of community support. The aims of these systems are to offer concrete supports in the critical areas of family life, housing, transportation, health care access, emergency care, social support, income, and employment to buffer the social and individual stressors that are created by the complex problems that justify the existence of these systems.

Rather than simply being composed of an array of fragmented services, these systems seek integration of their constituent elements so that recipients obtain the resources and supports they need and all of these elements embody a similar goal set and do not work at cross-purposes in serving and supporting recipients. Descriptors like "one stop shopping," "an integrated service system," "a responsive system of services," and "seamless services" are often invoked by administrative leaders and workers within these systems to characterize their vision and their aims. An emphasis placed on collaborative practice among diverse human service disciplines makes professional credentials a central attribute of these service systems. Interdisciplinary—and perhaps transdiscipli-nary—practice serves as another central and defining attribute. However, the principal defining attribute within this scenario is the creation of actual integrat-ed systems of service, an aim that has been most challenging in the history of social welfare and human services. The mission of these systems is to support community living of people whose functioning and quality of life would be jeop-ardized without these supports.

New service systems and arrangements begin to emerge around social problems that failed to receive systematic attention in the past. Individuals with Acquired Immune Deficiency Syndrome now have opportunities to become involved in systems of care that offer people a range of services that are inte-grated around the management of the illness and the promotion of well-being. Drug-exposed infants are targeted by comprehensive systems that offer an inte-grated array of intervention resources seeking to integrate health care with devel-opmental, social, and community support services. And perhaps youths who have engaged in gang activity or violent behavior are channeled into service sys-tems offering housing, developmental education, work opportunities, and career development.

Case management within a community support framework is seen as a core service although service systems may be struggling with how best to con-figure these services and the workloads and performance of case management components. The aim of case management is to coordinate and integrate services at the level of the individual recipient through the assurance that needs are iden-tified on a timely basis and that the recipient obtains responsive services, usual-ly defined as ones that are appropriate, accessible, and adequate.

Case management within this scenario must fit into a *human service model of community support*, a model committed to addressing social vulnerability and its consequences (Goodin, 1985). The organizing ethos of these human service systems means that they embody many of the functions of communities and pri-mary groups and must, therefore, offer services that meet a range of diverse needs. This organizing ethos places considerable stress on case management components as expectations among recipients, their family members, and com-munity stakeholders escalate. In situations where the human service system is unable to develop appropriate resources to respond to the needs of recipients, case managers are required to provide these services or supports, creating a con-fusing role set for individual case managers.

In situations where the role integrity of case management is respected, case managers are asked to identify and track needs and are placed into roles in which they can truly organize individualized services. The system recognizes that the effectiveness of case management is linked to the resource and service develop-ment of the system, and incumbents of these roles are not asked to engage in activities that take them out of their roles as organizers of individual-level services and as advocates for the fulfillment of the individual needs of recipients. Within innovative systems the case manager is recognized as the representative of the individual recipient.

Scenario 2: Management of the Economic Costs of Human Services

Broad commitment to human services within our communities and within our polities is on the wane as citizens and their elected officials become more frustrated with what is seen as waste, misuse of public dollars, and the misallocation of resources to people who are not seen as "deserving." Despite expectations of an expanded and enhanced array of public benefits and goods coming from government, there is strong citizen sentiment against paying for these and supporting these for other people or for the community at large. Human services are not seen as public goods designed to benefit everyone but as a discrete set of services that must be rationed and limited in time, scope, and quantity since the public is unable or unwilling to support human service expenditures. A growing conservative ideology reinforces the need to reduce these expenditures dramatically, the need to target a limited range of resources on those who are seen as most deserving, and the need to link expenditures to strict accountability measures, preferably by making providers of human services adopt market-like frameworks of performance.

Case management is embedded within this market-like framework. Case management is given a very clear purpose and set of aims. It seeks to control utilization, reduce the risk of inappropriate resource expenditures, and divert recipients to lower-cost forms of care and service. Human services increasingly come under the purview of managed care entities that are given public contracts to manage the resources that federal, state, and local governments have committed to human services. Managed care entities endorse quality, prevention, and cost management. But their primary concern is with reducing or controlling costs and with achieving cost savings compared to the former way of delivering services. Thus, within this scenario, quality and prevention may very well take a "back seat" to the management of expenditures.

Managed care entities increasingly take over the care of those individuals who have been traditionally the concern of state governments. These so-called public domain populations are defined rationally, perhaps using statistical tools to characterize sociodemographic attributes, clinical characteristics, and behavioral qualities in order to match groups or clusters to service consumption patterns. Packages of services are then designed to offer these individuals, and providers are identified who bid to deliver these packages according to standards defined by the managed care entity. This entity purports to embody the interests of the consumer and those of the ultimate customer (who is probably the actual funder or payer). Providers who are certified must operate under these standards and achieve a level of performance that is within the normative limits established by the managed care contractor.

The managed care entity is committed to close monitoring and scrutiny of expenditures. Thus, risk and utilization management are essential features of a managed care framework of human service delivery. Case management within this scenario is an essential element of this system and must embody *a business model of human service practice.* Within this scenario, the case manager acts as a benefits manager who is responsible for gatekeeping as well as for exerting control over the consumption, utilization, and perhaps funding of service provision to individual consumers. Unlike other forms of case management that emphasize the importance of a strong relationship between recipient and case manager, this approach to case management is most likely concerned with data and the management of data. Case managers who are probably selected for their technical expertise in a clinical discipline oversee data on needs, diagnosis, consumption patterns, and outcomes. These data are the basis of decisions to divert recipients from expensive services, to stop treatment or service, or substitute one form of treatment (e.g., medication) for another form of treatment (e.g., psychotherapy). Thus, the principal aim of case management is to achieve efficiencies in the treatment of a recipient in order to reduce risk to the system of managed care. Technologies relevant to diagnosis, information management, and outcome monitoring become very important to the effectiveness of case management within this scenario.

The possibility of creating performance-oriented and outcome-driven human service systems in which case management serves a proactive role is one positive attribute of this scenario. However, the question of whether "managed" human services can achieve both economic and consumer goals is a very serious one. The approach to human services operating within this scenario gives some recognition to the values of consumer choice, consumer dissent, and the achievement of meaningful outcomes. Yet there is ample possibility that these important values—essential to the realization of a consumer-driven system—will be subordinated to system-driven priorities valuing efficiency, cost reduction, and the elimination of aspects of services essential to the humanization of service delivery and to the buffering of the social reaction many recipients experience because of their assumption of deviant statuses.

A business mindset may increase the sensitivity of case managers to resource issues and to the achievement of a responsible use of limited funds. But there may be the assumption within this approach that case managers merely formulate a utility function that reduces the burden of the managed care system but fails to internalize so-called negative externalities created by conflicts emerging between consumers and direct service providers, a short-run approach to service delivery, and perhaps even the biasing of service delivery resulting from offering access to those recipients who are most acceptable to the system and/or who are seen as the best candidates for treatment and service.

Scenario 3: The Management of Undesirables

American society, according to some social critics, has created marginal subcultures in which some people have no homes, no jobs, and simply no place within a community that offers them positive identities and value. Szasz (1994) argues that services are explicitly organized to achieve social control under the guise of compassion so that those individuals whom the general community identifies as deviant are confined and isolated in the very community that wants protection from them (Kozol, 1995). We can find the headlines in daily newspapers that exemplify this sentiment: "The department of social services fails to alert police as mentally ill father goes on rampage"; "Homeless people threaten shoppers despite outreach by social workers"; "Social service agencies stand idle as park is threatened by retarded men." These headlines are reminders that human services are seen by citizens and officials as one way of controlling those individuals who have been deemed behaviorally, culturally, or physically problematic.

Human services within this scenario will increasingly take on the role of social control agent and perhaps serve a surrogate function within a society that increasingly prioritizes criminalization of social problems and a commitment to cold vindictiveness. Social problems, from this perspective, are seen as significant if not substantial threats to community life, beginning when people are seen as failing to conform to prevailing values and norms, and culminating when this failure is intepreted as creating a threat to the physical safety of community members (Dumm, 1987). Within this scenario, the public sees human services as a means of controlling or managing deviance, and its principal mission lies in the compassionate control of individuals who will only threaten the well-being and safety of the community if they are not supervised (Szasz, 1994).

Case management, therefore, is connected to the policing and safety functions of community life and, secondarily, to the function of care (Jacobs, 1992). Whereas in the previous scenario, economic costs are seen as particularly problematic, within this scenario social costs created by deviant individuals are seen as most problematic. A legitimate function of human services, within this scenario, is the assumption of social control responsibilities. There is considerable evidence that human services are becoming extensions of court systems, diversionary systems, and jails and prisons. There is substantial evidence illustrating the criminalization of mental illness found in the number of people with serious mental illness in jail, the demise of the verdict of "not guilty by reason of insanity," and court orders committing people to outpatient forms of behavioral management and oversight. In the wake of deinstitutionalization, and the increased visibility of so-called deviance within our communities, public opinion may require human services to become better managers of community safety and more competent champions of community values. Indeed, accountability may become linked to the demonstrated ability of human services to foster safe communities.

Case management in this scenario is based on a model of *criminalization and control*. It is devoted to operationalizing a compassionate oversight of recipients. Recipients are aware of the role of case management and the controls that are being placed on them. Case managers may incorporate electronic technology to monitor the physical movements of their charges. They may need to violate the privacy of recipients in the name of oversight or management of deviant behavior, or for accountability purposes, so that case managers can respond to their principal clients: a judge or other court officer.

Case management with recipients may be initiated in jail by corrections officers who are responsible for discharge planning and for assuring that recipients' needs are identified in order to support a smooth transition from jail to community. Contact with external human service professionals may be initiated at this time so that there is effective transition of case management roles and activities. The case management plan may actually be part of a larger plan supporting parole or probation.

With the proliferation of prison building and the diversification of alternatives to punishment (such as bootcamps, low security camps, confinement to households, and community options), human services take on a broader role in addressing the needs of people who have been adjudicated as criminals. Increased criminalization may itself lead to political and community concerns about costs of incarceration. This results in a movement to deinstitutionalize non-violent offenders, who are transitioned or diverted into systems of human services designed to control behavior, resocialize offenders, and reintegrate these offenders into community living.

The juxtaposition of community support and social control gives case management as a core element of these systems a very visible role in the deinstitutionalization of offenders. Case managers are responsible for the assurance that needs are identified and that appropriate services are in place to meet these needs. Case managers assume advocacy roles in helping offenders to achieve resocialization goals and reintegration into the community. These are very positive attributes of a system that has foresaken rehabilitation as an animating ideal—and that has embraced punishment as the principal aim—for at least the past twenty-five to thirty years.

However, the effectiveness of case management is compromised by its very organizing ethos. First, case managers have difficulty forming relationships with offenders because of a duality to their roles that can create substantial conflict for the effective implementation of case management. Case managers must be both advocates and enforcers. They must promote the interests of recipients at the same time as they must oversee and control the behavior of their charges. This role confusion recreates a classical limitation of case management: Is it driven by the perspectives and concerns of recipients, or by the system that seeks to serve or control the recipient? By failing to address this archetypal problem embedded in case management, programs designed to serve offenders proactively devolve into ones characterized by mistrust, control, and lack of commitment.

Second, the effectiveness of human services depends on the responsiveness of other providers of services and community supports. Yet many providers find unattractive both the recipients as well as the rules and standards of control they must operate within when they select to serve recipients who are offenders. Case managers may have little power or authority to motivate providers to respond to the needs of offenders, and most likely case managers resolve this dilemma by reducing their expectations about the quality of support offered to recipients or by creating systems of community support devoted only to serving offenders or ex-offenders. This makes it increasingly difficult to help recipients with criminal histories to reintegrate into community living, and creates systemic contradictions that case management may not be able to surmount.

Scenario No. 4: The Management of Clinical Pathways

The greater society's push to make human services accountable has created pressure on human service organizations to achieve predictability of outcomes and to specify the technical processes and inputs needed to deliver a service and achieve desired outcomes. Accreditation has adopted a strong outcome orientation. Human service organizations seeking recognition from accreditors like the Joint Commission on the Accreditation of Health Care Organizations (JCAHO) and the Council on the Accreditation of Rehabilitation Facilities (CARF) are working on the rationalization of service processes and the demonstration of effectiveness. Also, funders embrace outcome-based funding in critical areas of human service so that providers are reimbursed primarily for achievement of measurable outcomes for either the recipient or community. Commitment to this rationalization reflects the pressure human service organizations are experiencing both from the larger efficiency orientation of funders (either public or private), and consumers and their advocates who seek more predictable, competent, and effective service systems. A number of health and human service organizations are embracing research and development as a means of specifying the effectiveness of their service processes and concretizing desired outcomes. Many organizations also are adopting Total Quality Management as a strategy to improve core processes and critical outcomes.

As with some of the other scenarios (such as in Scenario No. 1) case management is not pervasive nor as broadly defined within this scenario of human services. Case management is connected to a technical notion of service provision in which a critical pathway of service is specified to achieve a desired outcome like management of symptoms, achievement of self-care, or maintenance of employment. Case management is seen as a means to steer the recipient through this pathway, to assure that the pathway operates in a correct manner and that service provision and outcomes are optimized.

Senior clinical practitioners assume case management activities as part of their overall clinical role set. Thus, case management is integrated into other service roles filled by physicians, nurses, social workers, and psychologists. Case management is seen as a highly professional activity. These individuals are chosen for their leadership skills as well as their knowledge and skills in a substantive area of human service practice. These individuals also possess the authority within their organizations to review all services, redirect these services as needed, oversee quality, standardize practice, and conduct utilization review. Pressure exerted by funders to achieve outcomes gives case managers a great deal of power to steer and, if needed, to reorganize the services offered by the human service organization.

This form of case management values knowledge about the problem that is the focus of service and the institutionalization of this knowledge into organizational routine and practice. Case managers formulate service protocols for various recipient profiles and use and enforce these protocols to achieve desired outcomes. For example, a psychiatrist within an acute care setting may implement a protocol to move a patient through a psychiatric unit within a week and on to another level of care. The psychiatrist as case manager is basically concerned with an appropriate diagnosis, quick and appropriate medication, and the coordination of care with discharge planning.

Case managers grapple with a dual accountability: an accountability to the "customer" who wants specific outcomes achieved and an accountability to the recipient who deserves a good service. However, consumerism is seen as the provision of good outcome-oriented service that is designed and implemented by the professional staff of the organization, and overseen or otherwise managed by senior practitioners who undertake case management activities as part of their role set.

Case management within this scenario is more professional than case management under some of the other scenarios, and its purpose and authority is more clearly defined, thereby reducing the ambiguity that often afflicts case management. Case management is seen as a limited aspect of the overall organizational service technology, but it occupies a critical role in orchestrating the necessary service activities and actors needed to create a desired outcome. This form of case management is most likely adopted by direct service providers operating in a managed service or care framework. The specification of discrete outcomes such as symptoms and functional behaviors as well as the centralization of authority in a specific role links this scenario of case management to a *clinical or medical model of management.*

This form of case management, however, can degrade into people processing when larger concerns created by a problem seen through another lens (such as through a social problem lens rather than through an illness lens) are ignored by the organization and attention is invested in specifying more concrete and immediate outcomes for resolution. The acute care setting identified above, for example, may concentrate on discharging people whose functioning has been stabilized through medication but who must grapple with serious problems created by housing deficiencies in the community or the absence of ongoing social supports. Advocates of this rationalized form of case management may argue that this criticism ignores the necessity to integrate a program and the case management that occurs within this program to a larger system of human services.

Yet, as with all human services that purport to be "outcome-driven," we must be concerned with the validity of these outcomes and their relevance to the overall problem that is the focus of the service initiative and case management. There is the possibility that what we prioritize as outcomes is trivial, is seen by consumers as lacking in relevance, or is merely short-run achievements that fail in the long run to add value to the lives of recipients. Validating outcomes and understanding their scope, utility, and limitations are important considerations in this scenario of human services and case management practice. What may be valued as an outcome by recipients may not be valued as an outcome by a human service organization or system. Thus, the very real possibility of value conflict can operate within this scenario as it can within many of the other scenarios presented in this chapter.

Scenario No. 5: Recipient Management of Services

Consumers of human services serve as the force for the expansion of case management. The founding of many case management programs and systems was a product of consumers wanting more accountable and responsive human services. The emergence of brokering, linkage, and rehabilitation forms of case management was based on consumer perspectives. Consumers have not abandoned this tradition. Indeed, they have become more assertive as consumers, and their advocates have increased in numbers on the boards of public and nonprofit human service organizations. The Americans with Disabilities Act, the long line of federal developmental disabilities policy, federal support for assistive technology, and the formation of service organizations run for and by people with disabilities underscore the necessity to strengthen case management as a frontline strategy for creating responsive human service systems.

As emphasis is placed by policy makers on the control and rationalization of human service budgets, and as managed service programs grow in response to this political disaffection with human services, consumers continue to organize and press for systems of organizing and purchasing human services that are controlled by consumers and not by professionals. Conflict emerges at local human service forums and hearings as consumers assert themselves, articulate their desires, and demand more control over human services. A tension emerges between local decision makers who want to control budgets, and consumers who want to control the organization and purchase of those services they see as essential to their well-being.

Consumers turn the rhetoric of managed care and Total Quality Management to their own use. Organized consumer groups argue that a progressive and responsive system of human services follows four principles. First, such a system assumes that consumers must control services and supports, and determine directly what is needed for them to prosper and what is essential to the achievement of their definition of quality of life. Second, outcomes are defined by the consumer, working, if needed, in close collaboration with an advisor or advocate. The determination of outcomes is seen as an extension of the value of control that is infused into the role of recipients.

A third principle recognizes that the consumer exercises discretion over the purchase of the services or supports that he or she determined to be of personal importance. In practice this means that consumers can venture into the marketplace of human services and obtain those services that have relevance, meaningfulness, and quality from the perspective of consumers. It also means that there is enough flexibility in this approach to purchasing services for consumers to come together into collaborative efforts to sponsor a new service or support system that better achieves the outcomes they seek, rather than merely purchasing services from existing but perhaps inadequate providers.

The fourth principle endorses dissent. Consumers have the option of continuing with the services or supports they are purchasing, or they may readily withdraw their financial support and seek what they desire elsewhere. Consumers can evaluate what they are receiving from a very personalistic but potent standpoint, using criteria that are relevant to any consumer within a market society: Are they getting what they want? Are they achieving outcomes that are personally important to them? Do providers reduce the social and personal costs of accessing and using services? Do service providers offer services and supports in a manner that is consistent with the values of the purchaser? The operationalization of dissent in practice means that consumers are empowered to determine whether the continuation of a market relationship is desired and worthwhile. Consumer needs and desires do not have to be met through established human service systems and organizations. Consumers can go outside community support systems, mental health systems, and other providers of human services and seek the supports they desire through nontraditional means and organizations.

Case management is linked to a progressive conception of consumerism, one that is truly more consistent with our market culture than what now exists within the broad arena of social and human services. A case manager becomes a consumer advocate and representative who is assisting a consumer or group of consumers to implement the four principles discussed above: the infusion of control into the role of consumer; the identification of needs and desired outcomes; the purchase of services; and the expression of dissent. Case managers adopt roles and organize resources that add value to the recipient as consumer and that empower the consumer to manage the services and supports that he or she has defined as important. "Adding value" means that case managers have information about the range of human services operating in a community and, more importantly, have data on the performance of the organizations delivering these services and supports, with performance validated in terms of values important to consumers. Case managers are very knowledgeable about those providers who truly value consumerism and operate in a manner that is responsive, sensitive, and committed to the perspectives and values of their purchasers. A commitment to innovation means that case managers are available to offer or obtain technical assistance that will help consumers to craft alternative services and supports.

In addition, case managers have expertise in helping consumers to craft performance contracts with providers, and in assisting consumers to monitor and evaluate these contracts from perspectives consumers define as important and meaningful. Case managers can assist consumers to resolve disputes or dissatisfaction and to shop for services if a provider is not performing at an acceptable level.

A principal negative consequence of this orientation to case management emerges from the strain between the autonomy of consumers and the adequacy of the benefits that is the basis of this autonomy. If the benefit is inadequate or trivial then the empowerment of the role of consumer as controller will be trivial. The actual level of the monetary benefit (i.e., how many dollars the consumer actually controls) and the actual discretion enjoyed by the consumer (e.g., the consumer actually has cash available as opposed to vouchers) are critical considerations in the achievement of recipient management of human services.

Another limitation here concerns the expertise and competence of case managers and of case management systems. Not all consumers will want to employ or involve a case manager. Yet many will most likely want the assistance of someone who is informed and competent in the individual management of human services using a consumer-driven model of service delivery. Performance pressure is heightened for the case manager who is committed to stewardship of consumers' perspectives and desires as opposed to trusteeship of a system's perspectives and desires. Case managers must perform in ways that promote self-determination and empowerment by collecting, organizing, and using consumer-relevant evaluation data; by forming relationships with consumers that allow them to take the lead in defining needs, outcomes, and values; and by absorbing for consumers the conflict that may emerge when provider organizations experience difficulties in responding to assertive and empowered consumers.

CONCLUSION: A FUTURE OF MIXED SCENARIOS

Throughout this volume I have consistently used the term case management even at the risk of alienating some of my readers who may perceive this term as pejorative and negative. I have not adhered to this practice for this purpose, and many people who know me professionally are aware of the failings I see in case management, including what we have chosen to call it.

But the term has stood the test of time, and we continue to come back to it perhaps more to articulate a vision that is difficult to capture in words, and less to achieve an accurate or precise label. The content of this book, especially the scenarios communicated in this chapter, illustrates the importance of this label when we consider what is meant by "case" and what is meant by "management." Those of us involved in the enterprise of human services, whether as policy maker, practitioner, or consumer, are seeking to manage something. All of the scenarios identified above have one thing in common: We seek to manage the individual provision of human services in order to achieve an outcome valued by someone. Return to the scenarios, peruse them again, and identify what you believe is meant by management within each scenario and what actually forms a case. By articulating what we mean by case and by management, we will better understand the value bases of each alternative way of thinking about case management and its purpose in human services.

The future of case management is linked to change in the human services, and this change will be viewed as either positive or negative, depending on one's values. The nature of this change, however, most likely will be an admixture of many different forces and factors creating systems characterized by the further elaboration of human services in certain problem areas (e.g., serious mental illness); the introduction of managed care strategies into new areas of health and human services; the use of human services to engage in social control; the responsiveness of human services to outcome-based funding; and the responsiveness of human services to empowered consumers. The future of case management will reflect this admixture, which means that case management will likely take on many different alternative forms, textures, emphases, and characters. Thus, when we speak of case management we must specify the form of case management we are referring to, the context in which case management is to perform, and the outcomes by which this performance should be appraised.

The form of case management we seek to implement in the managed care arena, for example, is very different from the form of case management we seek to implement in community support systems for people with serious mental illness. Differences in form will be explained by differences in purpose. And behind purpose lurks critical values that animate human services for better or worse. As the dictum of design suggests: the form of case management will embody the principal values of the designer (Petroski, 1992).

What scenario will be dominant? As I noted at the beginning of this paper, this is difficult to predict with certainty. Dominance of a particular scenario may be found in the prevalence and success of certain values that receive political endorsement and support within our social and economic institutions. Indeed, if efforts to balance the federal budget are successful, then change will likely reverberate throughout human services, and case management as a strategy for rationalization, cost control, and utilization control will likely gain in legitimacy, especially as state governments grapple with more responsibility for human services and have fewer resources to devote to this responsibility. Thus, scenarios two, three, and four may become dominant in the near future, and when the term case management is invoked, systems that are trying to get more out of less may come to mind. The case manager as "trustee" may be the future dominant form. Management in this dominant form will mean the efficient management of needs to fit within a resource base perceived to be finite and constrained.

But we cannot ignore those value packages and related programmatic elements that challenge the hegemony of efficiency within human services. These elements may not be dominant now. They may be small and lacking in salience. They may not receive a great deal of attention and yet, nonetheless, they may continue to be influential, and they may flourish within contexts that value efforts to forge meaningful responses to consumers. Case management did emerge, in part, from consumer activism, and there is good reason to believe that consumers will continue to grow in assertiveness, and will continue to expand their expectations about the responsiveness and performance of human services.

Thus, I assert that a consumer-driven form of case management with its commitment to the stewardship of consumer perspectives will continue to operate within many of our human service systems, and this form of case management probably will be more ambiguous, differentiated, and ambitious compared to case management based on trusteeship. Consumer-driven case management is not an end in itself but is a reflection of a larger-scale effort within human services to attain three ends:

- the responsiveness of human services to the characteristics, qualities, and desires of consumers.
- the subjugation of organizational and professional interests to the perspectives and desires of consumers.
- the impact of human services on the quality of community life among consumers.

These three ends may be antithetical to systems that are driven by cost containment as their principal organizing ethos. Coexistence between two different and conflicting archetypes of case management committed to substantively different ends is perhaps merely an expression of an archetypal value conflict operating within human services, one that reflects a societal ambivalence concerning the use of social and human services to fulfill human needs. Is case management an expression of a system preoccupied by costs? Or is case management an expression of consumers whose needs and desires must be amplified and passionately represented? Readers may be critical of such a dichotomy. Yet this dichotomy does reflect a very real conflict in trying to reconcile the fulfillment of needs with the containment of costs. And perhaps part of our dissatisfaction with case management as a small but important innovation in human services is embedded in its failure to achieve two very different aims, a failure that is not new to human services, and one that will most likely continue into our future given the current cultural and structural realities governing the organization of social welfare in the United States.

REFERENCES

Abrahams, R., & Leutz, W. (1983). The consolidated model of case management to the elderly. *Pride Institute Journal of Long-Term Health Care* 6(4), 29–34.

Abramson, N. S. (1986). Continuum of care for the chronically mentally ill elderly. In N. S. Abramson, J. K. Quam, & M. Wasow (Eds.), *The elderly and chronic mental illness.* San Francisco, CA: Jossey-Bass.

American Association on Mental Retardation. (n.d.). *Mental retardation: Definition, classification, and systems of support.* 9th ed. Washington, DC: American Association on Mental Retardation.

American Hospital Association. (1992). Case management: An aid to quality and continuity of care. In S. M. Rose (Ed.), *Case management and social work practice* (pp. 149–59). New York: Longman.

Anthony, W. A. (1979). *The principles of psychiatric rehabilitation.* Amherst, MA: Human Resource Development Press.

_____. (1993). Managed mental health care: Will it be rationed care or rational care? *Psychosocial Rehabilitation Journal* 16(4), 120–23.

_____. (1994). Recovery from mental illness: The guiding vision of the mental health system in the 1990s. In IAPSRS, *An introduction to psychiatric rehabilitation* (pp. 556–67). Boston, MA: Boston University Center for Psychiatric Rehabilitation.

Anthony, W. A., & Blanch, A. (1989). Research on community support services: What have we learned? *Psychosocial Rehabilitation Journal* 12(3), 55–82.

Anthony, W. A., Cohen, M., Farkas, M., & Cohen, B. F. (1988). Case management—more than a response to a dysfunctional system. *Community Mental Health Journal,* 24(3), 219–28.

Applebaum, R., & Austin, C. (1990). *Long-term case management: Design and evaluation.* New York: Springer.

Applebaum, R. & Christianson, J. (1988). Using case management to monitor community-based long term care. *Quality Review Bulletin,* 14(7), 227–31.

Applebaum, R., & Wilson, N. L. (1988). Training needs for providing case management for the long-term care client: Lessons from the National Channeling Demonstration. *The Gerontologist* 28(2), 172–76.

249

Arkansas Department of Human Services, Office on Aging. (1984). *Comprehensive case management guidelines*. Little Rock, AR: Arkansas Department of Human Services.

Aronowitz, S., & Giroux, H. A. (1991). *Postmodern education: Politics, culture, and social criticism*. Minneapolis: University of Minnesota Press.

Ashbaugh, J., Bradley, V., & Blaney, B. (1994). Implications for future practice and systems design. In V. J. Bradley, J. Ashbaugh, & B. Blaney (Eds.), *Creating individual supports for people with developmental disabilities: A mandate for change*. Baltimore, MD: Paul H. Brooks.

Ashley, A. (1988). Interdisciplinary update: Case management—the need to define goals. *Hospital and Community Psychiatry* 39(5), 499–500.

Austin, C. (1993). Case management: A systems perspective. *Families in Society* 74(8), 451–59.

Aviram, U. (1990). Community care of the seriously mentally ill: Continuing problems and current issues. *Community Mental Health Journal* 26, 69–88.

Axelson, L., & Dail, P. W. (1988). The changing character of homelessness in the United States. *Family Relations* 37, 463–69.

Bachrach, L. (1981). Continuity of care for chronic mental patients: A conceptual analysis. *American Journal of Psychiatry* 138(11), 1449–56.

_____. (1989). Case management: Toward a shared definition. *Hospital and Community Psychiatry* 40(9), 883–84.

_____. (1992a). Case management revisited. *Hospital and Community Psychiatry* 43(3), 209–10.

_____. (1992b). What we know about homelessness among mentally ill persons: An analytic review and commentary. *Hospital and Community Psychiatry* 43(5), 453–64.

Baerwald, A. (1983). Case management. In L. Wikler and M. P. Keenan (Eds.), *Developmental disabilities: No longer a private tragedy* (pp. 219–23). Silver Spring, MD: NASW.

Baier, M. (1987). Case management with the chronically mentally ill. *Journal of Psychosocial Nursing and Mental Health Services* 25(6), 17–20.

Baker, F., & Intagliata, J. (1984). Rural community support services for the chronically mentally ill. *Journal of Community Psychology* 5, 3–14.

Baker, F., & Weiss, R. (1984). The nature of case manager support. *Hospital and Community Psychiatry* 35, 925–28.

Ballew, J. R., & Mink, G. (1986). *Case management in the human services*. Springfield, IL: Charles C. Thomas.

Barker, R. L. (1987). Case management. *Social work dictionary*. Silver Spring, MD: NASW.

Barrow, S. M., Hellman, F., Lovell, A. M., Plapinger, J., & Streuning, E. L. (1989). *Effectiveness of programs for the mentally ill homeless*. New York: New York Psychiatric Institute.

_____. (1991). Evaluating outreach services: Lessons from a study of five programs. In N. L. Cohen (Ed.), *Psychiatric outreach to the mentally ill*. New Directions for Mental Health Services, 52 (pp. 29–46). San Francisco, CA: Jossey-Bass.

Bassuk, E. L. (1989). Homelessness: A growing American tragedy. *Division of Child, Youth, and Family Services Newsletter* 12.

References

Bassuk, E. L., Carman, R. W., Weinrebb, L. F., & Herzig, M. M. (1990). *Community care for homeless families.* Newton Centre, MA: Better Homes Foundation.

Bassuk, E. L., & Cohen, D. A. (1991). *Homeless families with children: Research perspectives.* Silver Spring, MD: National Institute of Mental Health and the National Institute on Alcohol, Abuse, and Alcoholism.

Bassuk, E. L., & Rosenberg, L. (1988). Why does family homelessness occur? A case-control study. *American Journal of Public Health,* 78, 783-788.

_____. (1990). Psychosocial characteristics of homeless children and children with homes. *Pediatrics* 85, 257–61.

Beatrice, D. F. (1981). Case management: A policy option for long-term care. In J. J. Callahan & S. S. Wallack (Eds.), *Reforming the long-term care system.* Lexington, MA: Lexington Books.

Belcher, J. (1988). Rights versus needs of the homeless mentally ill persons. *Social Work* 40, 398–402.

_____. (1993). The trade-offs of developing a case management model for chronically mentally ill people. *Health and Social Work* 18(1), 20–31.

Berk, R. A., & Rossi, P. H. (1990). *Thinking about program evaluation.* Newbury Park, CA: Sage.

Berkowitz, G., Halfon, N., & Klee, L. (1992). Improving access to health care: Case management for vulnerable children. *Social Work in Health Care* 17(1), 101–23.

Biegel, D. M., Tracy, E. M., & Corvo, K. N. (1994). Strengthening social networks: Intervention strategies for mental health case managers. *Health and Social Work* 19(3), 202–16.

Bogdonoff, M. D., Hughes, S. L., Weissert, W. G., & Paulsen, E. (1991). *The living at home program: Innovations in service access and case management.* New York: Springer.

Bond, G., Miller, L., Krumwied, R., & Ward, R. (1988). Assertive case management in three CMHCs: A controlled study. *Hospital and Community Psychiatry* 39(4), 411–18.

Bond, G., Pensec, M., Dietzen, L., McCafferty, D., Giemza, R., & Sipple, H. (1991). Intensive case management for frequent users of psychiatric hospitals in a large city: A comparison of team and individual caseloads. *Psychosocial Rehabilitation Journal* 15(1), 90–97.

Borenstein, D. R. (1990). Managed care: A means of rationing treatment. *Hospital and Community Psychiatry* 41(10), 1095–98.

Bradley, V. J., Ashbaugh, J., & Blaney, B. (Eds.). (1994). *Creating individual supports for people with developmental disabilities: A mandate for change.* Baltimore, MD: Paul H. Brooks.

Brager, G., & Holloway, S. (1978). *Changing human service organizations: Politics and practice.* New York: Fress Press.

Brennan, J. P., & Kaplan, C. (1993). Setting new standards for social work case management. *Hospital and Community Psychiatry* 44(3), 219–22.

Bricker-Jenkins, M. (1992). Building a strengths model of practice in the public social services. In D. Saleeby (Ed.), *The strengths perspective in social work practice* (pp. 122–35). New York: Longman.

Brindis, C., Barth, R. P., & Loomis, P. (1987). Continuous counseling: Case management with teenage parents. *Social Casework* 68, 164–72.

References

Brostoff, P. M. (1988). Ethical dilemmas facing private geriatric case managers. In K. Fisher and E. Woisman (Eds.), *Case management: Guiding patients through the health care maze.* Chicago: Joint Commission on Accreditation of Health Care Organizations.

Brown, R. I., & Hughson, E. A. (1987). *Behavioral and social rehabilitation and training.* New York: Wiley.

Brown, S. E. (1994). *Investigating a culture of disability.* Las Cruces, NM: Institute on Disability Culture.

Buckner, J. C., Bassuk, E. L., & Zima, B. T. (1993). Mental health issues affecting homeless women: Implications for intervention. *American Journal of Orthopsychiatry* 63, 385–99.

Bunker, D. R., & Wijnberg, M. H. (1988). *Supervision and performance: Managing professional work in human service organizations.* San Francisco, CA: Jossey-Bass.

Bybee, D., Mowbray, C. T., & Cohen, E. (in press). Evaluation of a homeless mentally ill outreach program: Differential short-term effects. *Evaluation and Program Planning.*

Cambridge, P. (1992). Case management in community services: Organizational responses. *British Journal of Social Work* 22(5), 495–517.

Capitman, J. A., Haskins, B., & Borstein, J. (1986). Case management approaches in coordinated community-oriented long-term care demonstrations. *The Gerontologist* 26, 398–404.

Chamberlin, J., Rogers, J., & Sneed, C. (1989). Consumers, families, and community support systems. *Psychosocial Rehabilitation Journal* 12(3), 93–106.

Chamberlin, R., & Rapp, C. A. (1991). A decade of case management: A methodological review of outcome research. *Community Mental Health Journal* 27(3), 171–88.

Cheung, K., Stevenson, K., & Leung, P. (1991). Competency-based evaluation of case management skills in child sexual abuse intervention. *Child Welfare* 70(4), 425–35.

Citizens Committee for Children of New York, Inc. (1992). *On their own—at what cost? A look at families who leave shelters.* New York: Citizens Committee for Children of New York.

Clark, K., Landis, D., & Fisher, G. (1990). The relationship of client characteristics to case management service provision: Implications for successful system implementation. *Evaluation and Program Planning* 134(3), 221–29.

Cnaan, R. A., Blankertz, L., Messinger, K. W., & Gardner, J. (1988). Psychosocial rehabilitation: Toward a definition. *Psychosocial Rehabilitation Journal* 11(4), 61–77.

Cohen, A., & Degraaf, B. (1982). Assessing case management in the child abuse field. *Journal of Social Service Research* 5(1, 2), 29–43.

Cohen, M. B. (1989). Social work practice with homeless mentally ill people: Engaging the client. *Social Work* 34, 505–9.

Cohen, M., & Anthony, W. A. (1988). A commentary on planning a service system for persons who are severely mentally ill: Avoiding the pitfalls of the past. *Psychosocial Rehabilitation Journal* 12(1), 69–72.

Cohen, N. L., & Tsemberis, S. (1991). Emergency psychiatric intervention on the street. In N. L. Cohen (Ed.), *Psychiatric outreach to the mentally ill.* New Directions for Mental Health Services, 52 (pp. 3–16). San Francisco, CA: Jossey-Bass.

Cohen, S., & Brand, R. (1993). *Total quality management in government*. San Francisco, CA: Jossey-Bass.

Coles, R. (1989). *The call of stories: Teaching and the moral imagination*. Boston: Houghton, Mifflin.

Corrigan, P., & Kayton-Weinberg, D. (1993). Aggressive and problem-focused models of case management for the severely mentally ill. *Community Mental Health Journal* 29(5), 449–58.

Creech, B. (1994). *The five pillars of TQM*. New York: Dutton.

Curtis, W. R. (1974). Team problem solving in a social network. *Psychiatric Annals* 4, 11–27.

———. (1979). *The future use of social networks in mental health*. Boston, MA: Social Matrix.

Dail, P. (1990). The psychosocial context of homeless mothers with young children: Program and policy implications. *Child Welfare* 64(4), 291–307.

Davis, I. (1992). Client identification and outreach: Case management in school-based services for teenage parents. In B. Vourlekis & R. Greene (Eds.), *Social Work Case Management*. New York: Aldine.

Degen, K., Cole, N., Tamayo, L., & Dzerovych, G. (1990). Intensive case management for the seriously mentally ill. *Administration and Policy in Mental Health* 17(4), 265–69.

DeJong, P., & Miller, S. (1995). How to interview for client strengths. *Social Work* 40(6), 729–36.

Deitchman, W. S. (1980). How many case managers does it take to screw in a light bulb? *Hospital and Community Psychiatry* 31(11), 788–89.

Del Togno-Armanasco, V., Hopkin, L. A., & Harter, S. (1993). *Collaborative nursing case management: A handbook for development and implementation*. New York: Springer.

Dennis, D. L., Buckner, J. C., Lipton, F. R., & Levine, I. S. (1991). A decade of research and services for homeless mentally ill persons: Where do we stand? *American Psychologist* 46, 1129–38.

Devore, W. (1995). Organizing for violence prevention: An African-American community perspective. In F. G. Rivera & J. Erlich (Eds.), *Community organizing in a diverse society*. 2d ed., (pp. 61–75). Boston: Allyn and Bacon.

DeWeaver, K. L., & Johnson, P. L. (1983). Case management in rural areas for the developmentally disabled. *Human Services in the Rural Environment* 8(4), 23–31.

Dietzen, L., & Bond, G. (1993). Relationship between case manager contact and outcome for frequently hospitalized psychiatric clients. *Hospital and Community Psychiatry* 44(9), 839–43.

Dill, A. (1987). Issues in case management for the chronically mentally ill. In D. Mechanic (Ed.), *Improving mental health services: What the social sciences can tell us* (pp. 61–70). San Francisco, CA: Jossey-Bass.

Dincin, J. (1990). Assertive case management. *Psychiatric Quarterly* 61(1), 49–55.

Dixon, T., Goll, S., & Stanton, K. (1988). Case management issues and practices in head injury rehabilitation. *Rehabilitation Counseling Bulletin* 31(4), 325–43.

Donovan, M. (1994). Introduction to outpatient case management. In M. Donovan &

T. Matson (Eds.), *Outpatient case management: Strategies for a new reality* (pp. 19–36). Chicago, IL: American Hospital Pub.

Donovan, M., & Matson, T. (1994). (Eds.), *Outpatient case management: Strategies for a new reality*. Chicago, IL.: American Hospital Pub.

Doyal, L., & Gough, I. (1991). *A theory of human need*. New York: Guilford.

Draine, J., & Solomon, P. (1994). Jail recidivism and the intensity of case management services among homeless persons with mental illness leaving jail. *Journal of Law and Psychiatry* 22(2), 245–61.

Drake, R. E., Osher, F. C., & Wallach, M. A. (1991). Homelessness and dual diagnosis. *American Psychologist* 46, 1149–58.

Ducanis, A. J., & Golin, A. K. (1979). *The interdisciplinary health care team*. Germantown, MD: Aspen.

Dumm, T. L. (1987). *Democracy and punishment: Disciplinary origins of the United States*. Madison: University of Wisconsin Press.

Durell, J., Lechtenburg, B., Corse, S., & Frances, R. (1993). Intensive case management for persons with chronic mental illness who abuse substances. *Hospital and Community Psychiatry* 44(5), 415–16.

Dvoskin, J., & Steadman, H. (1994). Using intensive case management to reduce violence by mentally ill persons in the community. *Hospital and Community Psychiatry* 45(7), 679–84.

Egan, G. (1993). *Adding value*. San Francisco, CA: Jossey-Bass.

Eggert, G. M., Friedman, B., & Zimmer, J. (1990). Models of intensive case management. *Journal of Gerontological Social Work* 15(3, 4), 75–101.

Eisenberg, M. G., Griggins, C., & Duval, R. J. (Eds.). (1982). *Disabled people as second-class citizens*. New York: Springer.

Elliott, R. L. (1994). Applying quality improvement principles and techniques in public mental health systems. *Hospital and Community Psychiatry* 45(5), 439–44.

Ellison, M. L., Rogers, E. S., Sciarappa, K., Cohen, M., & Forbess, R. (1995). Characteristics of mental health case management: Results of a national survey. *Journal of Mental Health Administration* 22(2), 101–12.

Endicott, J., Spitzer, R., Fleiss, J., & Cohen, J. (1976). The Global Assessment Scale: A procedure for measuring overall severity of psychiatric disturbance. *Archives of General Psychiatry* 33, 766–71.

Epstein, L. (1988). *Helping people: The task-centered approach*. Columbus, OH: Merrill.

Evans, M., Banks, S., Huz, S., & McNulty, T. (1994). Initial hospitalization and community tenure outcomes of intensive case management for children and youth with serious emotional disturbances. *Journal of Child and Family Studies* 3(2), 225–34.

Everett, B., & Nelson, A. (1992). We're not cases and you're not managers: An account of a client-professional relationship developed in response to the "Borderline" diagnosis. *Psychosocial Rehabilitation Journal* 15(4), 49–60.

Farkas, M. D., & Anthony, W. A. (1989). *Psychiatric rehabilitation programs: Putting theory into practice*. Baltimore, MD: Johns Hopkins University Press.

Farkas, M. D., Anthony, W. A., & Cohen, M. A. (1989). Psychiatric rehabilitation: The approach and its programs. In M. D. Farkas & W. A. Anthony (Eds.), *Psychiatric rehabilitation programs: Putting theory into practice* (pp. 1–27). Baltimore, MD:

Johns Hopkins University Press.

Feldman, J. L., & Fitzpatrick, R. (Eds.). (1992). *Managed mental health care: Administrative and clinical issues.* Washington, DC: American Psychiatric Press.

Finch, W. A. (1980). Social workers versus bureaucracy. In H. Resnick & R. J. Patti (Eds.), *Change from within: Humanizing social welfare organizations* (pp. 73–85). Philadelphia, PA: Temple University Press.

First, R. J., Greenlee, R. W., & Schmitz, C. A. (1990). *A qualitative study of two community treatment teams. Summary report.* Columbus, OH: Ohio Department of Mental Health.

First, R., Rife, J., & Krauss, S. (1990). Case management with people who are homeless and mentally ill: Preliminary findings from an NIMH demonstration project. *Psychosocial Rehabilitation Journal* 4(2), 87–91.

Flexer, R., & Solomon, P. (Eds.). (1993). *Psychiatric rehabilitation in practice.* Boston, MA: Andover.

Freddolino, P., Fleishman, J., & Moxley, D. (1987). Assessing client support and representation services: A progress report. Unpublished monograph. Michigan State University School of Social Work, East Lansing.

Freddolino, P., & Moxley, D. (1988). *Evaluation of the Mental Health Advocacy Services Division of Michigan Protection and Advocacy Service, Inc.* East Lansing: Michigan State University School of Social Work.

_____. (1992). Refining an advocacy model for homeless people coping with psychiatric disabilities. *Community Mental Health Journal* 28(4), 337–52.

_____. (1993). Wants versus needs: Finding an alternative to case management. Disabilities Studies Quarterly, 13(2), 28–32.

_____. (1994). *The road to empowerment: The mental health rights protection and advocacy movement in the United States.* East Lansing: Michigan State University School of Social Work.

Freddolino, P., Moxley, D., & Fleishman, J. (1988). Daily living needs at time of discharge: Implications for advocacy. *Psychosocial Rehabilitation Journal* 11(4), 33–46.

_____. (1989). A field tested advocacy model for people with long-term psychiatric disabilities. *Hospital and Community Psychiatry* 40(11), 1169–74.

Freire, P. (1968). *Pedagogy of the oppressed.* New York: Seabury Press.

_____. (1994). *Pedagogy of hope.* New York: Continuum.

Galbraith, J. K. (1996). *The good society.* Boston, MA: Houghton Mifflin.

Gerhard, R., Dorgan, R., & Miles, D. (1981). *The balanced service system.* Clinton, OK: Responsive System Associates.

Gerhart, U. C. (1990). *Caring for the chronic mentally ill.* Itasca, IL: Peacock.

Gibelman, M., & Demone, H. W. (1989). The evolving contract state. In H. W. Demone & M. Gibelman (Eds.), *Services for sale: Purchasing health and human services* (pp. 17–57). New Brunswick, NJ: Rutgers University Press.

Gil, D. (1976). *The challenge of social equality.* Cambridge, MA: Schenkman.

Gitterman, A. (Ed.). (1991). *Handbook of social work practice with vulnerable populations.* New York: Columbia University Press.

Gliedman, J., & Roth, W. (1980). *The unexpected minority: Handicapped children in America.* New York: Harcourt Brace Jovanovich.

Goodin, R. E. (1985). *Protecting the vulnerable: A reanalysis of our social responsibilities.* Chicago, IL: University of Chicago Press.

Gottesman, L. E., Ishizaki, B., & MacBride, S. M. (1979). Service management: Plan and concept in Pennsylvania. *The Gerontologist* 19(4), 379–85.

Granet, R., & Talbot, J. (1978). The continuity agent: Creating a new role to bridge gaps in the mental health system. *Hospital and Community Psychiatry* 29, 132–33.

Gutek, B. (1995). *The dynamics of service: Reflections on the changing nature of customer/provider interactions.* San Francisco, CA: Jossey-Bass.

Hagen, J. L. (1987). Gender and homelessness. *Social Work* 32(4), 312–16.

Hagen, J. L., & Hutchinson, E. (1988). Who's serving the homeless. *Social Casework* 69, 491–97.

Halfon, N., Berkowitz, G., & Klee, L. (1993). Development of an integrated case management program for vulnerable children. *Child Welfare* 72(4), 379–96.

Hancock, T. (1991). Healthy cities: The case of Canada. Paper presented at Building Health through Community conference, Boston, MA, April 1991.

Harrington, J. (1995). *Total improvement management.* New York: McGraw-Hill.

Harris, M. (1990). Redesigning case management services for work with character-disordered young adults. In N. L. Cohen (Ed.), *Psychiatry takes to the streets: Outreach and crisis intervention for the mentally ill.* New York: Guilford.

Harris, M., & Bachrach, L. (1988). *Clinical case management.* San Francisco, CA: Jossey-Bass.

Harris, M., & Bergman, H. (1993). *Case management for mentally ill patients: Theory and practice.* New York: Harwood Academic.

Hasenfeld, Y. (1983). *Human service organizations.* Englewood Cliffs, NJ: Prentice-Hall.

Hill, K., & Clawson, M. (1988). The health hazards of "street level" bureaucracy: Mortality among the police. *Journal of Police Science and Administration* 16(4), 243–48.

Hillyer, B. (1993). *Feminism and disability.* Norman: University of Oklahoma Press.

Hodge, M., & Draine, J. (1993). Development of support through case management services. In R. W. Flexer & P. L. Solomon (Eds.), *Psychiatric Rehabilitation in Practice.* Boston, MA: Andover.

Hurley, R. E. (1986). Toward a behavioral model of the physician as case manager. *Social Science and Medicine* 23(1), 75–82.

Hyde, P. S. (1989). *Memo on case management services.* Columbus, OH: Ohio Department of Mental Health.

Ignatieff, M. (1984). *The needs of strangers: An essay on privacy, solidarity, and the politics of being human.* New York: Penguin.

Ingram, R. (1988). Empower. *Social Policy* 19(2), 11–16.

Institute of Medicine. (1991). *Disability in America: Toward a national agenda for prevention.* Washington, DC: National Academy Press.

Intagliata, J. (1982). Improving the quality of community care for the chronically mentally disabled: The role of case management. *Schizophrenia Bulletin* 8(4), 655–74.

———. (1992). Improving the quality of community care for the chronically mentally disabled: The role of case management. In S. M. Rose (Ed.), *Case management and social work practice* (pp. 25–55). New York: Longman.

Isaac, R., & Armat, V. C. (1990). *Madness in the streets: How psychiatry and the law abandoned the mentally ill.* New York: Free Press.

Jacobs, D. R., & Moxley, D. P. (1993). Anticipating managed mental health care: Implications for psychosocial rehabilitation agencies. *Psychosocial Rehabilitation Journal* 17(2), 15–32.

Jacobs, J. (1992). *Systems of survival: A dialogue on the moral foundations of commerce and politics.* New York: Random House.

Johnson, A. (1990). *Out of Bedlam: The truth about deinstitutionalization.* New York: Basic Books.

Johnson, P. J., & Rubin, A. (1983). Case management in mental health: A social work domain? *Social Work* 28(1), 49–55.

Kane, R. A. (1988). Case management: Ethical pitfalls on the road to high quality managed care. *Quality Review Bulletin* 14(5), 161–66.

Kane, R. A., & Caplan, A. L. (1992). *Ethical conflicts in the management of home care: The case manager's dilemma.* New York: Springer.

Kanter, J. S. (1985). Case management of the young adult chronic patient. In J. S. Kanter (Ed.), *Clinical issues in treating the chronic mentally ill.* New Directions for Mental Health Services 27 (pp. 77–92). San Francisco, CA: Jossey-Bass.

_____. (1988). Clinical issues in the case management relationship. In M. Harris & L. Bachrach (Eds.), *Clinical case management.* New Directions for Mental Health Services 40 (pp. 15–28). San Francisco, CA: Jossey-Bass.

Kennedy, L. (1991). *Quality management in the nonprofit world.* San Francisco, CA: Jossey-Bass.

Kirkhart, K., & Ruffolo, M. (1993). Value bases of case management evaluation. *Evaluation and Program Planning* 16(1), 55–65.

Korr, W. S., & Cloninger, L. (1991). Assessing models of case management: An empirical approach. *Journal of Social Service Research* 14(1/2), 129–46.

Kozol, J. (1988). *Rachel and her children: Homeless families in America.* New York: Crown.

_____. (1995). *Amazing Grace.* New York: Crown.

Kretzman, J. P., & McKnight, J. L. (1993). *Building communities from the inside out.* Evanston, IL: Center for Urban Affairs and Policy Research, Northwestern University.

Lamb, H. R. (1984). *The homeless mentally ill.* Washington, DC: American Psychiatric Association.

Lane, H. (1992). *The mask of benevolence.* New York: Knopf.

Lappe, F. M., & DuBois, P. M. (1994). *The quickening of America: Rebuilding our nation, remaking our lives.* San Francisco, CA: Jossey-Bass.

Lauffer, A. (1984). *Strategic marketing for not-for-profit organizations.* New York: Praeger.

Levine, I., & Fleming, M. (n.d.). *Human resource development: Issues in case management.* Washington, DC: NIMH.

Like, R. C. (1988). Primary care case management: A family physician perspective. *Quality Review Bulletin* 14(6), 174–78.

Linz, M., McAnally, P., & Wieck, C. (1989). *Case management: Historical, current, and future perspectives.* Cambridge, MA: Brookline Books.

References

Lipsky, M. (1980). *Street-level bureauracy: Dilemmas of the individual in public services.* New York: Russell Sage Foundation.

Maluccio, A. N. (1974). Action as a tool in casework practice. *Social Casework* 55, 30–35.

_____. (1981). *Promoting competence in clients.* New York: Free Press.

Maternal and Child Health Bureau. (1994). *Integrating education, health, and human services for children, youth, and families: Systems that are community-based and school-linked.* Washington, DC: Maternal and Child Health Bureau.

Mayer, R. (1973). *Social planning and social change.* Englewood Cliffs, NJ: Prentice-Hall.

McGowan, B. G. (1987). Advocacy. *Encyclopedia of Social Work,* 18th Ed. (pp. 89–95). Silver Spring, MD: NASW.

McGrew, J. H., & Bond, G. R. (1995). Critical ingredients of assertive community treatment: Judgments of the experts. *Journal of Mental Health Administration* 22(2), 113–25.

McKnight, J. (1989). Organizing the community. In M. Linz, P. McAnally, & C. Wieck (Eds.). *Case management: Historical, current, and future perspectives.* Cambridge, MA: Brookline.

McQuistion, H. L., D'Ercole, A. D., & Kopelson, E. (1991). Urban street outreach: Using clinical principles to steer the system. In N. L. Cohen (Ed.), *Psychiatric outreach to the mentally ill.* New Directions for Mental Health Services, 52 (pp. 17–28). San Francisco, CA: Jossey-Bass.

Mechanic, D. (1987). Correcting misconceptions in mental health policy: Strategies for improved care of the seriously mentally ill. *Milbank Quarterly* 65(2), 203–30.

_____. (1991). Strategies for integrating public health services. *Hospital and Community Psychiatry,* August, 797–801.

_____. (1994). Integrating mental health into a general health care system. *Hospital and Community Psychiatry.* September, 893–97.

Meenaghan, T. M. (1974). Role changes for the parents of the mentally retarded. *Journal of Mental Retardation* 12, 48–49.

Meenaghan, T. M., & Kilty, K. M. (1994). *Policy analysis and research technology: Political and ethical considerations.* Chicago, IL: Lyceum.

Meenaghan, T. M., & Mascari, M. (1971). Consumer choice, consumer control in service delivery. *Social Work* 10, 50–57.

Meenaghan, T. M., & Washington, R. O. (1980). *Social policy and social welfare: Structure and applications.* New York: Free Press.

Mills, C., & Ota, H. (1989). Homeless women with minor children in the Detroit metropolitan area. *Social Work* 34(6), 485–89.

Mizrahi, T., & Abramson, J. (1985). Sources of strain between physicians and social workers: Implications for social workers in health care settings. *Social Work in Health Care* 10(3), 33–51.

Moore, S. T. (1987). The theory of street-level bureaucracy: A positive critique. *Administration & Society* 19(1), 74–94.

_____. (1992). Case management and the integration of services: How service delivery systems shape case management. *Social Work* 37(5), 418–22.

Morris, J. (1991). *Pride against prejudice: Transforming attitudes to disability.* Philadelphia, PA: New Society Publishers.

Mouth. (1995). *The voice of disability rights.* Rochester, NY: Mouth.

Mowbray, C. T. (1985). Homelessness in America: Myths and realities. *American Journal of Orthopsychiatry* 55(1), 4–8.

Mowbray, C. T., Bybee, D., & Cohen, E. (1993). Describing the homeless mentally ill: Cluster analysis results. *American Journal of Community Psychology* 21(1), 67–93.

Mowbray, C. T., Cohen, E., & Bybee, D. (1991). Services to individuals who are homeless and mentally ill: Implementation evaluation. In D. Rog (Ed.), *Evaluating programs for the homeless.* New Directions for Program Evaluation 52 (pp. 75–90).

Mowbray, C. T., Cohen, E., Harris, S. N., Trosch, S., Johnson, S., & Duncan, B. (1992). Serving the homeless mentally ill: Mental health linkage. *Journal of Community Psychology* 20, 215–27.

Mowbray, C. T., Moxley, D., Jasper, C., & Howell, L. (1995). Consumers as providers in psychiatric rehabilitation. Unpublished manuscript.

Mowbray, C. T., Moxley, D., Thrasher, S., & Associates. (1996). Consumers as community support providers: Issues created by role innovation. *Community Mental Health Journal* 32(1), 47–67.

Mowbray, C. T., & Tan, C. (1992). Evaluation of an innovative consumer-run service model: The drop-in center. *Innovations and Research* 1(2), 19–24.

Mowbray, C., Thrasher, S., Cohen, E., & Bybee, D. (1994). Challenges and barriers for staff working with persons who are homeless and mentally ill. Paper submitted for publication.

Moxley, D. (1983). Assessment of the social support networks of persons who have major psychiatric disorders: Development and investigation of an applied clinical instrument. Doctoral diss., Ohio State University.

———. (1986). Information needs of social work practitioners working with psychiatrically disabled persons. In J. Bowker & A. Rubin (Eds.), *Studies on chronic mental illness: New horizons for social work researchers* (pp. 83–94). Washington, DC: Council on Social Work Education.

———. (1989). *The practice of case management.* Newbury Park, CA: Sage.

———. (1994a). Outpatient program development. In M. R. Donovan & T. A. Matson (Eds.), *Outpatient case management: Strategies for a new reality.* Chicago, IL: American Hospital Pub.

———. (1994b). *Serious mental illness and the concept of recovery: Observations from a national forum.* Detroit, MI: Wayne State University School of Social Work.

———. (1995a). Case management and recovery: Community support in the paradigm of psychiatric rehabilitation. Paper submitted for publication.

———. (1995b). Clinical social work in psychiatric rehabilitation. Paper submitted for publication.

Moxley, D., & Buzas, L. (1989). Perceptions of case management services for elderly persons. *Health and Social Work* 14(3), 196–203.

Moxley, D., & Freddolino, P. (1990). A model of advocacy for promoting client self-determination in psychosocial rehabilitation. *Psychosocial Rehabilitation Journal* 14(2), 69–82.

———. (1991). Needs of homeless people coping with psychiatric problems: Findings from an innovative advocacy project. *Health and Social Work* 16(1), 19–26.

_____. (1994). Client-driven advocacy and psychiatric disability: A model for social work practice. *Journal of Sociology and Social Welfare* 21(2), 91–108.

Moxley, D., Mowbray, C., & Brown, K. (1993). Supported education. In R. Flexer and P. Solomon (Eds.), *Psychiatric rehabilitation in practice*. Boston, MA: Andover.

Moxley, D., & Taranto, S. (1994). Changing programmatic models: Issues in the transition from community mental health to community support and rehabilitation. Manuscript submitted for publication.

Myers, R., & Hall, O. (n.d.). Funding behavioral health care services: A case rate-outcome budgeting model. Unpublished paper.

National Association of Social Workers. (1992). *Case management in health, education, and human service settings*. Washington, DC: NASW.

National Institute of Mental Health. (1980). Announcement of community support system strategy development and implementation grants. Rockville, MD: NIMH.

Netting, F. E. (1992). Case management: Service or symptom? *Social Work* 37(2), 160–64.

Neugeboren, B. (1985). *Organization, policy and practice in the human services*. New York: Longman.

Nikkel, R., Smith, G., & Edwards, D. (1992). A consumer-oriented case management project. *Hospital and Community Psychiatry* 43(6), 577–79.

Oliver, M. (1990). *The politics of disablement*. New York: St. Martin's Press.

Osburne, D., & Gaebler, T. (1992). *Reinventing government: How the entrepreneurial spirit is transforming the public sector*. New York: Plume.

Parker, M., & Secord, L. J. (1988). Case managers: Guiding the elderly through the health care maze. *American Journal of Nursing* 88(12), 1674–76.

Percy, S. L. (1989). *Disability, civil rights, and public policy: The politics of implementation*. Tuscaloosa: University of Alabama Press.

Peterson, C. P. (1989). P. L. 99-457—Challenges and changes for early intervention. In M. Linz, P. McAnally, & C. Wieck (Eds.), *Case management: Historical, current, and future perspectives*. Cambridge, MA: Brookline.

Petroski, H. (1992). *The evolution of useful things*. New York: Vintage.

Piette, J., Fleishman, J., Mor, V., & Dill, A. (1990). A comparison of hospital and community case management programs for persons with AIDS. *Medical Care* 28(8), 746–55.

Pinderhughes, E. B. (1983). Empowerment for our clients and for ourselves. *Social Casework* 64(6), 331–38.

Poertner, J., & Ronnau, J. (1992). A strengths approach to children with emotional difficulties. In D. Saleeby (Ed.), *The strengths perspective in social work practice* (pp. 111–21). New York: Longman.

Prager, E. (1980). Evaluation in mental health: Enter the consumer. *Social Work Research and Abstracts* 16(2), 5–10.

Prottas, J. M. (1979). *People processing: The street level bureaucrat in public service bureaucracies*. Lexington, MA: Lexington Press.

Rago, W. V., & Reid, W. H. (1991). Total quality management strategies in mental health systems. *Journal of Mental Health Administration* 18(3), 253–63.

Raider, M. (1982). Protecting the rights of clients: Michigan sets a model for other states. *Social Work* 27(2), 160–63.

Raiff, N., & Shore, B. (1993). *Advanced case management: New strategies for the Nineties*. Newbury Park, CA: Sage.

Rapp, C. (1992). The strengths perspective of case management with persons suffering from severe mental illness. In D. Saleeby (Ed.). *The strengths perspective in social work practice*. New York: Longman.

_____. (1993). Client-centered performance management for rehabilitation and mental health services. In R. W. Flexer & P. L. Solomon (Eds.), *Psychiatric rehabilitation in practice* (pp. 173–92). Boston, MA: Andover.

Rapp, C., & Hanson, J. (1988). Towards a model social work curriculum for practice with the chronically mentally ill. *Community Mental Health Journal* 24(4), 310–27.

Rapp, C., & Wintersteen, R. (1989). The strengths model of case management: Results from twelve demonstrations. *Psychosocial Rehabilitation Journal* 13(1), 23–32.

Rehfuss, J. A. (1989). *Contracting out in government*. San Francisco, CA: Jossey-Bass.

Rifkin, J. (1995). *The end of work: The decline of the global labor force and the dawn of the postmarket era*. New York: Tarcher/Putnam.

Rivera, F. G., & Erlich, J. L. (1995). *Community organizing in a diverse society*, 2d ed. Boston, MA: Allyn & Bacon.

Roessler, R., & Rubin, S. (1982). *Case management and rehabilitation counseling*. Baltimore, MD: University Park Press.

Rog, D., Andranovich, G., & Rosenblum, S. (1987). *Intensive case management for persons who are homeless and mentally ill: A review of community support program and human resource development program efforts*. Washington, DC: Cosmos Corporation.

Rose, S. (1992). *Case management and social work practice*. New York: Longman.

Rose, S. M., & Black, B. L. (1985). *Advocacy and empowerment: Mental health care in the community*. Boston, MA: Routledge & Kegan Paul.

Rossi, P. (1978). Some issues in the evaluation of human services delivery. In R. C. Sarri & Y. Hasenfeld (Eds.), *The management of human services*. New York: Columbia University Press.

_____. (1990). The old homeless and the new homelessness in historical perspective. *American Psychologist* 45, 954–59.

Rossi, P. H., & Freeman, H. E. (1993). *Evaluation: A systematic approach*. 5th ed. Newbury Park, CA: Sage.

Rothman, J. (1989). Client self-determination: Untangling the knot. *Social Service Review* 63(14), 598–612.

_____. (1992). *Guidelines for case management: Putting research to professional use*. Itasca, IL: Peacock.

Rothman, J., & Thomas, E. J. (1994). *Intervention research: Design and development for human service*. New York: Haworth.

Rubin, A. (1987). Case management. *Encyclopedia of Social Work* 18 (pp. 212–22). Silver Spring, MD: NASW.

_____. (1992). Is case management effective for people with serious mental illness? A research review. *Health and Social Work* 17(2), 138–50.

Sashkin, J., & Kiser, K. (1993). *Putting total quality management to work*. San Francisco, CA: Berrett-Koehler.

References

Saleeby, D. (Ed.). (1992a). *The strengths perspective in social work practice.* New York: Longman.

_____. (1992b). Introduction: Power in the people. In D. Saleeby (Ed.), *The strengths perspective in social work practice* (pp. 3–17). New York: Longman.

Sampson, E. M. (1994). The emergence of case management models. In M. Donovan & T. Matson (Eds.). *Outpatient case management: Strategies for a new reality* (pp. 77–94). Chicago, IL: American Hospital Pub.

Schein, E. H. (1992). *Organizational culture and leadership.* 2d ed. San Francisco, CA: Jossey-Bass.

Seltzer, M., Ivry, J., & Litchfield, L. (1987). Family members as case managers: Partnership between the formal and informal support networks. *The Gerontologist* 27(6), 722–28.

Senge, P. (1990). *The fifth discipline.* New York: Doubleday.

Shapiro, J. P. (1993). *No pity: People with disabilities forging a new civil rights movement.* New York: Times Books.

Sheridan, M. J., Gowen, N., & Halpin, S. (1993). Developing a practice model for the homeless mentally ill. *Families in Society* 74, 410–21.

Sieverts, S. (1994). The private payers' perspective. In M. Donovan & T. Matson (Eds.), *Outpatient case management: Strategies for a new reality* (pp. 37–52). Chicago, IL: American Hospital Pub.

Skarnulis, E. (1989). Issues in case management for the '90s. In M. Linz, P. McAnally, & C. Wieck (Eds.), *Case management: Historical, current, and future perspectives.* Cambridge, MA: Brookline.

Smart, B. (1993). *Postmodernity.* London: Routledge.

Smith, J. G. (1984). Consumers evaluate their needs and agency programs. In V. J. Bradley, M. A. Allard, V. Mulkern, P. Nurczynski, & E. A. Cravedi (Eds.), *Citizen evaluation in practice: A casebook on citizen evaluation of mental health and other services.* Rockville, MD: National Institute of Mental Health. (DHHS Publication No. [ADM] 84-1338)

Smith, M. K., Brown, D., Gibbs, L., Sanders, H., & Cremer, K. (1984). Client involvement in psychosocial rehabilitation. *Psychosocial Rehabilitation Journal* 8(1), 35–43.

Solarz, A. L. (1988). Homelessness: Implications for children and youth. *Social policy report: Society for research in child development.* Washington, DC: Committee on Child Development and Social Policy.

Solomon, P., & Draine, J. (1995). The efficacy of a consumer case management team: 2-year outcomes of a randomized trial. *Journal of Mental Health Administration* 22(2), 135–46.

Solomon, P., Draine, J., & Delaney, M. (1995). The working alliance and consumer case management. *Journal of Mental Health Administration* 22(2), 126–34.

Steadman, H. J., McCarty, D. W., & Morrissey, J. P. (1989). *The mentally ill in jail: Planning for essential services.* New York: Guilford.

Steinberg, R. M., & Carter, G. W. (1983). *Case management and the elderly: A handbook for planning and administering programs.* Lexington, MA: Lexington Books.

Streuning, E. L., & Padgett, D. I. (1990). Physical health status, substance use and abuse, and mental disorders among homeless adults. *Journal of Social Issues* 46(4), 65–81.

Stroul, B. (1989). Community support systems for persons with long-term mental illness: A conceptual framework. *Psychosocial Rehabilitation Journal* 12(3), 9–26.

———. (1993). Rehabilitation in community support systems. In R. Flexer & P. Solomon (Eds.), *Psychiatric rehabilitation in practice* (pp. 45–62). Boston, MA: Andover.

Stufflebeam, D. L., & Shinkfield, A. J. (1986). *Systematic evaluation.* Boston, MA: Kluwer.

Sullivan, W. P. (1992). Reconsidering the environment as a helping resource. In D. Saleeby (Ed.), *The strengths perspective in social work practice.* (pp. 148–57). New York: Longman.

Surber, R. W. (Ed.). (1994). *Clinical case management: A guide to comprehensive treatment of serious mental illness.* Newbury Park, CA: Sage.

Susser, E., Goldfinger, S. M., & White, A. (1990). Some clinical approaches to the homeless mentally ill. *Community Mental Health Journal* 26, 463–80.

Susser, M., Hopper, K., and Richman, J. (1983). Society, culture, and health. In D. Mechanic (Ed.), *Handbook of health, health care, and the health professions* (pp. 23–49). New York: Free Press.

Szasz, T. (1994). *Cruel compassion: Psychiatric control of society's unwanted.* New York: Wiley.

Taylor, S. J. (1987). Continuum traps. In S. J. Taylor, D. Biklen, & J. Knoll, *Community integration for people with severe disabilities.* New York: Teachers College Press.

Tessler, R. C., & Dennis, D. L. (1989). *A synthesis of NIMH funded research concerning persons who are homeless and mentally ill.* Amherst, MA: Social and Demographic Research Institute, University of Massachusetts, and Policy Research Associates (Delmar, NY)

Tessler, R. C., & Goldman, H. H. (1982). *The chronically mentally ill: Assessing community support programs.* Cambridge, MA: Ballinger.

Thomas, E. J. (1984). *Designing interventions for the helping professions.* Beverly Hills, CA: Sage.

Thompson, T. (1996). Wisconsin's revolutionary welfare program is working. *The National Times,* 21–23 April.

Thrasher, S. P., & Mowbray, C. T. (in press). A strengths perspective: Homeless women with children from ethnography. *Health and Social Work.*

Turner, J. C., & TenHoor, W. J. (1978). The NIMH Community Support Program: Pilot approach to a needed social reform. *Schizophrenia Bulletin* 4, 319–48.

Vourlekis, B. S., & Green, R. R. (Eds.). (1992). *Social work case management.* New York: Aldine de Gruyter.

Wehman, P. (Ed.). (1993). *The ADA mandate for social change.* Baltimore, MD: Paul H. Brookes.

Weick, A. (1992). Building a strengths perspective for social work. In D. Saleeby (Ed.), *The strengths perspective in social work practice* (pp. 18–26). New York: Longman.

Weick, A., Rapp, C., Sullivan, W. P., & Kisthardt, W. (1989). A strengths perspective for social work. *Social Work* 34(4), 350–54.

Weil, M., & Karls, J. (Eds.). (1985). *Case management in human service practice.* San Francisco, CA: Jossey-Bass.

References

West, J. (1991). The social and policy context of the act. In J. West (Ed.), *The Americans with Disabilities Act: From policy to practice* (pp. 3–24). New York: Milbank Memorial Fund.

Wieck, C. (1989). A new way of thinking for case managers. In M. H. Linz, P. McAnally, & C. Wieck (Eds.), *Case management: Historical, current, and future perspectives.* Cambridge, MA: Brookline.

Williams, B. (1992). Caring professions or street level bureaucrats? The case of probation officers' work with prisoners. *Howard Journal of Criminal Justice* 31(4), 263–75.

Williams, M., Forster, P., McCarthy, G., & Hargreaves, W. (1994). Managing case management: What makes it work? *Psychosocial Rehabilitation Journal* 18(1), 49–59.

Williams, P., & Shoultz, B. (1982). *We can speak for ourselves: Self-advocacy by mentally handicapped people.* Cambridge, MA: Brookline.

Witheridge, T. F. (1992). The assortive community treatment worker: An emerging role and its implications for professional training. In S. Rose (Ed.), *Case management and social work practice* (pp. 101–11). New York: Longman.

Witkin, B. R. (1984). *Assessing needs in educational and social programs.* San Francisco, CA: Jossey-Bass.

Wodarski, L. A., Bundschuh, E., & Forbus, W. (1988). Interdisciplinary case management: A model for intervention. *Journal of the American Dietetic Association* 88(3), 332–35.

Wolfensberger, W. (1972). *The principle of normalization in human services.* Toronto: National Institute on Mental Retardation.

Wolfensberger, W., & Zauha, H. (Eds.). (1973). *Citizen advocacy and protective services for the impaired and handicapped.* Toronto: National Institute on Mental Retardation.

Wolk, J., Sullivan, W., & Hartman, D. J. (1994). The managerial nature of case management. *Social Work* 39(2), 152–59.

Wray, L., & Wieck, C. (1985). Moving persons with developmental disabilities toward less restrictive environments through case management. In K. Lakin & R. Bruininks (Eds.), *Strategies for achieving community integration of developmentally disabled citizens.* Baltimore, MD: Paul H. Brookes.

Yeich, S., Mowbray, C. T., Bybee, D., & Cohen, E. (in press). Exploring dimensions of consumer housing and support preferences. *Adult Residential Care Journal.*

INDEX